Twayne's United States Authors Series

EDITOR OF THIS VOLUME

David J. Nordloh

Indiana University

Frank R. Stockton

TUSAS 374

Frank R. Stockton

FRANK R. STOCKTON

By HENRY L. GOLEMBA

Wayne State University

TWAYNE PUBLISHERS
A DIVISION OF G. K. HALL & CO., BOSTON

Library of Congress Cataloging in Publication Data

Golemba, Henry L
Frank R. Stockton.

(Twayne's United States authors series ;
TUSAS 374)
Bibliography: p. 173– 79
Includes index.
1. Stockton, Frank Richard, 1834–1902—
Criticism and interpretation.
PS2928.G6   813′.4   80-26587
ISBN 0-8057-7288-X

For Timothy,
Jason, Justin,
and Peter Henry

Contents

About the Author

After receiving a bachelor's degree from Monteith College of Wayne State University in 1965, Henry L. Golemba taught in experimental programs at junior colleges in Warren, Michigan, and Fort Worth, Texas, before pursuing graduate work at the University of Washington in Seattle where he received a doctorate degree in 1971. His graduate studies focused on Transcendentalism and resulted in a dissertation on Margaret Fuller's criticism and esthetic. While doing research on Fuller, Dr. Golemba became interested in George Ripley as a paramount force in nineteenth-century American culture and wrote a book on Ripley which appeared in 1976. Currently, Dr. Golemba is associate professor of American literature at Wayne State University in Detroit. He has published articles on John Steinbeck, Walt Whitman, Edgar Allan Poe, Caroline Kirkland, Herman Melville, and Charles Ives in such magazines as *Modern Fiction Studies, The American Transcendental Quarterly, Criticism, Midwestern Miscellany*, and *Studies in the Novel*. Dr. Golemba has read papers before the Society for the Study of Midwestern Literature and the Modern Language Association on subjects ranging from science fiction to late nineteenth-century Realism. His interest in the relationship between science and the arts has led him to write a novel about the future called *And by Confusion* and to investigate the impact of scientific theory upon early nineteenth-century writers, particularly Herman Melville and Edgar Allan Poe.

Preface

At all levels from the most popular to the most critical, Frank (Francis Richard) Stockton was greatly esteemed in his era. In 1893, librarians reported that only Mark Twain and F. Marion Crawford were more in demand than Stockton among practicing American writers. In 1895, Stockton's *The Adventures of Captain Horn* outsold all other American novels. A poll conducted in 1899 by *Literature*, a respected literary journal, awarded him fifth place, preceded only by William Dean Howells, John Fiske, Mark Twain, and Thomas Bailey Aldrich, placing him ahead of Henry James, S. Weir Mitchell, and Bret Harte. Stockton's admirers among writers included Mark Twain, William Dean Howells (who said Stockton was, after Twain, America's finest humorist), Edward Eggleston, Rudyard Kipling, Arthur Quiller-Couch, Robert Louis Stevenson (whose novel, *The Wrong Box*, Stockton was asked to complete after Stevenson's death), Edmund Gosse, Robert Browning, and, in the twentieth century, author Gertrude Stein, illustrator Maurice Sendak, and critic Edmund Wilson.

Yet, except for the dim bell that rings when one hears "The Lady, or the Tiger?" mentioned, Stockton is all but unknown today. One aim of this book is to resurrect Stockton as Kenneth Eble and Robert Cantwell reintroduced Kate Chopin in the 1950s, not on the basis of nostalgia but of merit. Stockton is a capable, conscientious literary artist whose work, with respect to humor alone, rivals Mark Twain's and compares favorably with that of Edward Eggleston, Bret Harte, and Joel Chandler Harris.

Consider for a moment Stockton's achievements. His children's story *What Might Have Been Expected* (1874) foreshadows Mark Twain's *The Adventures of Tom Sawyer* by two years and *The Adventures of Huckleberry Finn* by ten. His development of the fairy tale with mature themes and sinister forces captivated Maurice Sendak, who in the 1960s illustrated "The Griffin and the Minor Canon" and "The Bee-Man of Orn." His experimentation with point-of-view narration inspired Gertrude Stein's technique in telling *The Autobiography of Alice B. Toklas* (1933). His stories about the complexities and frustrations of ordinary middle-class life as expressed in "Our Fire Screen" and "A Piece of Red Callico," published in the 1880s, were duplicated in James Thurber's stories of the 1940s and 1950s. His anti-imperialist and anti-war sketches like "The Skipper and El Capitan" (1898) and "The Governor-General" (1898) anticipate Leonard Wibberley's popular success with *The Mouse That Roared* (1955).

While Kate Chopin in one novel, *The Awakening* (1899), captured a woman's frustration in trying to fulfill her potentiality, Stockton in a series of novels investigated the subject in its many dimensions: from *The Late Mrs. Null* (1886) in which an independent woman does quite handily without a husband, to *Ardis Claverden* (1890) in which the title heroine's motivation is as Oedipal as it is genteel, to *The House of Martha* (1891), a reverse rendition of the *Pygmalion* or *My Fair Lady* theme, to *Mrs. Cliff's Yacht* (1896) which suggests what middle-aged women might do with the world had they possession of its wealth and power, to *The Girl at Cobhurst* (1898) which shows how superior women are spurned if not politely resented by society, to *Kate Bonnet* (1902) wherein a woman's sense of civilization appears in unequal battle with what may be called the Imp of the Perverse, and finally to *John Gayther's Garden* (1902) where the various aspects of self-growth and self-culture as they pertain to women are calmly explored.

These facts alone should win Stockton some credit, even without considering his historical importance as perhaps the first American science-fiction novelist, or his originality in the detective genre in "Struck by a Boomerang" (1900) where the ratiocinative narrator deduces that he himself is the murderer. Nevertheless, except perhaps for the continuing popularity of his "The Lady, or the Tiger?" (1882), Stockton, whose name was a household word in his day, is virtually unknown in ours. His sudden and complete descent into obscurity is as astounding as if a modern writer who combined the popularity of a Kurt Vonnegut with the literary experimentation of a Robert Coover should become forgotten in the next generation. Yet such is Stockton's story. In this book's conclusion I analyze eight primary reasons for Stockton's neglect which relate not only to Stockton but to the history of literary criticism over the last hundred years. I hope this analysis and the rest of this study help to elucidate the value of Stockton, whose career spans the cultural and literary epoch from 1870 to 1902.

Most of the available material on Stockton, with the notable exception of four fine essays by Howells published between 1887 and 1901, is biographical. The score of contemporary reviews are actually interviews, from which one is more likely to learn about Stockton's collection of rare pipes than about his next novel, more about where he wrote "The Griffin and the Minor Canon" than about why he wrote it. One of my major aims is to interpret this biographical material, to show for example how Stockton's upbringing influenced his writing—in a family with an aged father, a fire-and-brimstone Methodist who despised art as frivolous and profane; a much older step-brother who as a famous preacher shared the podium with Abraham Lincoln at Gettysburg; a mother who was so staunch a Southerner she was almost caught behind the lines in the Civil War; two younger brothers, who with Frank as chief instigator, played Tom Sawyer–like pranks on their Philadelphia neighbors. Stockton's peculiar brand of humor, his view of the world as absurd, his reluctance to become acerbic in his satire, his droll sense of wit, and his appreciation of eccentric behavior were all shaped by his youthful experiences.

Another objective is to make the first close and extended examination of Stockton's art, especially in relationship to the middle-class, middle-brow audience which made his literary career possible. Martin Griffin's *Frank R. Stockton: A Critical Biography* (1939) is a useful record of biographical and bibliographical fact, but his subtitle is misleading, for he seldom attempts interpretation and usually rests content with plot summary. Howells's essays are brilliant in themselves, but piecemeal. My study is meant to be a thorough analysis, one that synthesizes Stockton's personal experience with his art. Even a simple matter like his recipe for "Cold Pink" is shown to mirror his esthetic position. A major event—as when his cousin blew up the Secretaries of the State and the Navy—is demonstrated to have affected Stockton's ironic perception of society.

Since Stockton was a prolific popular writer, his relationship with the publishing industry, his audience, and his fan clubs will be examined. For much of the extrinsic material and some of the methodology, I am indebted to the advances in American literary criticism of the past twenty years, particularly with respect to popular culture, women's studies, and apperceptive criticism. For special notice I should single out William C. Spengemann's work on the domestic novel in *The Adventurous Muse: The Poetics of American Fiction, 1789–1900* (1977) and Ann Douglas's study of the link between feminism and religious leaders in *The Feminization of American Culture* (1977).

Several other aims are also of importance, such as defining the uniqueness of Stockton's style—which is not exclusively Realism nor Fantasy but a combination of the two modes—and locating the common thread that binds into a coherent whole Stockton's impressive diversity—ranging from science fiction to local color, from satire to sentimentalism to satires on sentimentalism, from gay humor to grim philosophy. The study of Stockton also helps to explain such puzzling literary questions as, why did women and children replace men as major characters in the last quarter of the nineteenth century? how accurate are the stereotypes of the era as "The Gay 90's," "The Gilded Age," and "The Mauve Decade"? and to what extent could a journeyman writer devoted to the tastes, values, and expectations of his readers maintain a commitment to quality in his art?

Two main limits restrict this study. One is my attitude of advocacy criticism, whereby the best that Stockton has to offer is garnered without, I hope, plunging into exaggeration or ignoring his faults and disappointments. Since he is relatively unknown today, I am more sympathetic than I would be with an author whose reputation is firmly established. Even with that avuncular attitude, I find Stockton inferior as an artist to the giants of his day—James, Crane, and Twain—though his work is far superior to popular writers such as Horatio Alger, Richard Harding Davis, and Francis Marion Crawford. I believe Stockton's art can stand alongside that of Kate Chopin, Bret Harte, and Hamlin Garland; but even here Stockton, bent on originality, diversity, and production in nearly fifty volumes, wrote no single novel that without the support of the rest of his canon can equal *The Awakening* or *Main-Travelled Roads*.

The other limit is length. Some of the subjects which can be only adumbrated here deserve book-length treatments in themselves. Among these I include the character and composition of the book-buying readership of the era and the popular writer's full relationship to it; a complete description of all the nuances of female characterization in Stockton as it compares with other literature and cultural phenomena of the times; a specialized study of the impact of "the reviewing public"—which Stockton's wife in 1902 described as still "quite a new thing"—on the popular writer who began to have four masters besides his own esthetic: the public, the magazine editor, the book publisher, and the critical reviewer. My forays into these and other areas are only exploratory. The field if not quite virginal is still largely innocent and for that reason exciting.

The generous efforts of many people must be acknowledged with my fond thanks. Foremost are my friends and colleagues, Dr. Joanne Creighton and Dr. Vern Wagner, whose standards of elegant prose and

Preface

direct style I hope I have not failed too sadly to meet. My student, Steven Sabo, located two articles relevant to Stockton in modern science-fiction magazines that I on my own would have missed. Librarians of many institutions have my gratitude, and four deserve special mention: Joan St. Clair Crane of the rare book division of the Alderman Library, University of Virginia at Charlottesville, and Mardel Pacheco, Assistant to Curator of Manuscripts, Princeton University, encouraged me in my research; Mary V. Gaver, formerly head librarian at Rutgers University and a Stockton scholar herself, assisted me in locating Stockton resources; Dr. Arnold Pings, chief librarian at Wayne State University, permitted me free use of the rare twenty-three volume Shenandoah edition of Stockton's writings. A sabbatical leave from Wayne State University gave me the time to do the work. Letters and other unpublished documents from Box 145 of the Scribner's Authors Files are published with permission of the Princeton University Library and Charles Scribner, Jr. Letters and other unpublished documents from the Clifton Waller Barrett collection of Stockton material are published with permission of the University of Virginia Library, Charlottesville.

HENRY L. GOLEMBA

Wayne State University

Chronology

1834   Born April 5, to William Smith and Emily Drean Stockton, Philadelphia.

1839   Becomes lame; forms "A.O.B."; attends Zane Street School.

1844   Father dismissed as Alms House superintendent; cousin inadvertently blows up Secretaries of State and the Navy.

1852   Receives B.A. from Philadelphia Central High School; joins "Forensic and Literary Circle"; studies wood engraving.

1859   December: publishes "Kate" in *Southern Literary Messenger*.

1860   Marries Marian E. Tuttle, April 30; privately prints "A Northern Voice Calling for the Dissolution of the Union"; establishes engraving office in New York; father dies, November 20.

1864   Writes journalism for Philadelphia *Press* and *Post;* supports Jay
1867   Cooke's banking plan.

1872   Supports Horace Greeley for president; with wife, writes *The Home;* contributes to J. G. Holland's *Punchinello,* Edward Eggleston's *Hearth and Home,* later to *Puck.*

1873   Becomes Mary Mapes Dodge's assistant on *St. Nicholas;* writes first novel, *What Might Have Been Expected.*

1874   First installment of *Rudder Grange,* November, which appears as novel, 1879.

1876   Temporarily blind, takes recuperative trip to Virginia, then to Florida and Nassau.

1877   November 3; brother John dies.

1878   Quits *St. Nicholas;* vision permanently impaired.

1882   Visits Europe for two years; "The Lady, or the Tiger?" appears, November.

1884   Wins *Youth's Companion's* best-story prize; seriously ill.

1885   *The Late Mrs. Null,* November; resides in Morristown, New Jersey, near Edison's Menlo Park.

1886   *The Casting Away of Mrs. Lecks and Mrs. Aleshine.*

1887   *The Hundredth Man.*

1890   Buys "The Holt"; supports International Copyright Law; *Ardis Claverden.*

1894   Returns in March from Chicago and the West.

1895   *The Adventures of Captain Horn* outsells all American novels.
1897   Contributes to *The Critic's* symposium, February, on the Venezuelan Question between America and Great Britain.
1898   *The Girl at Cobhurst;* "The Skipper and El Capitan."
1899   *The Associate Hermits;* is voted fifth place among best living American writers by *Literature,* April; buys "Claymont."
1900   *A Bicycle of Cathay.*
1902   *Kate Bonnet;* while guest of National Academy of Science, dies of cerebral hemorrhage, April 20; Mark Twain attends funeral; *John Gayther's Garden* and *The Captain's Toll-Gate* published posthumously.

CHAPTER 1

Youth to Maturity

I   *"The Secret Society of the A.O.B. (1834–1843)"*

WHEN two respectable ministers came to call on a Sunday, William Smith Stockton, Frank's father, served them his wife's locally famous mincemeat pie. They took one bite and puckered their mouths. An amazed expression crossed the ministers' faces. Someone had substituted cold mush for the mincemeat filling. William gazed sternly at his ten-year-old son, Francis Richard Stockton; Frank and his two younger brothers glanced at each other and bolted from the house.

When a Bucks County, Pennsylvania, farmer saw two boys trespass into his barn to hunt cats, he sneaked up on them and jumped through the front door with a loud yell. The frightened boys scrambled away through the rear door. The farmer watched their flight in satisfaction, for his carefully crafted image of dangerousness had protected his property from the pranks of boys. To his surprise, the boys—Frank Stockton and his brother—came right back. They had noticed his brood of pigs, they said, and wanted to buy one. Selling a shoat for the exorbitant sum of one dollar, the farmer thought he had struck a good bargain, but two years later when Frank sold the pig, now grown plump, for eight dollars, he was not quite so sure.

One night after everyone had presumably gone to sleep, Frank's mother heard a great tumult upstairs and knew precisely whence it came. She marched to Frank's room, opened the door, and saw a large blanket draped almost from the ceiling. From the top of the blanket peeped two small faces. One was Francis Richard's. He had convinced his brothers to upset the heavy, old-fashioned, high-posted bedstead and to place the mattress and bedclothes on the underside which was now the upperside.

Had Emily Dream Stockton known such relativity of perspective would one day make her son Frank famous, it would have been small consolation, for the "Secret Society of the A.O.B." which Frank had founded was causing her gray hairs. And he was the son of one of the

17

most respected and conservative Methodist pamphleteers in the world, a man who spoke with fiery eloquence against Jesuits, alcohol, and slavery, a man who split the Methodist Church in 1830 to promote lay representation and who split it again in 1858 over abolition, a man who authored respected biographies of John and Charles Wesley, and who would cross to the sunny side of the street on a hot summer day to avoid walking in the shadow of the Arch Street theater. Even the injured leg which lamed five-year-old Francis slightly for the rest of his life did not make the boy more prudent.[1]

The antics of the "A.O.B.," which rivalled the pranks of the Gang of Pirates and Outlaws in Mark Twain's *The Adventures of Tom Sawyer* (1876) and the juvenile practical jokes recorded in George Wilbur Peck's *Peck's Bad Boy and His Pa* (1883), were an embarrassment to Frank's mother as a poor reflection on her household and also on generations of Virginia Dreans, New Jersey Gardiners, and Pennsylvania-New Jersey Stocktons. In 1656, Richard Stockton had come to America from Cheshire, England. His eldest son, Richard, settled in Princeton, New Jersey, and founded an influential family—one of whom, also named Richard, signed the Declaration of Independence. Another son of the patriarch, named John, settled in Burlington, New Jersey, which, though closer to Trenton, used Philadelphia as its metropolitan center. John's great-grandson was Samuel, Francis's grandfather.[2] This man married Hannah Gardiner, whose great-grandfather was the first Speaker of the General Legislature for the colonial Jerseys, and whose great-great-grandfather was a member of the General Assembly and of the Governor's Council.

Francis's father, William Smith Stockton, was noted as one of the most militant and independent of the Methodist laity. All other interests were subservient to his religion. The Stockton family claimed that in his entire lifetime William had read only one whole novel and part of another. He was deeply impressed by Harriet Beecher Stowe's *Uncle Tom's Cabin* (1851–52) and it satisfied any craving he may have had for light reading. He dipped into Eugene Sue's *The Wandering Jew* (1844–45) in order to comprehend his Jesuit opposition, but recoiled from the novel in horror.[3] Had he known his puckish son Francis was to become one of America's most popular writers, he would have considered the tribute the trial of Job. Religion absorbed all his thoughts; his only relaxation was in gardening, which also became one of Francis's favorite pastimes and a major metaphor of his literary art.

William's first wife was a young Quakeress, Elizabeth Sophia Hewlings of Burlington, whose esteemed ancestors included Aaron Burr. Of their eleven children, only three survived to adulthood. The eldest, Thomas Hewlings Stockton, born on June 4, 1808, became one of the most respected Methodist preachers of his day. During the Civil War he was chaplain to both houses of Congress, shared the podium with Abraham Lincoln when he delivered the Gettysburg Address, and was said by Henry Clay to be the greatest pulpit orator Clay had ever heard.[4] In continuing the tradition of his father's missionary zeal, he published a sermon in 1865 imploring that the enthusiasm that had succeeded in rooting out the institution of slavery in the late Civil War be now channeled toward the eradication of other equally evil problems—particularly those that violated the third commandment that the Sabbath be kept holy. No newspapers should be sold and no shops should be open on Sunday, he argued. A committee note added: "The foregoing argument will apply with equal force to the running of the [street] cars on Sunday."[5]

Such examples of an overzealousness which placed purchasing a Sunday newspaper on the same level with selling slaves helped hone Frank Stockton's appreciation of the absurd. His affection for his half-brother kept the tenor of that appreciation at the level of amused tolerance and prevented it from becoming venomous. In 1861, when Thomas published a collection of antiquated and fervent religious poems complete with an impassioned autobiographical sketch, Frank was glad to cut seven and design two of the illustrations for the volume.[6] If Frank harbored any jealousy toward his older half-brother, it would have emerged in "The Battle of the Third Cousins," but in that story the animosity and rivalry are explained away as a misunderstanding, and the two cousins become friends.[7] The fact is that since Thomas was twenty-six years Frank's senior the age difference was too great for much sibling rivalry. Indeed, Thomas was closer to his father's age than to Frank's, and in 1834, the year of Frank's birth, Thomas and William rivalled each other for fame as the most eminent Methodist in America.

Frank's other half-siblings were Elizabeth, who had limited success in publishing poems in magazines in the 1850s, and Emily, whose romantic nature is responsible for Frank's names—"Francis" for King Francis I and "Richard" for Richard the Lion-Hearted. Likewise, Emily dubbed Frank's younger sister "Marie-Louise" (born 1838) after Napoleon's second wife and in honor of Frank's mother's French ancestry. Frank's other full siblings—his closest brother John Drean (1836), William S., Jr. (1841), and Paul (1843)—escaped such historically laden sobriquets, but Frank carried on her penchant for fancy names by calling his pet dog "Fax Mentis Incendium Gloria" or "Fax," for short.

William Stockton's first wife, Elizabeth Sophia Hewlings Stockton, died of tuberculosis on August 10, 1826. Four years later, at the age of forty-five, he married twenty-year-old Emily Hepzibeth Drean of Leesburg, Loudon County, Virginia, which is halfway between Washington, D.C., and Harpers Ferry. Emily Drean's French ancestry from her mother's side was held responsible for the whimsical, fanciful tone of many of Frank Stockton's stories. This odd notion was reinforced by Stockton himself in a collection of instructive essays and stories for schoolchildren called *Tales Out of School* (1875), in which he reviewed Jules Verne's *From the Earth to the Moon* (1865) and commented that the scene where the three space travelers while away time playing dominoes is one which "only a Frenchman could have imagined."[8]

Setting aside the specious theory of "French blood," one can safely say that Emily Drean had a great influence on her son. The pity is so little is known about her; none of the important Stockton biographies tells anything beyond the superficial.[9] Yet she clearly inspired the strong-willed, lively, principled, and kind women characters he depicted in his works, perhaps especially in what Stockton considered his best novel, *Ardis Claverden* (1890), "Ardis" being a favorite name in the Drean family.[10] Or perhaps her life is more accurately portrayed in Stockton's *The Girl at Cobhurst* (1898) in which the woman of genius and generosity is misunderstood, distrusted, and abused.

Emily Drean definitely caused Frank to feel fondly toward the South, culminating in his pitifully unsuccessful attempt in 1860 to forestall the Civil War. The woman he married was a Southerner who had been a literature teacher at his mother's school. Although he wrote many stories about New Jersey, New England, New York, and other Northern locales, many of his best local color efforts dealt with Virginia. In the last years of his life, the Stocktons' favorite home was located only twenty-two miles west of his mother's birthplace.

Probably her greatest gift was to allow her son a life of freedom and security from the time of his birth in Philadelphia on April 5, 1834, at least until 1844. Since her husband was engaged in church affairs, busy writing biographies and pamphlets, active in his new position as Superintendent of a Methodist Alms' House (where the Philadelphia General Hospital now stands), and was old enough to be Frank's grandfather, Emily presided over the household and permitted Frank his secret society of the A.O.B. and other childhood pranks. The large household was considered a blessing wherein children were deemed a more sure sign of God's favor than money. The varied and genially eccentric personalities delighted Frank, a delight expressed in his *The Squirrel Inn* (1891), which depicts a group of Dickensian characters as idiosyncratic as the oddly designed house at which they room.

Frank's education began under his mother's tutelage, but he had ample time for games, gymnastics, and his favorite pastime—fishing. Though slightly built and partially lame, he developed a strong, wiry physique and excelled at vaulting. His brother John was even more athletic and was fond of breaking the ice for an invigorating winter dip. In 1840, Frank was sent to the Zane Street School in West Philadelphia where he received a solid basic education. In all, his childhood was replete with halcyon days. In 1844, two events were to alter that situation.

II *School and Scandal (1844–1860)*

Two shocking events rocked the Stockton clan in 1844. One involved Frank's cousin, Robert Field Stockton (1795–1866), a descendant of Richard, the signer of the Declaration of Independence, the Stockton branch that had always been more prestigious. Robert had distinguished himself as a naval officer in the War of 1812 and in the conflict with the Barbary pirates (1815), and in 1821 he had secured Liberia for the American Colonization Society which planned to settle former American slaves there. President John Tyler had asked him to be his Secretary of the Navy. John Ericsson, who later designed the ironclad *Monitor* of Civil War fame, helped Robert design and build the *Princeton*, the first warship driven by a screw propeller. But in 1844, when Robert Stockton was demonstrating a new cannon he had invented, the largest in the American fleet, to a group of assembled officials, a disastrous event occurred. One gun exploded, killing the Secretary of State, the Secretary of the Navy, the father-in-law of President Tyler, and wounding several other passengers. Robert was exonerated of the mishap and went on to become a hero of the Mexican War (1845–1848) second only to John Charles Frémont, and to serve as a United States Senator (1851–1853).

Picture the scene: a group of eminent dignitaries in full formal dress stands on the deck of America's finest warship to observe soberly—ironic in itself—the performance of a death-dealing cannon virtually on the eve of war. The gun explodes, killing several. One almost envisions Robert turning to the slain Secretaries to offer his sincerest apologies. Somehow he composes a telegram informing the President of the event. The ship sails on, and Robert serves his country well in both peace and war, as both appointed and elected official. When two New England ladies in *The Casting Away of Mrs. Lecks and Mrs. Aleshine* (1886) suffer shipwreck and treat the ocean-going catastrophe as though it were rain on a picnic, the situation is parallel. Though the *Encyclopaedia Britannica* for 1971 records the event under "Stockton, Robert Field," it omits one further irony which Frank was sure to seize: Robert had dubbed the lethal cannon "The Peacemaker."[11]

Even though Frank includes a sketch of Robert as the concluding chapter of his *Stories of New Jersey* (1896), no biographer has discussed this episode; yet it reveals much about Stockton's temperament and art.[12] On the obvious level, Robert's career is partly responsible for Frank's fascination with pirates and history (*The Stories of New Jersey, Buccaneers and Pirates of Our Coasts* [1898], *Kate Bonnet* [1902], his last novel) and for the lifelong interest in science, inventions, and war which inspired both his science-fiction stories and his invention of a parallel-line engraving tool which was patented in 1862 and widely used.[13] More significantly, this event dramatizes the peculiarity of Stockton's writing, a quality so difficult to define that William Dean Howells struggled in the attempt and Edward Eggleston simply conceded that "Stockton's mind possessed one chamber that had been denied to the rest of mankind."[14] Though Eggleston does not name it, that one chamber houses an absurdist philosophy, not as the nineteenth century understood it, equating absurdity with nonsense or wrongness, nor in the twentieth-century sense of spiritual anguish. Rather, Stockton viewed mankind as sailing along in an incomprehensible and unpredictable universe in which at any moment disaster might explode to shatter the serenity of clear skies. Then man, like ants whose hill has been crushed by a careless boy's heel, busily returns to recreating what he considers normality. Stockton's characters are as natural as Alice or Dorothy, but instead of Wonderland or Oz they enter the real but equally fantastic streets of New York City or the backroads of Virginia. Whether buying a piece of cloth or falling in love, they experience adventures as whimsically astonishing as any caused by the Queen of

Hearts or the Wizard of Oz, or, for that matter, by Robert Field Stockton and his fatal "Peacemaker."

The other scandal of 1844 struck closer to home. Frank's father, though a conscientious Alms House superintendent since 1831, was either a very poor businessman or a worse judge of character. In either case, the trustees of the charitable institution discovered that, among other items, twenty-seven tons of meat were unaccounted for.[15] As with Robert, William was not held personally to blame for this fiasco, but on June 24, 1844, his resignation was accepted. William sought no other employment, preferring instead to devote his time to writing voluminous tracts on Methodism and Temperance, equating the latter with total abstinence. Income from his mother's large farm on North Broad Street, where Temple University now stands, allowed his family to live modestly, and this budget was supplemented by tuition from a school for young ladies which his wife Emily founded and administered successfully.

From 1844 on, William spent his time at home, and Frank's home-life immediately quieted. William was not a tyrant, but the children had to be kept still while he worked in his study. Moreover, his general disapproval of the arts must have created a repressive atmosphere. At the age of ten, when Frank was beginning to read novels, his father might come downstairs, read a paragraph or two of his copy of Ann Radcliffe's *The Mysteries of Udolpho* (1794), and shake his head in disappointment over this waste of time.[16] William had been a bookstore clerk, and his son Thomas records that he felt reading to be a sacred activity, but religion was the only subject sacred enough to read about. Any other reading was frivolous or worse.[17] In adult life, Frank was personally noted for two idiosyncrasies: his meticulous neatness and his soundless laughter, traits of inhibition resulting from the days his father stayed at home.[18] His father's influence might also account for the fact that Frank when an adult did not attend church except for funerals of relatives or friends.[19]

The ministers Stockton portrays in his fiction are "all right fellows," but they are always incidental when not downright impotent. When Mrs. Cliff in *Mrs. Cliff's Yacht* (1896) takes fourteen reverends sailing on her steamship designed as a charitable institution, her niece defends her action by saying, "if Mrs. Cliff takes out poor children from the slums, and hardworking shop girls and seamstresses, why shouldn't she take hard-working ministers and give them some fresh air and pleasure?"[20] Such association certainly wounds the prestige of the clergy, and more so when they all become seasick. Yet two prove useful—as Mrs. Cliff's assistants in a charitable organization she forms and directs. In *The Captain's Toll-Gate* (1903), when John Asher is plagued by a vicious gossip, he takes the problem not to the Methodist minister but to the minister's wife, who with the aid of the ladies in her Dorcas Society sets matters right.[21] In *The Girl at Cobhurst* (1898), one of Stockton's most interesting novels for its satire of the Romance genre, the rector, Mr. Ames, seems to exist solely for the brilliant Dora Bannister to marry on the rebound, and the reference may reveal Stockton's opinion of his parents' marriage. As a wedding gift, Dora's best friend and cicerone gives her a corkscrew; whether a Freudian allusion or a reference to seeking consolation in drink, the gift is indeed a negative comment.[22] The minister aptly named "Bishop" in *The Associate Hermits* (1899) is a far more positive character, but even he settles for becoming a rich man's librarian. Stockton's ministers are never more than genial frills.

With a sense of relief from his too tranquil home, Frank entered Philadelphia's Central High School in 1848. Established only ten years earlier, Central High offered a curriculum equivalent to the best junior colleges today and was empowered to grant a bachelor of arts degree.[23] Frank, with a vague notion of becoming a physician, took many science courses, an education that would serve him well in his writing career. Science's stress on logic tells in Frank's consistent plot, close observation, and realistic style. He did well at his studies but not exceptionally, for he graduated nineteenth in his class in February, 1852. His classmates had diverse interests and would become judges, physicians, financiers, and philanthropists.[24]

During his high school years, Stockton's interest in writing grew. Walking to and from school, he would "take up the thread of a plot and carry it on from day to day until the thing became a serial story."[25] At home, he or John would begin a story, the other would add to it, and the two would toss it back and forth until it was completed.[26] This oral practice served Stockton well in middle and late age when his sight was impaired and he could not depend on manuscript revision.

One of Stockton's first attempts at poetry began, "My love she hath a black eye;/ Her lips are cherry red." His friends ridiculed the verse, wanting to know just how Frank's girlfriend came to get her eye punched. Another poem written when Frank was fourteen celebrated the American victory over Mexico at the battle of Monterey.[27] In 1893, at the height of his fame, Stockton told a minor poet, Edith M. Thomas, in a flirtatious interview that he recalled merely the first and last pairs of lines to what he claimed was the only poem he ever wrote.[28] Thomas shifted his last line to second place and added lines that inverted Stockton's ironic meaning: "We walked in a garden of roses,/ Miss Jane, Sir Cupid, and I./ The next time I looked in the garden,/ The rascal was walking with her." Edith Thomas then adds, "Then softly I crept in, and caught her;/ She blushed, but would not be free./ By keeping Sir Cupid between us,/ There was room in those alleys for three."

Yet Stockton did write other poems, though he apparently forgot them. One called "Tickled by a Straw" is from an early work full of moralistic stories and instructive natural history sketches for young people:

> From his dreams of tops and marbles,
> Where the soaring kites he saw,
> Is that little urchin wakened,
> Tickled by a wheaten straw.
>
> How do you suppose he likes it,
> Young one with annoying paw?
> If I only were your mother,
> I'd tickle you with birchen straw.
>
> Soon enough, from pleasant dreaming,
> You'll be wakened by the law,
> Which provides for every vision
> Some sort of provoking straw.
>
> In dreams of play, or hope, or loving,
> When plans of happiness you draw,
> Underneath *your* nose may wiggle
> Life's most aggravating straw.[29]

Like Mark Twain and unlike Frances Hodgson Burnett of *Little Lord Fauntleroy* fame (1886), Stockton seized upon children's literature to present gloomy truths in a youthful context, such as the conviction that a fact of life as inviolable as the law of gravity (tops, marbles, kites) will shatter "dreams of play, or hope, or loving" and "happiness." His belief that dreams are relatively safe only in childhood and that the threat to "pleasant dreams" comes from primitive impulses ("annoying paw") explains his obsession with children's stories, which he insisted were meant for mature interpretation.

His wife claimed Frank was fond of telling about a backfired prank he and John perpetrated when Frank was fourteen. Miffed because a Baltimore religious weekly had rejected their poetic efforts, the brothers decided to copy an excerpt from John Milton's *Paradise Regained* and submit it with their own names affixed. When the magazine published the verse, the boys concluded that editors were indeed able to recognize good poetry when they saw it.[30] The boys also learned that their best talents lay in prose not poetry, and John Drean went into journalism while Frank concentrated on fiction.

But the application of literary interest and talent took much time. A deterring factor was their father's disapproval even when one of his sons won some success. While still in high school, Frank supposedly won a prize for a story submitted in a contest held by the *Boys' and Girls' Journal*.[31] On September 1, 1855, his first published story, a trivial satire that mocked the chivalric genre of Alexander Dumas, appeared in the Philadelphia-based *American Courier*.[32] But father William insisted that if his sons were bent on going into the arts, it should be one of the more practical, reliable, and prestigious of them. Upon Frank's graduation from high school in 1852, the three compromised on engraving—wood engraving for Frank, steel engraving for John—an art much esteemed in those days. Ironically, this "reliable" trade was in twenty years to be made obsolete by technological advances, especially in the process of photographic transference.[33] The one example of Frank's ability in Martin Griffin's biography and the two specimens in brother Thomas's *Poems* show Frank to have been competent but not original in his craft.

The eight years after graduation were fairly uneventful. Frank plied his engraving trade at the southwest corner of Sixth and Chestnut Streets in Philadelphia with no great success or failure. He joined the forty-member "Forensic and Literary Circle," which consisted of men who would make their marks in diverse fields and who debated such topics as "Female Influence."[34] He socialized with the women at his mother's West Philadelphia School for Young Ladies. But Frank's desire for a career in literature grew despite his father's disapproval and editors' rejection of his efforts.

One such manuscript, "What Can I Do for an Old Gentleman," which had many rejection slips pasted to it, reveals Frank's dilemma and commitment: "the pursuit in life which Tom considered himself so well qualified to follow was Literature—his ideas, however, were somewhat peculiar,—and he thought philosophical. . . . Everyone knows there are two ways by which a man can make money by the joint labor of his brain and pen. One is to learn the business, as you would a trade, and become a journalist, employed by those who will harness your Pegasus, but will at the same time provide him with oats—the other is to write what one pleases, as one pleases, and endeavour to find someone who will also be pleased with it, and—pay for it."[35]

As his first sentence reveals, while the Pegasus of his imagination could go unbridled, Tom-Frank's concept of the writer for a popular audience was one in which the Socrates of his philosophy must speak guardedly, a standard that would insure his contemporary popularity but would cause posterity to neglect him. Tom-Frank seems agreeable to this choice ("Tom wished to enjoy life as he worked, not after his work was done."), and his only desires are a chance to write, an opportunity to travel, and the possession of a place in the country. The means to these ends are to find an "Old Gentlemen," as the title suggests, to take him as protégé, perhaps suggesting Stockton's sense that his present old gentleman, his father, was unhelpful if not obstructive.

In the story, Tom rejects the absurd possibilities of securing his guardian by rescuing his daughter from drowning or runaway horses; such improbabilities for allowing a young man to find his niche in the world would emerge as the mainstay of Horatio Alger's popular stories beginning in 1866. Stockton had rejected them ten years before. He wanted to be a popular writer, but he set limits on how much he would compromise in order to sell. Stockton felt no attraction to Herman Melville's defiance of his audience; yet his pride in himself and in his art would not permit him to stoop to Alger's too easy, too mechanical, crowd-pleasing formulas.

Frank wrote other stories in his spare time, some downright poor. "The First Beefsteak" is one example. Similar to Charles Lamb's "A Dissertation on Roast Pig," it describes how Adam and Eve accidentally discover that broiled beef is delicious.[36] Stockton's story is unoriginal, immaturely conceived, awkwardly and sentimentally executed. Other efforts were more successful, and the best was "Kate," in which an ineffectual but well-meaning hero wins Kate from a summer-colony strong man despite his own bumbling actions. "Kate" was accepted for publication (without payment, much to Frank's surprise) by the prestigious *Southern Literary Messenger* and appeared in the December, 1859, issue, thus becoming Stockton's first important published short story on record.

The next year brought success to Stockton's first long story, "A Story of Champaigne," which was sold again to the *Southern Literary Messenger*, this time for thirty dollars; it appeared in the January, February, and May issues for 1861[37] "Champaigne" capitalizes on the growing interest in historical chivalry begun by Alexander Dumas' *The Three Musketeers* (1844), which later continued in America with Mark Twain's *The Prince and The Pauper* (1882), Charles Major's popular *When Knighthood Was in Flower* (1898), and even in *Yvernelle, A Tale of Feudal France* (1892) by Frank Norris, who is better known as a Naturalistic writer.

Stockton's story has typical twists which are of more interest biographically than esthetically, except for the fact that his hero, Rupert, is as in "Kate" a nonhero. The main moving force and source of action is a character named Tiberius Caesar (recalling Stockton's regal names), who is a dwarf (Frank himself was short, slight, and partially lame). Caesar takes the side of young Madame Celeste (Frank's mother?) against that of her abusive guardian, Count Maurice (Frank's father?). When Celeste's father dies, bequeathing his wealth to the count, Caesar breaks into a lawyer's study and burns all the lawyer's papers in his own fireplace to be sure that the father's will and other testaments are included in the conflagration.

The burning of the father's will is decidedly symbolic; on November 20, 1860, Frank's father died, thus freeing Frank from actual and psychological restrictions. On April 30 of the same year he had married Mary Ann Edwards Tuttle of Georgetown, South Carolina, who had been a literature teacher in his mother's school. Together they had left his father's house when Frank moved his engraving office to 160 Fulton Street in New York. The death of Rupert's father in the story, told with sincerity and restrained grief, demonstrates the ambivalence of love and resentment in Frank's relationship with his father. With a wife, with some publishing success, with a new office, and freedom from his father's influence, Stockton at the age of twenty-seven was his own man and ready to pursue his second career. The period 1860 to 1881 marks Stockton's real commencement.

III   *A New Beginning (1860–1881)*

Stockton's first important action of this period was to confront the institution of slavery which threatened America with civil war. In late 1860 he wrote an eight-page pamphlet called *A Northern Voice for the Dissolution of the Union of the United States of America* and published it in the spring of 1861 at his own expense. His argument was that America until 1860 had to remain unified for defense because the new country was weak. Now it was powerful enough to become two separate nations, especially since, Stockton believed, the North and the South were two distinct cultures: "two different and new varieties of the Anglo-Saxon family."[38] Conflict between North and South need not be feared because mutual economic interests would prevent it. The North, for example, required forty million dollars worth of the South's cotton alone each year.[39] Nor would the government buildings at Washington, D.C., be wasted, for they could be converted into a sort of United Nations' conference center where the North and South could meet.

Because of his visits to his mother's relatives in northern Virginia and his wife's reports of slavery in South Carolina, Stockton did not consider slavery to be as cruel as depicted in Harriet Beecher Stowe's *Uncle Tom's Cabin, or, Life Among the Lowly* (1852). Personally he did not favor nor benefit from slavery; practically, of course, the position of *A Northern Voice* if adopted would have perpetuated the institution. At any rate, the fall of Fort Sumter on April 13, 1861, began the Civil War and rendered Stockton's *Voice* irrelevant. Apparently, Stockton persisted in his opinion and wrote a six-thousand-word manuscript called "A Real Union" in 1864 which reiterated the basic points of *A Northern Voice*. But he must have realized its futility, for he did not trouble to publish it.[40]

More interesting than the content of these essays is the voice: strident, aggressive, almost hysterical. It was the first and last time he would use the frenzied style of the pulpit orator by which his father and older brother had gained renown. Ruefully, he must have noted his total ineffectuality. Personally, he must have been embarrassed over this topical outburst. He would never try the "deadly serious" authorial voice again. He could not adopt the tone of the Naturalistic writers nor of Mark Twain in more somber pieces like *The Man That Corrupted Hadleyburg* (1900). Balanced, genial, avuncular humor was to be his forte, the principal voice with which he felt most comfortable. His fiction would attempt to tease humankind from its folly, coax it into some reform. Never again would he preach, proselytize, or mutter dark warnings.

His later life is marked by apolitical activity. Crucial and exciting social issues he addressed only obliquely. The Alaskan Gold Rush, the growth of industrialism, the rise of organized labor, the consolidation of monopolies, which made Edward Bellamy's *Looking Backward: 2000–1887* (1888) and its scores of imitations widely popular, Stockton handles only tangentially in his fiction.

With respect to personal appearances, he delivered a ten-thousand-word lecture on "Female Influence" (1884) but avoided controversy; he spoke to the Society of Colonial Dames on "Early Women of New Jersey" (in 1891) and focused on personal qualities of outstanding women, thus eluding political questions of women's rights.[41] When given the opportunity to discuss the spirit of the American Revolution on its centennial, he transformed the "spirit" into the "ghost" of Washington whom he meets one night, and entertained his audience by explaining how Washington learned the trick of passing through walls from the Polish Colonel Pulaski. The only statement critical of American culture is slight: Washington is frightened by the roar of the Dover express which Stockton had not noticed. "I had forgotten," Stockton says, "the diabolical and infernal modes of conveyance of the present day."[42]

Stockton's biographer, Martin Griffin, claims the only political issue he supported with "wholeheartedness" was passage of the International Copyright Bill (1891) which had a vast influence on book publishing, distribution, and profits through royalties.[43] Even discounting the fact that this bill was greatly favorable to his income because of Stockton's enormous popularity by 1891, his letters show that even here his political efforts were meager. On December 29, 1889, he declined to give a lecture "for the good of the cause"; on March 7, 1890, he would attend the American Copyright League Convention only if it were combined with a dinner meeting of the Aldine Club of writers of which he was president. Even should he attend, he predicted his behavior in mock-heroic tones: "I shall try hard to be there and help *kill* the Adversary and afterward glory over his destruction at the genial board."[44]

Stockton's greatest contribution was to originate the idea of sending out postcards to drum up support. After passage of the bill, Stockton in two letters punningly praised Robert Underwood Johnson, who through his romantic poetry was known as the unofficial poet laureate of the United States, as the one most responsible for the law: "We made you bear our cross while we did the crow'n. Excuse me; I have a sore throat."[45] Five years later, in 1896, when severe loopholes were discovered in the law, Johnson tried to muster support to plug them, but

Stockton missed the spring meeting because he was in Louisiana on vacation; to the September meeting held when he was nearby in New Jersey he said simply that he "can't go."[46]

But he did address one political issue directly—his old hatred, war. In 1898, when the Spanish-American War, America's first extracontinental conflict, broke out, Stockton, along with Nathaniel Hawthorne's son Julian, Caroline Ticknor, and Nathan Haskell Dole, was assisting Harry Thurston Peck in compiling a thirty-volume collection of *The World's Great Masterpieces*. To represent his own best art, Stockton selected not "The Lady, or the Tiger?," "Mr. Tolman," or any other well-known story; he chose "The Governor-General," a satire on war and international politics whose theme and plot are identical to Leonard Wibberley's later *The Mouse That Roared*, which was immensely popular in the 1950s and was made into a Peter Sellers movie in 1959. In "The Governor-General," the governor of a tiny island who would rather collect specimens of parrots for the sake of science and esthetics is defeated by an imperialist power; he gains more advantages for himself and his island through defeat than had he been victorious or left alone. The best single line from the story comes when the aggressor's ship fires a warning shot from a cannon, and the governor mistakes it for a salute: the iron ball "flew over the marshes where the cryptograms grew in wild profusion."[47] The sentence captures Stockton's belief that war was a simple-minded attempt to solve the world's baroque complexities.

In "The Skipper and El Capitan," first published in *Cosmopolitan Magazine* for November, 1898, Stockton handles the same theme, but he adds a layer of romantic interest. The Yankee skipper's daughter is in love with the enemy "El Capitan"; war and the male sense of false honor associated with war interfere with the real, important matters of life—that a man and woman fall in love, found a family, progress toward a happier and more peaceful world. On a personal level, Stockton remembered well how once during the Civil War his younger brother William had fought, been taken prisoner by, and then escaped from his wife's half-brother, Dr. M.F.T. Evans. After each engagement one would search the battlefield to see if the other had been killed or wounded.[48] Stockton had received a bayonet as a memento of that internecine war and, true to his philosophy, he had it converted into a candlestick, something domestically useful.[49] In these efforts against war, Stockton contributed to a solid anti-imperialistic front of writing which included the verse of Henry Blake Fuller, the letters of William

James to the *Boston Evening Transcript*, "The Conquest of the United
States by Spain" of William Graham Sumner, "To a Person Sitting in
Darkness" by Mark Twain, and the sketches of Peter Finley Dunne
and William Vaughn Moody.[50]

Stockton tried to avert war through essays as well as fiction. With
respect to the Philippine controversy, he suggested satirically that the
natives be made slaves, thus claiming that imperialism would cause
America the same problems it had just fought a bloody Civil War to
solve.[51] Two years earlier, in 1897, war with the world's greatest imper-
ialistic power, Great Britain, seemed inevitable, specifically over the
question of the Venezuelan boundary line, but many other issues could
have served as ready excuses. In February, 1897, a literary magazine,
The Critic, held a symposium on this subject, inviting comment from
such writers as John Burroughs, Mary Mapes Dodge, Edward Eggleston, Edward Everett Hale, Julia Ward Howe, Robert Underwood
Johnson, and Moses Coit Tyler. Stockton's "domestic" as opposed to a
militaristic view was that if this conflict could be settled through peaceful arbitration, it would mark "the beginning of an advance in true
civilization and enlightenment which is shown by no other event in
this century."[52]

The peaceful settlement of this particular controversy consoled
Stockton, but he had no illusion that international power struggles
involving the United States were postponed forever. When he wrote a
science-fiction novel, *The Great War Syndicate*, in 1889, he abandoned hope that government could or would prevent war, and, like
Edward Bellamy, placed faith in business interests as a possible deter-
rent to strife. But he knew that his stories and essays promoting peace
and domesticity over aggression and violence were as impotent in
forestalling America's rising position as a world power as his *A Northern Voice* had been in preventing the Civil War.

Back in the 1860s, when Stockton was making the transition from
engraver to writer, his other political involvements were equally
unproductive. Journalism was the logical means of transition, and
Stockton's brother John was successful in this career at the Philadelphia
Press and helped Frank secure minor reportorial assignments at such
affairs as a flower show held by the Sanitary Commission. Wanting to
succeed on his own, Frank went briefly to New York and supported
Jay Cooke's plan of a debit economy whereby a national debt was
urged. Cooke's plan was partly responsible for the nation's economic
depression known as the Panic of 1873. Returning to Philadelphia to

work for *The Morning Post*, which brother John and John Russell Young had started, Stockton supported Horace Greeley's 1872 presidential campaign.[53] Greeley bears the dubious distinction of being the only major presidential aspirant not to receive even one electoral-college vote. Such experiences hinted to Stockton that politics, economics, and journalism were not his domain. He wisely devoted himself to creative writing, for which markets had opened with the vast increase in the number of magazines after 1865.

Before the Civil War, religious and political interests dominated the magazines; after the war, humor and romance. Before the war, the cry for distinctly American materials known as the Young America movement was all the rage; after the war, many American periodicals were patent imitations of European journals, especially British. *Puck*, *Vanity Fair*, and J. G. Holland's *Punchinello* were three of these, and Stockton contributed sporadically to all three.

Another market was the "How to" books, and Frank and his wife Marian (no longer called "Mary Ann") published one called *The Home—Where It Should Be and What to Put in It* (1872). Years later, when the Stocktons tried to buy and furnish a home themselves, they found their "practical handbook" virtually useless. However, *The Home* is of historical interest for insights into domestic life of the times; its six-page list of prices tells that a screwdriver then cost a quarter, a walnut sideboard forty dollars, a rocking chair three dollars. Washing and ironing were considered the worst chores, especially "puffing, crimping, and fluting of bias tucks and interminable lengths of ruffling." The book also includes cultural observations, such as the remark that American children have already become the prodigal members of the family: "It is only in America that society is so exclusively given up to the boys and girls."[54] Adults should mingle, *The Home* humorously urges, because they are after all the stabilizing force of civilization.

Stockton's first modest success, however, was as an editor with Edward Eggleston's *Hearth and Home* (from 1872 until the magazine's demise in 1875) for which he wrote a regular humorous column called "That Reminds Me." While at *Hearth and Home*, he met Mary Mapes Dodge, who was in charge of the children's section and was one of the best-known authors of children's stories in America primarily because of one book, *Hans Brinker; or, the Silver Skates* (1865). Dodge took a liking to Stockton because he was a hard worker whose literary talents were beginning to show, especially in stories he wrote for Horace Scudder's Boston-based *Riverside Magazine* and in his first novel,

Ting-a-ling (1870), a queer book in that it is *prima facie* a children's fairy tale and yet parodies the genre and inverts its formulas.[55]

Though *Ting-a-ling* has the obligatory princes and princesses, the main human character is a maid, Nerralina, who in trying to rescue a prince falls into a trap he has set for intruders and is decapitated. She is taken to the Fairy Queen who restores her head, but an ugly dwarf causes it to be replaced backwards. The focus on a maid not a princess and the absurd twist on the otherwise happy ending must have delighted or baffled juvenile readers. The principal nonhuman characters are Ting-a-ling, a two-inch fairy whose lover, Ling-a-ting, was drowned by a human tear, and his friend "a good but too violent giant" called Tur-il-i-ra, whose name is so similar to a popular Irish melody that Stockton might have been making an oblique statement about this immigrant group. At any rate, after many madcap adventures, Ting-a-ling and Tur-il-i-ra conclude they like humans but that humans are too small for the giant and too big for the fairy to be at ease in their presence.

When, in 1873, Mary Mapes Dodge had the opportunity to establish a children's magazine, she asked Stockton to be her chief assistant. They agreed that *St. Nicholas Magazine*—which for sixty years would be the best known in America and would make Dodge the single most influential force in this field—would be, unlike previous purportedly children's magazines, exclusively for children, would not consist of adult stories watered down for juveniles, and would not sermonize to its youthful readers. Its list of contributors reads like a "Who's Who" of literature and illustration. It published artists like Frederick Remington and Nathaniel Hawthorne's grand-daughter, Hildegarde Hawthorne, and writers like Longfellow, Rudyard Kipling, Bret Harte, Robert Louis Stevenson, Laura Ingalls Wilder of the *Little House on the Prairie* series, Gelett Burgess, Joel Chandler Harris ("Uncle Remus"), Alfred Tennyson, Louisa May Alcott, Theodore Roosevelt, William Dean Howells, and many others.[56] Despite these contributors, eking out quality material for every large issue was a problem. Stockton offered a few solutions. He translated poems and stories from French and German and published them under the pseudonyms of Paul Fort ("Paul" for his youngest brother, "Fort" for his brother-in-law, Fort Evans) and John Lewes.[57] Besides his own forty-four entries, he also encouraged his relatives to write; his wife contributed, as did his sisters Louise and, at the age of eight, Helen.[58] He also began four long serials which were later published as separate books. With his wife's help, he wrote *Roundabout Rambles in Lands of Facts and Fancy* (1872), consisting of about seventy stories and essays on scientific, natural, and historical oddities, and *Tales Out of School* (1875), which emphasizes story-versions of natural history.

The latter is rarely didactic. When it is, it counters the American materialism and anxiety to succeed represented by Horatio Alger's novels. In a story called "Two Happy Men," for example, Stockton advises that, "When a man's business is in any branch of what we call Art he is, perhaps, happier than he could be at anything else; for, beside the satisfaction of doing the work, it is a pleasure to see beautiful things grow under our hands."[59] In the final story of the collection, "The Jolly Cabordmen," a clever artist saves the "remarkably genial people who knew no evil and would not have practiced it if they had known it" from invasion by the cruel and rapacious Voldorites. As with his more serious anti-war writings, Stockton wished wit and art could outmaneuver physical might.

A Jolly Fellowship (1878), a collection of *St. Nicholas* stories set in Savannah, St. Augustine, and Nassau, offers little more than boyish adventures, but its locale, exotic in these pre-tourist boom days, made it popular. The case is far different with *What Might Have Been Expected* (1874), a remarkably good book that antedates Mark Twain's *The Adventures of Tom Sawyer* by two years and, more pertinently, Twain's deft combination of humor, realistic depiction, and gloomy undercurrents in *The Adventures of Huckleberry Finn* (1884). Located in his mother's Virginia country, Stockton's novel gives insights to costs (a quarter for a peck of corn meal, half dollar to rent a horse), customs (children outgrow Christmas trees at the age of twelve), and work activities (collecting sumac for use in tanning). It includes a sketch of a Cooperesque Natty Bumppo in Tony Kirk, a hunter in love with the peace and comfort of the woods, and a contrasting portrait of a "Southern cracker," mean George Mason from Mississippi. The complexities of race relations and sexism are also explored, and questions are raised about the conflict between elite education and humane impulses, hunting and ecology, orthodox and skeptical religious views. The main plot involves a sinister theme: a boy and girl, seeking to save an old black woman from the poorhouse, establish a telegraph line across a river to a mine. It turns out the mine owners had wanted the line all along, but felt they could not get the farmer's property rights. So the mine owners have let the children do their work for them as their unwitting agents, and then bought them out. The irony of the title is that, had the farmers been more alert, a capitalistic con game is "What Might Have Been Expected," a game that exploits the spirit of individualistic American enterprise. The novel is excellent, worthy of college-level study. That it was not as popular as the lesser *Ting-a-ling* is just what might have been expected.

With these and other contributions primarily to *St. Nicholas*, Stockton began to establish himself as a writer, but the price he was paying was high. He received many benefits, the chief perhaps being introduced to Mark Twain, Rudyard Kipling, and other writers at Dodge's summer house in the Catskill Mountains, but the arduous work was ruining his health. He said he feared a nervous or physical breakdown which would cause people to say: "just 'What Might Have Been Expected!'"[60] But he kept hard at the work until his eyes gave out and he lost much of his vision, a problem that would plague him the rest of his life. In the journal his wife kept, Marian records on January 31, 1885, that new glasses allowed Stockton to begin "reading and writing a little, after three years' abstinence."[61] To recuperate, the Stocktons took a vacation in the year of the nation's centennial, first to Virginia to visit relatives, then to Florida and Nassau.

Upon their return, Stockton's sight had somewhat improved, but other matters were disheartening. His health continued poor, at one time forcing him to bed for thirty-five hours with "a ten-pound boil—more or less," and Marian did some of his editorial work under his name.[62] On November 3, 1877, his brother John, the man closest to Stockton, died at the age of only forty. On a less personal, more professional level, Stockton for five years had been seeking without success a publisher for his first adult novel, *Rudder Grange*, whose first installment had appeared in *Scribner's Magazine* for 1874. When the novel finally appeared in 1879 and was a best seller for over a dozen years, Stockton learned a lesson about the vagaries of the book trade.

Equally capricious was the fate of his third children's novel, *A Jolly Fellowship* (a *St. Nicholas* serial he began in November, 1878), which Stockton considered far inferior artistically to *What Might Have Been Expected*. Since the latter had not sold well, Stockton imagined *Fellowship* would do even worse and expressed this apprehension in 1880 to Charles Scribner, when he estimated the novel would not sell more than a thousand copies.[63] The next year Scribner conveyed to Stockton the dubious praise that *Fellowship* proved to be "the most popular of our juvenile publications for 1880."[64] Upon Stockton's death in 1902, *St. Nicholas* praised the man and his work, especially *A Jolly Fellowship*.[65] Fortunate for Stockton that he saw life as absurd.

Finding the youthful, carefree, cheerful *St. Nicholas* a hazard to his health, Stockton resigned his five-year post as Dodge's assistant editor in 1878 and immediately accepted an associate editorship with *Scribner's Monthly Magazine* (renamed *Century Magazine* in 1881) and continued serialization of *Rudder Grange,* his first adult novel, incidents of which were inspired by his search for a house around Rutherford, New Jersey, when coming to work for *St. Nicholas* in 1873. "Rudder Grange" had been a boat that was now a house, but it was not a houseboat. It was fixed firmly to the Hudson River bank and was not meant to float. Such quirky twists govern the humor throughout the book as some of the chapter titles indicate: "A Novel Style of Dwelling-house," "A Novel Style of Boarder," "A Novel Style of Burglar," "A Novel Style of Girl." This last title, more than the humor of the skewed plot incidents, was the essence of *Rudder Grange's* success. The novel is told from the author's point of view, his wife's name is changed to Euphemia, and the "girl" or maid-of-all-work, based on a German girl the Stocktons had hired from a New York orphanage, is named Pomona.

As soon as Pomona enters, Euphemia becomes a very minor figure and the author evaporates as a character into a mere narrative necessity. Nearly every event then springs from Pomona's idiosyncratic mannerisms, as when she cuts a garbage hole above the water line, forgetting that landlocked boats do not rise with the tide, or when her reading of dime-thriller novels syllable by syllable drives the household mad: "The la dy ce sel i a now si zed the weep on and all though the boor ly vil ly an re tain ed his vy gor ous hold she drew the blade through his fin gers and hourl ed it far be hind her dryp ping with jore."[66]

The reason for the novel's popularity among middle-class readers is that it captured the ethos of the time. Henry James's characters in *The Portrait of A Lady* (1881) expressed fear that the old social order was crumbling. Thomas Beer in *The Mauve Decade* (1926) explains that one major bourgeois concern of the 1880s and 1890s was the Servant Question, meaning that the middle-class had difficulty obtaining obedient, tractable, reliable, and docile lower-class people glad for the chance to serve. Stockton carries this issue one step further, as the titles of some of the *Rudder Grange* stories indicate: "Pomona takes the Helm at Rudder Grange" and, even more telling, "Pomona Produces a Partial Revolution in Rudder Grange."

By 1880, the epically individualistic heroism of the antebellum American Renaissance had faded into a sappy sentimentality of

Romanticism as represented by Lew Wallace's *Ben-Hur* (1880). Henry Thoreau, Nathaniel Hawthorne, and Edgar Allan Poe were dead; Ralph Waldo Emerson was senile; Herman Melville was not publishing; Walt Whitman was partially crippled by a stroke. The age had suffered the Civil War, the Panic of 1873, political corruption of the 1870s, failure of religious leaders, industrialization, the rise of the cities, and the undercutting of religious dogma by scientific theory. "Grand, ungodly, godlike" heroes like Ahab in *Moby-Dick* (1852) were replaced by women like Isabel Archer and children like Huck Finn; males seem crippled or impotent. Emerson's lofty call to heroic living became the quiet wisdom through defeat in James and the humorous mask over life's problems in Twain and Stockton. Stockton stories covering other social phenomena show the sense of upheaval and the impossibility of complete heroism. In "On the Training of Parents" (*Century*, May, 1884) Stockton pretends to address children since they now are the decision makers in families, parents having lost confidence in their authority and defaulted on their responsibility. "Be firm but kind," Stockton ironically advises child masters, because parents are often innocently ignorant. In "The Transferred Ghost" (1884) it takes a genial ghost—a voice from the past—to trick the "hero" into finally admitting his love to a woman who has been waiting impatiently for her lover to "act like a man."

Whether by intuition or happenstance, Stockton struck a cultural nerve, and the probe was palatable since that nerve was the funny bone. Although *Rudder Grange* was rejected with thanks by several publishers, when Scribner's risked publishing it in 1879 it was an immediate hit. Stockton had proven he could capture the reading public's attention; Pomona's name and her creator's became household words; Stockton could now strike out for independence as an author in demand. On another recuperative vacation in the winter of 1881— again to Florida, this time from *Scribner's* instead of *St. Nicholas*— Stockton wrote back that, "Hard work last Fall made it advisable for me not to do my own writing for a time."[67] He decided to quit being a staff writer in order to pursue his own craft. His choice skyrocketed him to international fame the next year, a blessing that was not unmixed.

IV   *A Reigning Favorite (1882–1902)*

Standing on the deck of *The City of Berlin* bound for London on August 15, 1882, Stockton was filled with anticipation. Nearly fifty, he was a bit old to begin a new career, but the tri-part dream of his early sketch "What Can I Do for an Old Gentleman?" was about to become reality—a demand for his writings, a chance to travel, and, after Europe, the purchase of a country home with an all-important garden. The Stocktons were off to Europe for several reasons. In these pre-international copyright days, it was essential for an American writer to secure a reputable European publisher, and Stockton would establish contacts with the Edinburgh publishing house of David Douglas whose "American Authors Series" would print many of Stockton's stories. Stockton also wanted to visit the Italy of his favorite painter, Joseph M. W. Turner, one of whose Venetian paintings he had rendered into a wood engraving.[68] Turner's technique of absorbing solid reality into fog, mist, and light paralleled Stockton's art, where the commonplace swirls into all but chaotic topsy-turviness. James Herbert Morse says that Stockton also went to study English backyards to obtain ideas for his own, and—given Stockton's love of gardens and their domestic connotations—Morse is probably correct.[69]

Most of all, of course, Stockton's purpose was to gather fictional material, especially for novels like *The Rudder Grangers Abroad* (1891) and *Pomona's Travels* (1894). Unable to climb the Swiss Alps because of illness, Stockton conceived two fantasy pieces—the science-fiction story "A Tale of Negative Gravity" (1884), in which a man invents a backpack device that allows him to ascend and to hover over the ground, and "A Borrowed Month" (1886), a psychological study in which the lame hero through extrasensory perception transfers his affliction to his American friends, one friend per day, so that he can wander in the mountains.

Stockton could look forward to these adventures with a clear mind, for he had accumulated enough stories before leaving America so that, supplemented by those he mailed from Europe, he would appear regularly in the magazines. One of these stories, one he had already revised five times, caused a minor difficulty. William Carey, a *Century* editor, cabled Stockton that the title of "In the King's Arena" was rather pedestrian; would he mind, Carey asked, if it were changed to, say, "The Lady, or the Tiger?" Stockton did not object, and the story under its new name was published in *Century* in November, 1882. No one was prepared for the public's response.

"The Lady, or the Tiger?" a forerunner of modern recreative fiction in which the reader is expected to recreate the story just as the author created it, ends in total ambiguity. A young man in love with a princess is sentenced by his king to choose between two doors. Behind one is a vicious tiger; behind the other, a beautiful lady whom the man must wed. The princess, having discovered the secret, signals him to open the door on the right, which he does. Has the princess, jealous over the lady, consigned him to the tiger, or, out of kindness and mercy, to the lady? Stockton leaves the choice to the reader.

The public was mad to know. In America and then internationally people discussed the topic among family and friends; debating societies were formed; an operetta setting the story in Sparta was presented in 1888; political cartoonists used the dilemma to satirize government and society for decades; critics called it "a great link in the development of the short story." By the hundreds people wrote to Stockton all his life for the right answer. Rudyard Kipling threatened him with torture unless he "fess'd up." Robert Browning, who had established a similar device with "In a Balcony," wrote an analysis explaining how the story's context made the choice of tiger inevitable. An English friend reported that in the backlands of India he came across a group of Hindu men gravely debating the issue.[70] To Kipling's threat of torture, Stockton replied that if forced he would give the wrong answer. Good, Kipling averred; then the other answer will be the correct one. "Maybe," Stockton drawled, "but maybe not." His public response was more frank, less teasing: "If you decide which it was—the lady, or the tiger—you find out what kind of person you are yourself."[71] But America, a pragmatic culture, wanted answers, not ambiguities. As recently as March, 1964, a writer wishing to pacify the public's appetite on this subject rewrote the story as science fiction and gave the hero both—a lady who was a tigress.[72]

Stockton welcomed this hysterical excitement at first, but he soon discovered disadvantages. Instead of riding the crest of fame, he found that his stories were rejected either because they were in a different vein or because they did not appear to guarantee the same response. In "His Wife's Deceased Sister" (January, 1884) he discusses this problem, when an author finds he has written another "The Lady, or the Tiger?" and secrets it under lock and key. When he published "The Remarkable Wreck of the *Thomas Hyke*" in August, 1884, and Charles L. Webster of Mark Twain's publishing house wanted to include it in *Mark Twain's "Library of Humor"* as one of "the best selections from most of the well known American authors," Stockton feared "The Wreck" too might restrict his career.[73] Not until July, 1885, did Stockton feel safe enough from "The Lady" to write again on the theme in "The Discourager of Hesitancy"; in this the hero must choose the princess from a line of beautiful damsels, his only guide an ambiguous smile. Fortunately, the public's hysteria was not aroused.

The cults that surround "the reigning favorites of the day" are an important element of literary history. Besides the stir caused by "The Lady," other works captured the public imagination. In 1894 Stockton reported to his publisher that *The Great War Syndicate* (1889), a story wherein America and Great Britain are saved from war by an anti-war business consortium, was still famous: "I saw Captain Zolinski, the dynamite man, the other day, and he said that the people who were fitting out the Brazilian warships in New York had received several copies [of the novel], he himself sending one; and when people were most talking of the fleet, the *New York Recorder* printed a four-column review of the book with extracts."[74] On August 4, 1899, a businessman from Bradford, Massachusetts, wrote to Stockton to tell him that his "The Buller-Podington Compact" (1897), about two friends, one hating the sea but loving land activities and the other reversing these preferences, had inspired "a pass-it-on society so that [fans] may be induced to tell others about the good things in literature they have enjoyed."[75] Mrs. Frederick Gotthold, an amateur artist, asked his permission to print one gift copy of his juvenile story "The Bee-Man of Orn" (1883) on eighteen sheets of parchment accompanied by her illustrations. Years later, the United Workers of Greenwich, Connecticut, published a Gotthold-Stockton version of "The Lost Dryad" in which the dryad, whose single kiss can make someone ten years younger, creates a world of complications in a town: the proceeds from the book were earmarked to build a children's clubhouse and playground "in a very poor little village."[76]

Besides all this, of course, were the usual translations. In Germany, for example, Robert Lutz of Stuttgart printed *Rudder Grange* along with Twain's *Innocents Abroad;* Deutsche Verlags-Anstalt published Stockton's "Buller-Podington Compact" with Kipling's ".007"; Margaret Jacobi translated six of his stories into German.[77]

Eleven years after Stockton's death, Etta De Camp, a self-styled seeress, published a collection of stories that she claimed were dictated to her by Stockton from the spirit world.[78]

Even a quarter of a century after his death, his works were in demand and from a new source—the movies. At least three Hollywood agents and directors wanted to buy film rights to his stories, chief among whom was Andrew Lysander Stone, who achieved fame in the silent era with the two-reeler "The Elegy" and in talking pictures with

Cry Terror, The Song of Norway, and many others.[79] Interested in "ethics and psychology as well as drama," Stone wanted to film a version of Stockton's "Old Applejoy's Ghost" (1900) in order, he said, to do "something truly artistic." In 1942, Fred Zinnemann, who later won Oscars for *From Here to Eternity* (1953) and *A Man for All Seasons* (1968), directed a short film version of "The Lady, or the Tiger?" for M-G-M studios.

During Stockton's life, his role as a cult figure, all the more remarkable since he preferred a reclusive life, encouraged people to write to him requesting he suggest names for their boats. A hotel on the Hudson River named itself after one of Stockton's novels, *The Squirrel Inn* (1891), a queerly designed caravansary full of eccentric residents.[80] Even Stockton was caught up in cultism, as when he named three generations of cows "Marjorie Daw" after Thomas Bailey Aldrich's excellent story about an ideal but nonexistent woman. Of the many reviews of Stockton, more space—and by "more" is meant a proportion of thirty to one—was spent describing his books, his study, his home and surroundings than in discussing his art. At least a dozen drawings and photographs of him appeared in the magazines. Anyone who read Stockton knew about his old-fashioned mustache and his quirk of being the last American author to write with a quill pen.

The writer as celebrity was also a boarder, a household companion; he and his works became an integral part of everyday life. Such fascination with artists today seems to have shifted to other media—to music, television, and movies—and exists in literature to the same degree only with the science fiction fan clubs. But still the comparison is different, because in Stockton's cults the relationship was one of friendship, of pleasure in the visit of a genial uncle or aunt; today the basis is awe, envy, or reverence. The difference is the difference between love and adoration.

Cult interest included Stockton's homes, for homes were significant status symbols to middle-class America, and the choice of home was of monumental importance, as William Dean Howells shows in the first chapters of *A Hazard of New Fortunes* (1890). Stockton had three, and a wealth of detail surrounds them. From about 1877 to 1882, the Stocktons vacationed at Lego, once one of Thomas Jefferson's houses, visible from Monticello (Marian even wrote down Stockton's stories on a lap desk that had belonged to Jefferson).[81] The first home they owned was a twelve-acre property with a twenty-room house, an apple orchard, and several cottages and sheds which Mary Mapes Dodge

named The Holt, near Morristown, New Jersey.[82] Theodore Roosevelt
had played there as a child, and The Holt's tower had been used as an
astronomical observatory by Dr. Charles Kitchell. Stockton's last home,
called Claymont (1899–1902), was in the Shenandoah Valley near his
mother's country on land once owned by George Washington at
Charles Town, West Virginia, where John Brown was hanged and near
the old road where General Edward Braddock marched to his celebrated defeat. Describing these years at Claymont, Marian said, "Truly
life was never sweeter to him than at its end, and the world was never
brighter to him than when he shut his eyes upon it."[83]

After a business trip to New York, Stockton stopped in Washington
to attend a banquet of the National Academy of Sciences on April 16,
1902. He became ill and died in his room at the Willard Hotel of a
cerebral hemorrhage on April 20, 1902. Thus ended the life of a writer
whom a contemporary critic included with Mark Twain and Joel
Chandler Harris as "the reigning favorites of the day."[84] When still a
teen-ager, Stockton had described his tri-part dream of an ideal life in
"What Can I Do for an Old Gentleman?" At the age of sixty-eight, he
had fulfilled all the hopes of this youthful dream.

V *In the Garden (Post 1902)*

Though Stockton reigned with the public, he did not rule publishers.
Today a famous author can often publish any book regardless of quality, but Stockton could not ride this crest of popularity. When in 1899
he sent a story suggested by Rudyard Kipling to Scribner's, his old publishing house, and offered it for three hundred dollars, two hundred
dollars less than his normal fee, Scribner's rejected it. When he offered
The Girl at Cobhurst, which may be one of his best novels, to Horace
E. Scudder of *The Atlantic Monthly* in 1893, it was rejected because
it was "milder, paler" than Stockton's *The House of Martha,* his least
exciting novel to a modern reader. When in 1889 he offered *Ardis
Claverden,* which he considered "the most important work of my literary career," it was rejected, not to be published for nearly two years.
On March 9, 1886, Stockton complained that his books were not being
"pushed" as much as they should: "to think that I had only 104 more
purchases in my own country than in England, is rather humiliating."
Today we worry that television is converting Americans into illiterates;
in 1896 writers shared the same fear directed toward a different source,
as Stockton humorously compained to Charles Scribner: "My recent

royalty returns—the smallest I have ever had from your house—have made me fear that there may be some truth in the statement that the bicycle rage has had a bad effect upon the book trade. I suppose that that cannot be helped unless books are protected by a heavy tax on bicycles."[85]

Nor could Stockton use his influence among publishers to promote other novelists he respected. When John Ford Bemis wrote a novel about a preacher who becomes an agnostic and is slaughtered along with his innocent wife in a Georgia swamp by a religious mob, Stockton, who had written not one word the public might find offensive, told Bemis: "You had best get the couple out of the swamp alive, but your conclusion is logical and right." He recommended the novel to *Century*, but its editor, Richard Gilder, informed Bemis that the *Century's* large domestic circulation would not receive this story placidly.[86] And that was that.

The major cause for this attitude, one that would delay publication of Stephen Crane's *Maggie: a Girl of the Streets* and Theodore Dreiser's *Sister Carrie*, was that, as F. L. Pattee comments, "the old idea of a publishing house as a happy family of authors and publishers associated to advance the great cause of literature and to be of mutual service . . . was giving way now to the one idea of a publishing house organized for business only."[87] Business was based on market sales and the market was bifurcated. At one extreme were the dime novels and adventure stories which caused the New York *Newsdealer* for September 1, 1891, to lament that Stockton sold less well than he should because "'Gore' and 'realism' seem still to pay both author and publisher better than genuine literature." At the other extreme was the middle-class woman reader, "the Titaness" in Thomas Beer's phrase, whose careful morality and sense of etiquette any publisher, especially a magazine publisher, was loath to offend.

Business demanded the widest distribution possible, and this in turn involved two phenomena. First is the rise of magazines. Today movie rights to a novel are the best guarantee of profit; then it was magazine serial rights. In 1885 Stockton informed Scribner that he regularly received more money from the magazines proportionately than from a publishing house for a novel; in 1889 he exclaimed over the "high price paid by . . . *Once-a-week* for *The Great War Syndicate*"; in 1891 he noted that he could command a flat $5,000 as a regular magazine price but had to depend on a risky fifteen percent for book royalties.[88] Since well-paying magazines consumed material voraciously, they made it possible for a large number of Americans to make their living as professional writers. In his *Literature and Life* (1902) Howells mentions hundreds of these writers, a new breed which fifty years earlier could not have sustained themselves as literary professionals. Many of these, such as Henry Harland, whom Howells groups with Henry James and Bret Harte, are known only to the most dedicated scholars of the period; others, such as Edith Wyatt and Will Payne, are barely recognized even by them.[89]

While many could place stories in magazines, not all could then succeed as novelists, but those who did encountered the second phenomenon—that of multiple editions intended to reach as many different book budgets as possible and thus offset international copyright problems. "I am a believer in cheap books," Stockton wrote, "and believe that this is the only method by which the American author can combat the flood of English reprints."[90] In 1900, for example, Stockton's more popular stories like *Rudder Grange* and "The Lady, or the Tiger?" were available in six different forms, including two inexpensive hardbounds, the "uniform" and the "popular" editions; an American paperback version costing fifty cents; and a British paperback for thirty-five cents. The other two editions were part of a project which Marian Stockton called "a sort of monument to my husband's genius; and he so considered it, and was justly proud of it."[91] Stockton wanted the project to be called "the Magnolia Series," since he considered the flower "by natural right our national flower"; but was converted by Scribner's to accept "the Shenandoah" edition.[92] Printed in two editions, the very handsome "regular" and the even fancier "Japan" version, with an embossed magnolia on each title page, photographs of Stockton and his homes, illustrations by Frank O. Small, Albert Herter, A. I. Keller, Peter Newell, and Arthur B. Frost (Stockton's friend, neighbor, and purported model for Mr. Rudder Grange), the Shenandoah edition collected most of his best novels and stories into twenty-three volumes, and was issued between 1899 and 1904.[93]

This project exposed more readers to Stockton's better works. His favorite, *Ardis Claverden,* for example, sold second only to *The Late Mrs. Null* from August, 1900, to February, 1903, in the Shenandoah edition whereas it was on the bottom of the popular edition sales for the same period.[94] But another purpose of this "monument to his genius" was to reward Stockton by creating a further source of income for his family in case of his death. The reward turned out to be picayune: in the two and one half years before and after his death in 1902, the combined sales for all Scribner's volumes amounted to less than $5,000, the amount that in his prime Stockton could command for a single story from a magazine. In England, matters were equally bad, even discounting the hyperbole used when publishers talk to each other. His English publisher, Cassell and Company, told Scribner's that *John Gayther's Garden* was published posthumously in 1902 at "a substantial loss. It was only because of our admiration of Mr. Stockton's powers as a writer . . . that we undertook to publish this last volume from his pen."[95]

A standard pattern involving extremely popular writers is that their books do not sell for a period immediately after their death. That pattern held true for Stockton. The Boy Scouts of America in 1913 wanted to print 5000 fifty-cent copies of his *The Adventures of Captain Horn*, movie agents wanted to purchase his copyrights, and people were transposing his stories into musicals and stage plays, but these sources did not pay much.[96] Marian might report in 1905 that Stockton's books were still "well-thumbed in the children's department of Carneghie Library" in Washington D.C., but they were not being bought. In fact, his brother William, co-executor with Marian of his estate, complained that royalty income by 1907 was down to one hundred dollars per year.[97]

Taxation also became a problem, with the New York tax assessor in 1905 claiming a percentage of $12,000 in royalties, an injustice that was not solved until after Marian's death in 1912.[98] To obtain money, she was forced in 1902 to sell both their beloved homes, Claymont and The Holt, and Stockton's relatives housed together to economize. By 1905, childless Marian tried to write children's stories to make money, a notion she had dismissed as "absurd" three years earlier; she was unsuccessful, she felt, because her ideas were "so terrifically unorthodox" and her heroines were "poor little heretics."[99] On March 28, 1909, Stockton's niece, Louise, who had been his amanuensis while he lived at The Holt and who may have inspired his concept for *The House of Martha* (1891), died young and poor. By 1911, his surviving siblings, William and Louise, were poverty-stricken, with no hope that matters might improve.[100]

One fresh insight about Marian comes in a letter from William to Charles Scribner for August 16, 1910, marked "Personal and Confidential." Marian was "not fully responsible," according to William: "she has never been able to live in peace, with any member of the family, for any length of time, because of her strange hallucinations and eccentricities, but she always gets over these in time, and will go back and act as if nothing has occurred, and is as sweet and pleasant as any one could be, until something new happens." While this assessment must be qualified by possible family squabbles over Stockton's dwindling estate and by advancing age, William's opinion suggests Stockton's marriage was not as staid as one might assume.

Throughout his career, Stockton's marriage was presented as a happy one, partly to preserve the image of "a reigning favorite" whose contented home life was the picture enthusiasts demanded just as today they demand news of arguments and extramarital affairs. The bulk of Stockton's stories deals with courtship and marriage and the attendant themes of independence, self-growth, and character evaluation.

On July 31, 1893, Marian wrote to Charles Scribner to give her opinion on marriage occasioned by a book on divorce by Robert Grant: "we think on the whole his 'reflections' are in favor of the marriage state in spite of its drawbacks, although it may not answer the question 'Is marriage a failure?' to the satisfaction of those who think—or pretend to think it is." Marian enjoyed this divorce novel and admitted the drawbacks of marriage. One wonders if she included herself among those who thought, or pretended to think, the institution was a failure. If William's account of her strangeness is at all reliable, perhaps Stockton did not have to look far for a model of his willful, destructive, or eccentric heroines. Wrapped in a cloak of gentility, the age does not tell beyond William's "Personal and Confidential" letter.

In a personal assessment of a quite different sort—his own career—Stockton offered his most revealing feelings in a letter of November 5, 1900, to Robert Underwood Johnson:

It seemed very odd to me that your letter should have arrived just when it did. Last night, I dreamed a dream, to the following effect; my house and everything I possessed burned down and I had nothing left but one suit of clothes. There being no reason why I should stay here, I went to New York and proceeded immediately to the Century office. There I gathered all of you around me; you, Gilder, Buel, and I think Carey, was there. I then told you I had assembled you in order to inform you that I had determined to give up humorous writing. You, with one accord, exclaimed that you thought that would be a bad thing, that you had no doubt, if I were to try, that I could write in a humorous vein, as well as I ever did. To this I replied, "Oh, it is not that! I can write humorous stories if I want to, but the readers of to-day do not care for them; the public taste has altered; humor is no longer fashionable. I shall write no more humorous stories." Seeing that I was in earnest you ceased to try to persuade me.

Now, is it not very strange that, the next morning after a dream like that, I should receive from you a letter asking for a humorous story?

Well, we shall see. If you can take care of the reading public, I will see what can be done about a story.[101]

Two years before his death, Stockton was quite aware that his writings, like his mustache and use of a quill pen, would soon be thought quaint and antiquated. History proved him right for a variety of causes. First, the "Gay 90's" was long considered a frivolous age with no literature of any great importance. It was not until the 1930s that Henry Seidel Canby declared in *The Age of Confidence* that, "the time has come to think of the nineties as more than a small town joke."[102]

Second, the same problem that dogged Stockton during his life trailed him afterwards—the eclipse effect of "The Lady, or the Tiger?" People who know that story feel they know the writer and do not read more of his work, though they enjoy and admire "The Lady." Even those who are familiar with *Rudder Grange* and *The Casting Away of Mrs. Lecks and Mrs. Aleshine* are unaware that if a complete collection of Stockton's works were assembled, it would amount to more than thirty, perhaps even fifty volumes.

Finally, best-selling writers until the 1970s have been disdained as beneath critical attention and have been written off as "pop lit." Science fiction especially has suffered from this contempt, and a reprint of Stockton's science fiction was not produced until 1976—and even so it is incomplete. Today, however, some American critics like John Cawelti, Ann Douglas, William Spengemann, Leslie Fiedler, and Russell Nye are turning their attention to the field of popular literature in general and the domestic novel in particular. The methodologies, perspectives, and formulas they are refining provide the tools for the first time to do the work of evaluating adequately a once-reigning favorite. The time is ripe to test the appraisal made by *Harper's Weekly Magazine* upon the occasion of Stockton's death: "he was as distinct an embodiment of the American spirit in one sort as Mark Twain was in another."[103]

CHAPTER 2

"A Master Workman"

AS a journeyman writer, one dependent on the popularity of his books, Frank Stockton's concepts of the function and purpose of art were tightly interlaced with the reading, cultural, and publishing facts of his times. Hence the logical way to approach his art is first to study briefly the era in which he flourished; then to examine his "artist's models" from literature and life; then to explicate his own special esthetic as set forth in his stories, letters, and essays; and finally to assess the culmination of all this as it emerges in his art as a peculiar combination of the realistic and the absurd, which may be called "The Garden of the Grotesque."

I *"The Great Public"*

In 1934 Henry Seidel Canby concluded his *Age of Confidence* by saying that the time had come to consider the pre-Naturalist period from 1876 to 1900 as something more than a small-town joke. Since then, studies have ameliorated the situation, but they still tend to concentrate on those literary giants like Henry James and Stephen Crane who eclipse the period, or on the popularity of writers like Horatio Alger and F. Marion Crawford, or on vast social, political, and economic influences.[1] Today, as a consequence, much good information exists about the great artists and the dime novelists, but the most original and telling phenomenon of the era has been ignored—the "middle-brow" reader who was Stockton's principal audience, the same audience that made Mark Twain's lectures successful.

Today this readership is primarily responsible for causing "serious writers" like Saul Bellow, Robert Coover, John Updike, Joyce Carol Oates, Tom Robbins, and others to appear on best-seller lists. They constitute a readership that expects good writing and demands an entertaining story. They might grow impatient with the subtleties and indirections of a Henry James, and they are quite aware that the adventure stories they read are no more than potboilers or pleasantries perused to pass time. As Warner Berthoff explains, this middle-brow reader in the 1880s was a new phenomenon made possible by the growth of the American middle class as a result of industrialization and urbanization.[2]

While an entire book could be written about this readership, I shall focus on seven characteristics relevant to Stockton's work. First, as Howells's *The Rise of Silas Lapham* (1885) shows, readers were heirs of the Genteel Tradition and were concerned with conscience, morality, improvement, and uplift. Magazine editors who considered themselves this audience's spokesmen deplored the fact that novels like Stockton's did not sell as well as cheap thrillers, and complained that "'Gore' and 'realism' seem still to pay both author and publisher better than genuine literature."[3] To promote superior writing, people like Mrs. Bobbs of Bobbs-Merrill publishers in 1905 wanted to print Stockton's "A Piece of Red Calico" and "The Lady, or the Tiger?" in her volume of "representative American humor," and a Chicago schoolteacher in 1893 wanted to include some Stockton to insure "a better class of readers [i.e., of school anthologies] for the schools of the West."[4]

The obvious problem with this improvement concern is its encouragement of censorship, a second important element of the age. As editor for *St. Nicholas,* Stockton himself protected the public by rejecting one story for "a less painful" one, exactly what later happened to his own *The Girl at Cobhurst.*[5] Since to insure maximum income a practicing writer had to serialize his story in the magazines before publishing it as a novel, he had to pass through the sieve of the restrictive magazine editors. A middle-brow writer, then, had in fact three masters, as Stockton explains in an 1896 essay: the reading public, the magazine editor, and the book publisher. All had different conceptions of the nature and function of literature.[6] All apparently agreed that a writer could introduce sinister snakes into his literary gardens, but they must be handled with silk gloves. As a consequence of such unwritten censorship, personal libraries of the day were notable for what they excluded. Henry Canby (1878–1961) describes what reading material was available to him as a youth in his family's library: "no [Thomas] Hardy; no Whitman (naturally); no Mark Twain except *Innocents Abroad*—he was a cheap and flippant writer; only a little Poe; . . . quantities of Longfellow; no Melville of course; no Emerson and Thoreau—it was not until my college days [c. 1898] that I came under their pervasive influence in the original texts!"[7]

In the preface to his collection of stories called *Afield and Afloat* (1900), Stockton mentions that one tentative title had been "Love and Water," but he feared the phrase would be misconstrued to mean diluted love as in "scotch and water." The fear was real, for love and all other subjects risked dilution to suit public taste. Writers like Alger, Crawford, and Davis accepted dilution. Others like Stockton chose the alternative of including sinister truths but camouflaging them with pleasantries. As Stockton specified in the same preface, "on the edges of the most dreadful precipice fair vines and blossoms often grow, and we are lucky if we can pick the flowers and blossoms without tumbling into the deep ravine."[8]

Canby calls this era the Age of Confidence, for the middle class was confident that individuals of character would continue to rise in society. Since the vast middle class was new, they were intrigued with themselves as shown by the lack of demand for "soap operas." That fascination constituted a third literary concern. There was no need to transform "ordinary life into the luxuriantly romantic," to use Manuela Soares's phrase, because middle-class life was considered fascinating in itself. Members would instead buy tickets to see Howells's more realistic plays about "the drama of a broken tea cup."[9] While Thoreau in *Walden* boasts of returning an axe sharper than when he borrowed it, women in *The Casting Away of Mrs. Lecks and Mrs. Aleshine*, one of Stockton's more popular novels, take equal pride in leaving a borrowed house cleaner than it ever was. "I could see by the proud light in their eyes," says the narrator, "that they felt their superiority to ordinary women, although they were properly resolved not to show such feeling."[10]

The rich, such as the banker and restaurateur J. Weatherby Stull in *The Hundredth Man,* are usually evil. The rich man is denounced to his face by middle-class heroes as "a coward of a proprietor, with a ham sandwich for a soul, and a stale one at that."[11] Strikers in the same novel are absurd or misguided. Lower-class individuals, when obedient and aware of their place, are fine, but akin to thieves when not. In *The Adventures of Captain Horn* and its sequel *Mrs. Cliff's Yacht* a lower-class man turns robber and is tortured to death. The good middle-class folk on whom he preyed send money to ease the lot of his poor, uncomplaining mother. The name Stockton bestowed upon this man is "Banker," thus striking two class targets with one pointed barb. Pomona, the heroine of several novels spanning twenty years of Stockton's career and his first popular adult character, is a diamond in the rough. The diamond is her potentiality to become a staunch middle-class person; the rough is her lower-class servant background.

In a sketch that Howells considered one of Stockton's finest, the title character, Mr. Tolman, vacations from his successful business by opening a bookshop which he then bequeathes to a young married couple, thus making them happy. This act of charity allows him to return refreshed to his business, much to the chagrin of his clerk, who had hoped to become manager. Yet the story is structured so that the reader's heart is entirely with Tolman and the newlyweds; the disappointment of the working-class man is without interest, and the reader would have to read carefully indeed to uncover this one serpent in the general happiness of the story. Even in fantasy stories like his still-popular children's story, "The Griffin and the Minor Canon," the lower and upper classes are equally detestable; only children and those in middle-class positions like the minor canon are kind, truthful, and trustworthy.

The middle class's self-pride sometimes became arrogance as its contempt for the rich and disdain for the poor indicate. It expected that business, which made the vast middle class possible, could solve all social ills as in Edward Bellamy's *Looking Backward* (1888); corporations could stop war as in Stockton's *The Great War Syndicate* (1889). In Stockton's *The Captain's Toll-Gate* the son of Captain John Asher's best friend is in the theoretical-mathematics department of a "freshwater college" whose president is a professor of mental and moral philosophy. Asher comments, "Even the head Professor of Theoretical Mathematics would never get to the top of the heap. He is not useful enough for that."[12] The Captain dismisses speculative subjects as useless and sees administration, a form of business, as "the top of the heap."

Yet this business orientation is complex. The Captain sees no anomaly in a philosopher-businessman. He may not know the worth of theoretical mathematics, but he values the humanities as a necessary complement to business instincts. He is a utilitarian but no cultural slob. Even with private property, that *sine qua non* of the middle class, business transcends mere selfishness and involves moral and philosophical considerations so that the issue develops complex problems that occupy many pages of *The Casting Away, The Hundredth Man, Captain Horn,* and *Mrs. Cliff's Yacht.*

The middle class might be property, business, self, and class centered, but it had a strong sense of social responsibility and propriety lumped under the heading, Duty—and writers had to deal with this interplay of business and morality. However, as Canby says, this concept was more a sense of personal honor than a fear of what neighbors might think.[13] Those like the greedy banker J. Weatherby Stull, who is more concerned with appearances than morality, are inferior in character though their social position is high. Influenced by American Transcendentalism with its emphasis on self-reliance and spiritual law, the American middle class could not embrace that stultifying sense of social pressure that John Galsworthy and others depict as the hallmark of English Victorianism. Stockton's heroes and heroines are obsessed with harmonizing the tricky antitheses of a personal sense of right with conventional mores, a tension felt even in the domain of etiquette. Since being refined seemed to verge on being British, nationalistic pride therefore suspected refinement as patriotic disloyalty.

Thus Stull in *The Hundredth Man* gives his restaurant an English ambience, but the American farmer who battles Stull, Enoch Bulripple, hires American waiters as strikebreakers: "With a bold, undaunted air they strolled up and down the rows of tables . . . like volunteer firemen . . . with the peculiar intrepidity of shuffle known only to waiters of this class. In strong untrammeled tones they rang out the orders . . . tossing to each diner his pasteboard check with an accuracy of aim that was sure to deposit it upon some restive article of food."[14] Stull sees such action as "ruinous profanation"; the strikers, led by Bencher, who punningly claims the restaurant seeks "to lay its vile yokes [yolks] upon the necks of its employees," view it as scab labor. The entire point of *Pomona's Travels*, besides its opportunities for humor and travelogue, is for Pomona to figure out how to accept the best in British culture, whose literature she loves, while retaining her American character.

Such complexities qualify Canby's label for the age. Certainly Americans had confidence, but their confidence was in themselves, not in their era—a sense of impending doom formed a fifth major characteristic of the age. The personal resources of Mrs. Lecks from New England and Mrs. Barb'ry Aleshine from Meadowville, Pennsylvania, are strong enough to weather any catastrophe. The first disaster occurs when their ship sinks, and the ladies are not surprised. Impending shipwreck was a constant possibility, whether involving an actual ship or a metaphorical ship of state or of society. Half of Stockton's fiction takes place on the water, and to be "at sea" seemed a fitting depiction of the times. Of the many causes of this malaise, two in particular deserve reiteration—the loss of faith in male leadership and the fear of war.

The first is aptly demonstrated in *The Hundredth Man* when Enoch Bulripple retires to his hotel room. On his wall a "large lithographic picture of the death-bed of Jonathan Edwards" is conspicuously displayed, but Enoch could spare no thought for the expiring religious leader because his mind was occupied with business plans.[15] Even strong male leaders seem fragile, and women must shield them. In *The Captain's Toll-Gate* the heroine, Olive Asher, saves both her uncle ("the only hero I have ever met") and the President of the United States from an anarchist by shooting the anarchist through the head with his own pistol. A woman must protect the official leader (the President) and the natural leader (her uncle) from society's dangerous elements. For her services, she is rewarded by "being sacrificed to the stock market," in that her motivation for murder is kept secret.[16]

The incident is a reflection of the unsteady times. In the decade prior to *The Toll-Gate*'s publication in 1903 the following political leaders were assassinated: the mayor of Chicago (1893), the president of France (1894), the governor of Kentucky (1900), the king of Italy (1900), and the President of the United States, William McKinley (1901). The Gay 90's may be characterized by madcap bicycle riders called scorchers, but the cyclists pedaled over rickety bridges at full flood. If they ever stopped pedaling, they would quickly realize the unsteadiness of the vehicle. Only one's own motion kept the bike steady, kept it moving. In one of Stockton's last novels, *The Bicycle of Cathay* (1900), the hero is overwhelmed by events whenever he rests his bike. His only safe respite is provided by a physician's daughter.

The strongest endangering blast to the bicycle ride of the era blew from the winds of war. As Angus Wilson explains, from 1893 to 1895 war with England seemed inevitable; after 1900, war with France appeared probable.[17] While these particular wars were averted, the Spanish-American War of 1898 was not. Aware individuals knew that future wars were linked with America's international prestige. War was good for business, and business propped up the middle class, but war was also anathema to the middle-class's domestic values. Moreover, even the concept of war with England as the erstwhile "mother country" was moot. In 1860, in his *A Northern Voice*, Stockton had spoken of "the two great Anglo peoples" of North and South. But the population of the United States, thirty-one million in 1860, had swollen to fifty million by 1880 and seventy-six million in 1900, many of whom were not of Anglo background. In 1885 the Statue of Liberty was dedicated, its famous motto welcoming "the teeming masses." Plurality of ethnicity had meant only two "nationalities" in 1860, but by 1900 it included at least two dozen varieties.

Hence six main concerns of Stockton's readership have been described: a campaign for moral improvement; a practice of censorship; a fascination with middle-class, middle-brow lifestyles; confusion over the interplay of business interests and moral or spiritual values; a sense that society faced impending wreck; and the loss of faith in leadership models. The seventh issue—woman—is integral with the other six and is paramount in Stockton's art. The painter, James McNeill Whistler, cited another name by which the epoch is known, the Mauve Decade: "Mauve?" he said, "Mauve is just pink trying to be purple."[18] The traditional connotations of these two colors—femininity and royalty—are suggestive.

During and after the Civil War women were becoming more self-reliant. In 1865 Vassar College opened; in 1875, Smith. Stockton's stories constantly promote college education for women in contrast to the prevailing chauvinist notion that it was a waste. In 1890 social reformers like Lucy Stone, Elizabeth Cady Stanton, and Susan B. Anthony were living, public forces to be reckoned with. Pursuing a different but no less public tack, Jane Addams founded Hull House in 1889 and later became renowned for several books on politics and sociology. Social pressure combined with legal clout to aid less activist women, as when Harry Thurston Peck, with whom Stockton had collaborated on *The World's Greatest Masterpieces,* suffered a nervous breakdown and committed suicide over the humiliation resulting from a breach of promise suit in 1910.

With respect to literature, women readers dictated what sold, causing Thomas Beer to complain of their repressive influence that squelched serious writing. William Dean Howells, concurring that women were influential, felt male repression would be worse:

> The man of letters must make up his mind that in the United States the fate of a book is in the hands of the women. It is the women with us who have the most leisure, and they read the most books. They are far better educated, for the most part, than our men, and their tastes, if not their minds, are more cultivated. Our men read the newspapers, but our women read the books; the more refined among them read the magazines. If they do not always know what is good, they do know what pleases them, and it is useless

to quarrel with their decisions, for there is no appeal from them. To go from them to the men would be going from a higher to a lower court, which would be honestly surprised and bewildered, if the thing were possible.[19]

Stockton was always conscious of this feminine audience. The gardener-narrator of *John Gayther's Garden* is well aware that the anonymous Mistress of the House is his real master, not her oft-absent husband who is merely the nominal head of the household. Gayther-Stockton pays close attention to his Mistress's reactions to his stories. He seeks to provoke her without alienating her, to evoke her better qualities without sounding didactic. When he realizes he has crossed the boundaries of his Mistress's sense of good taste, he appeals to the Daughter of the House, who represents the next generation of reader, one who Stockton expects will allow the writer greater freedom to pursue his art.[20]

To illustrate here the subject of women as readers and characters two examples may be cited: *Mrs. Cliff's Yacht* (1896) and *The House of Martha* (1891). Of the former, William Lyons Phelps in *The Advance of the English Novel* (1916) said that although he read and enjoyed *The Adventures of Captain Horn* four times, he found this sequel poor because "it represents a mental attitude flatly contrary." Yet Stockton's main interest was in Mrs. Cliff's mentality, to which *Captain Horn* was something of a preface. From the adventures that made Mrs. Cliff rich, he moved to a consideration of how this middle-aged woman would handle her wealth. Instead of investing her money in stocks to make more money, she spends her funds on charities that benefit people as near as her neighbors and as far away as peasants in Peru. Instead of ridiculing this type of woman as Charles Dickens does with Mrs. Jellyby in *Bleak House* (1853), Stockton extols the virtues of middle-class, middle-aged, middle-brow womanhood, much as he did with the less wealthy Mrs. Lecks and Mrs. Aleshine. Mrs. Cliff would have been Stockton's answer to Kate Chopin's criticism of motherly women in *The Awakening* (1899).

The House of Martha, an even greater accomplishment for its time, would probably strike a modern reader as boring. That reader would then be surprised to discover that Stockton's audience found the novel "racy and entertaining," with "vivid characterization."[21] Not much happens. A reclusive young man, wishing to record his memoirs, hires a secretary from the House of Martha, a religious order on Roman Catholic lines. When he falls in love with her, her mother superior sends her away. After searching for her for two hundred pages, *she* finally finds *him*, and they marry. To understand why it was considered "racy," even when one knows that the relationship mirrors that between Stockton and his niece when they lived at The Holt, one must examine the novel's era.

In 1912 George Bernard Shaw was to write *Pygmalion* (later famous as *My Fair Lady*) wherein an uncouth flower-girl is trained to be a lady. Compared to Shaw's story, Stockton's is indeed racy, for it involves not the transition of a flower-girl into a lady, but just the opposite—the transformation of a nun-like lady into full flowering womanhood. The amanuensis had been recording the man's notes in a niche behind a screen. A wasp scares her from her recess into the open, and her nun's cap falls to reveal luxuriant hair. The nun's femininity ripens with each chapter, and her maturation energizes the hermetic male into becoming an active, forceful person. Women in the nineteenth century, as Ann Douglas says, learned to turn their sterotype of saintliness to their advantage, although the price was a loss of individuality.[22] Douglas would be impressed with Stockton's inversion of the stereotype, in which the saint becomes an earthy woman.

Such daring, complexity, and originality are not the mark of a mere hack. Stockton's contemporaries, like Davis, Crawford, Burnett, Susan Warner, Mary Jane Holmes, and Alger, would not have made the attempt. At the other extreme, Stockton's female characters may equal Crane's or Howells's, but they never match the sensitivity and complexity of James's or even Chopin's women. They tend to operate as role models rather than as individual psychologies. The issues they face may be more diverse socially, but their inner portraits usually lack personal life.

II   *Literary Models*

William Dean Howells's *Literature and Life* (1912) claims there is often no difference between literature and life, a notion seconded by other members of the Realist and Naturalist movements which began in Stockton's day. Stockton subscribed to this idea so enthusiastically that one suspects he was being satirical. He told an interviewer that writers, like painters, should have professional models, a point that Henry James had seriously explored the same year in "The Real Thing" (1893). In "My Bull-Calf" Stockton's artist becomes successful only after he drags a real bull into his studio in order to paint it. In

"Our Story," which is about the literary process, the author-hero says that characters should "be drawn from life, for it would be perfectly ridiculous to create imaginary characters when there were so many original and interesting personages around us." The story ironically becomes Stockton's self-portrait.[23]

One pastime of interviews was to ferret out living models. C. C. Buel believed the book illustrator, Stockton's friend, Arthur B. Frost, was Mr. Rudder Grange, and he makes Stockton assure him that Mrs. Lecks and Mrs. Aleshine were ladies Stockton knew in New England and that his black characters were based on real blacks in Virginia. William Werner is glad to discover that the male boarder in *Rudder Grange* was a Mr. Francis Boardman. Howells asserts that Roland Clewe, the hero of Stockton's science-fiction novel *The Great Stone of Sardis* (1897), is modelled on Thomas Alva Edison, and the laboratory at Sardis, New Jersey, is really the wizard's Menlo Park. When Stockton wins an archery contest, he quickly exploits his experience through literature.[24]

Though there is some worth in viewing Stockton as a Realist, one can be misled. One of Robert Louis Stevenson's favorite Stockton stories was "The Wreck of the *Thomas Hyke*," wherein a ship submerges but does not sink and the passengers make themselves quite comfortable aboard this vertical ship, which is neither technically afloat nor gone to the bottom. Stockton explained he got the idea for this story by asking himself, "With all the many sea stories written, is there any kind of shipwreck not yet discovered?"[25] Such questions of invention naturally lead Stockton away from reality as a model into fantasy.

In *The Stories of the Three Burglars* Stockton satirizes writers like Crane and Davis who felt they must experience firsthand the events they describe. In "The Pilgrim's Packets" a Stockton persona complains, "My story . . . has been objected to by the Realists. In fact, they have gone so far as to call it absurd. . . . The Materialists and Rationalists of literature will have none of me. . . . They object to my machinery and send me to the children. But I have nothing for the children. There is a moral purpose running through my story—a purpose for maturest minds." The moral of this story is essentially absurd, as the hypothetical Rationalists and Materialists warn: problems that are the result of ignorance are sometimes "solved" by solutions based on another, perhaps greater, ignorance. Stockton's contribution to fantasy, a technique that Frank Baum would later develop in his Wizard of Oz series (1900–1917), was to displace unearthly beings with more familiar ones: a fairy is the child-reader's persona, the giant a loving uncle, the genies representatives of adult strangers. Or, as Stockton said in 1896, his work can be divided into two general types involving the interplay of Fantasy and Realism: "The world of fancy invaded by the real; the world we live in as seen through spectacles of more or less fantastic colors."[26]

Hence Stockton was no thorough-going Realist, for he loved the fanciful. Nor was he a Romancer, because, as William Lyon Phelps explains, his droll humor acted on the Romantic genre "like prussic acid."[27] Stockton was essentially an absurdist humorist, but his times had not yet invented such terms. Critics consequently were baffled. Was *Captain Horn* a burlesque or an adventure novel? Was his pirate story *Kate Bonnet* serious or satirical? They could not decide, for the novels did not neatly fit any conventional form. Howells admitted in 1897 that after twenty years he finally developed a feeling for when Stockton was joking and when not, although he still was not always sure.

Still, when Stockton was asked by *Munsey's Magazine* to contribute an essay on his favorite novelist, he chose two Realistic writers—Daniel Defoe and Charles Dickens—in order "to join in the work of the great forces of evolution by promoting the survival of what it considers the fittest."[28] Daniel Defoe's great contribution, according to Stockton, was that Crusoe "owed his human existence to his surroundings. He was an outgrowth of a story." Defoe's organic technique inspired Stockton's method of painting the scene so realistically that the characters seem a natural part of their setting. When the characters behave oddly, their behavior seems plausible because of the realistic backdrop.

This is the "solid rock" Stockton admired in Mark Twain's art: "Mark Twain is a high jumper, but he always jumps from the solid rock of fact and is not afraid of breaking his neck by falling back upon it."[29] According to Stockton, Henry Rider Haggard's *She* (1887) is less successful artistically because its exotic setting fails to achieve a realistic base. Howells interprets this idea with respect to Stockton's art, using the metaphor of an airplane: "His aeroplanes take their flight from the solid earth, from a firm basis of reasonable fact, and then sweep through space with all the apparent ease of the bird [in contrast to Twain's "high jumping"] that sails on sleeping wings. You rest safe in their impossibility, and are as delightedly content in their power to bring you to the earth again as if you had never left it. . . . You admit the premises, and the rest inevitably follows, as you desire it should."[30]

Dickens, who had lapsed in popularity in the 1890s, was esteemed by Stockton because his characters seemed representative types of humanity. "Sarah Gamp is seen beside you on the ferry, though you can't recall what novel she's from," Stockton says. Whereas Henry James developed strong personalized characters, Stockton was more concerned with types which reflect essences of psychological or social models. The main theme of *The Hundredth Man* clarifies this point. Its hero, Horace Stratford, a Francis Stockton persona, "was not an idler."

He was a man of ideas, and his principal business in life was to work out these ideas, either to please or benefit himself, or for the pleasure or benefit of others.

At present he was engaged in the study of a character, or it might be better said, in the search for a character. It had come to him, in the course of his reading and thought, that in every hundred books on a kindred subject, in every hundred crimes of a similar kind, in every hundred events of a like nature, and in every hundred men who may come within one's cognizance, there is one book, crime, circumstance, or man which stands up above and distinct from the rest, preëminent in the fact that no one of the others is, or could have been like it.[31]

Stockton's characterization ran counter to the Naturalists, who depicted their characters as insects, depersonalized forces, or as straws in the wind. In seeking authorial objectivity, the Naturalists maintained an emotional distance from their characters, an effect which violates what Stockton calls "the great principle" of literary art, whereby "the author who believes in his characters and loves them will make them real beings, who shall live with his readers and be held by them always as companions and friends."[32]

Stephen Crane was noted for consuming one cigarette after another; Stockton for his "rare collection of pipes." The one image suggests self-destruction and burning out; the other, serenity and and tolerance. Where Twain decided, "Man is the cruellest of the animals and Life a tragic mistake," Stockton's version might have been, "Man is the quirkiest of animals and life an amusing absurdity." That is the sentiment of *The Squirrel Inn* when a woman complains that the plot is becoming bewilderingly complicated and puts the blame on the queer design of the house, the reality in which they live. "Things didn't turn out as I expected them to," she says, "and I suppose they never will; but it always was my opinion, and is yet, that nothing can go straight in a crooked house." Another Stockton persona answers, looking "reflectively in front of him":

> "It strikes me, Susan, that our lives are very seldom built with a hall through the middle and the rooms alike on both sides. I don't think we'd like it if they were. They would be stupid and humdrum. The right sort of a life should have its ups and downs, its ins and outs, its different levels, its outside stairs and its inside stairs, its balconies, windows, and roofs of different periods and different styles. This is education. These things are the advantages that our lives get from the lives of others.
>
> "Now, for myself, I like the place I live in to resemble my life and that of the people about me. And I am sure that nothing could be better suited to all that than the Squirrel Inn." (198)

Stockton's love for his characters and his desire to make them "friends and companions" are partly responsible for his success—and for his one great failing. An obituary puts it kindly: his characters are not as "strung up" as in Sarah Orne Jewett or Mary Wilkins Freeman. How-ells is more outspoken: "It is, perhaps, an inevitable consequence of [Stockton's] view of human life which concerns itself but little with the great moments of emotion, that there are frequent failures in proportion."[33]

Such is the danger of taking Defoe and, to an extent, Dickens as one's models. Such, too, is the effect of having a father and older brother famous for the emotionalism and severe seriousness against which Stockton rebelled. Moreover, Stockton evidently distrusted those "great moments" as being Romantic if not sentimental self-indulgence parallel to Arthur Thorne's obeisance to "seriousness" in *The Hundredth Man*. Although Thorne preferred the novels and ballads of Thomas Babington Macauley, he "read [Herbert] Spencer and [Thomas] Huxley and [John] Ruskin, and was a steady student of [Dante Gabriel] Rosetti and [Robert] Browning. The Proper, in his eyes," says Stockton, borrowing a scene involving Little Jo and a Bobbie in Dickens's *Bleak House,* "was a powerful policeman, leading by the collar a weeping urchin, who represented the personal inclinations of Arthur Thorne."[34]

Stockton names other writers in "My Favorite Novelists": Victor Hugo, Honoré de Balzac, Alexander Dumas, Alphonse Daudet, Thackeray, and Cervantes. Toward the first three Stockton bears little affinity, except for the record of society that he attempted, as did Hugo and Balzac, and for the attraction to a Dumas-type romance only to satirize the genre. With the last three the link is more sure, for they all employed a seriocomic method glossed by a good-humored authorial tone. The name of the ship that brings the hero home to start a wild series of science-fiction adventures in *The Great Stone of Sardis* is the *Thalia-Euterpe*—the muses of comedy and lyric poetry—and Stockton and the other three writers are noted for daring to mix these seemingly unblendable modes.

Stockton mentions a great many other writers in his prose. Some, like Mark Twain, Charles Dudley Warner, Emile Erkmann-Chatrian, are recommendations to his reading public; others, like Frances Burney and Mrs. Radcliffe, are cited as fine early reading from which his public's taste should have been weaned. Sometimes he makes suggestions for further reading. If readers liked his "The Lady in the Box," he suggests they might enjoy Edmund About's similar story. Occasionally, literature is a test, as in *The Captain's Toll-Gate* when Olive learns that the mind of her schoolgirl idol is neither wide nor deep because he is unfamiliar with Charles Lamb's essays. Also, he cites writers to chide his audience, as when they prefer Elizabeth Barrett to Robert Browning, because she is easier to understand, and when they decline to read Eugene Sue's *Wandering Jew* (as his father had declined to do) because its theme is unpleasant.

Then again, Stockton will use references to other writers to exercise his wit, as when he says in *The Vizier of the Two-Horned Alexander*, a tale of an immortal man, "Ah, Maria Edgeworth—there will never be another!" and does not explain if that is good or bad. In *The Squirrel Inn* a schoolteacher, wishing to preserve Dickens for all ages and cultures, translates him into Latin and then back into prosaic, uncolorful English. The result is hilariously bland, with Dickens's style shorn of all vitality. Finally, of course, he uses literature as allusion to enrich his own art, as when he gives his main character in *The Associate Hermits*, who is anything but heroic, the epic name of Hector.

Stockton's broad list includes classical and modern, foreign and domestic writers, and his eight favorite novelists are Spanish, French, or English. But Stockton's art is strictly within an American tradition, though not the traditions represented by Melville, Emerson, or Edwards. Puritanism, in Stockton's writings, is simply irrelevant, as illustrated by Jonathan Edwards's neglected death-portrait in *The Hundredth Man*. Transcendentalism is useful only to the lower classes who would profit from more self-reliance. To the middle class, a Whitman converts to a rich man's librarian, a Margaret Fuller settles down to marriage, and a Thoreau goes west to work for the railroad in *The Associate Hermits*. Melville's heroic symphonies sound discordant to the Mauve Decade. His great white whale becomes Stockton's "crab" in *The Great War Syndicate*, a submarine which immobilizes warships by grabbing their rudders with a mechanical pincer. The reclusive temperament of the lawyer that Melville criticized in "Bartleby, the Scrivener" becomes sensible behavior in Stockton's detective story "Struck by a Boomerang." Melville's noble savage Queequeg becomes a loyal, domesticated servant, Cheditafa, in *The Adventures of Captain Horn*.

While Stockton was uncomfortable with the heroic traditions of Melville, Emerson, and Edwards, he fit well, as did Twain, into the tradition of human limits, a tradition whose leading lights are Charles Brockden Brown, Hawthorne, and Poe. A brief analysis of two fantasy stories, "The Lady in the Box" and "The Magic Egg," and one novel, *Ardis Claverden*, should show Stockton's partnership in this tradition of limits and his uniqueness within it.

In "The Lady in the Box" (1899) electrical shock awakens the heroine from a forty-year sleep induced by hypnotism. While these plot devices are similar to H. G. Wells's *When the Sleeper Wakes* (published the same year) and to Edward Bellamy's enormously popular *Looking Backward*, the story's themes are more similar to Brown's *Wieland* and Hawthorne's "The Birthmark" in being more individualistic and philosophical than sociological and political. His issues are those of the individual sacrificed in "the interest of science and for the advance of the World," of the heroine's belief that she has been used "shamefully and wickedly" by her husband, of the conflict between head and heart, reason and love, science representing rationality and poetry representing imagination, and nature versus science where nature ultimately reigns supreme: "nature was resuming her authority over the lady."[36] These issues are keynotes of the Brown-Hawthorne-Poe tradition of limits in which Stockton worked.

"The Magic Egg" (1894) is a solid example. Herbert Loring, returning from the Far East, organizes a show of his souvenirs for "a private few" (students, idlers, friends—i.e., Stockton's imagined readership). After forty-five minutes of fireworks from Korea, he places an egg on a plain pine table. The egg grows huge, cracks, a cock emerges, crows, struts, and then returns to the egg which becomes whole again. The crowd is ecstatic, but decides the next day that the display was merely a trick, a rather dull trick at that. Indeed, as soon as the novelty wears off, the "private few" forget all about the magic egg and remember only the fireworks, much as history would remember "The Lady, or the Tiger?" and forget "The Magic Egg."

Loring's fiancée, Edith Starr, who had come to the demonstration late, knows that the egg was only an egg, and that the transformation only seemed to take place because the fireworks had hypnotized the crowd. Her assessment is even more harsh than in Sherwood Anderson's similar story "The Egg" (1921). "Everything was a sham and an illusion," she decides. "Every word you spoke was untrue." You would have "taken away my reason and my judgment, as you took them away from all those people and . . . made me a tool of your will— glaring and panting with excitement at the wonderful things you told me to see where nothing existed. . . . But now I know that nothing was real, not even the little pine table—not even the man!"[37]

Like Brown, Hawthorne, and Poe, Stockton is concerned with questions of illusion and reality, absurdity and nothingness, will and manipulation, especially with respect to woman's fear of being manipulated by males. Moreover, like so many of his stories, this one is about his own art and art in general. The "private few," his readership, would forget the wonderful creation of life (the entire drama of life in an eggshell) which the artist-magician manages. The audience remembers only the pyrotechnics, the superficiality of plot, humor, and character type.

But most importantly, Edith is more right than she knows. Her assessment pertains not only to Loring's show but to art and reality. The artist does create an illusion of condensed life in order to make his readers "pant and glare with excitement," but the show is an illusion. The cock in the story is imaginary, but in terms of the story's reality the pine table is meant to be taken as actual; yet the story itself is a fiction, an illusion. Indeed, all reality may be illusory, in that everything people deem important may be merely a pretense of significance. Perhaps meaning is merely a trick of the eye; perhaps nothing in reality is "real, not even the little pine table—not even the man." Literally speaking, that is true, for there is in fact no egg upon the printed page, just as there is no real windmill which Don Quixote takes for a real giant. The possibility of total illusion, the story suggests, may be true for Reality at large.

This point is Stockton's firmest link with Poe, even though he only once commented directly on Poe in declining an invitation to speak at the fiftieth anniversary of Poe's death: "To do honor to Poe, is an honor to every man who honors him. A half century has passed since the death of our poet and romancer and no man has not yet [*sic*] appeared who is worthy to stand beside him in his chosen field of literature, but the stars of his intellect—and they are many—shine all the brighter."[38] A single story reveals Stockton's debt to "our poet and romancer." When an artist couple, the Chiverleys, fall on hard times in *Ardis Claverden*, the usually gentle husband badgers his wife until she breaks down in tears. He captures her misery on canvas and creates a painting that far surpasses anything he has done. "Do you mean to say," his wife exclaims, "that you spoke to me as you did to make me look that way?" He answers, "Not to make you look so, only to keep you so until I caught the angelic woe." Stockton pushes right up to the dreadful theme of Poe's "The Oval Portrait," but where Poe's story ends in death, Stockton returns the lovers-artists to a life of renewed harmony. "And now," Mr. Chiverley continues, "for joy, peace, rapture!"[39]

Poe's major depiction is of the nothingness of existence, the void of life, what he called "the blackness of darkness." In this same novel, Stockon presents parallel scenes of nothingness in black and in white. The first occurs in a cave where the stalactites, pits, damp, and dark cause a boisterous city braggart to "feel the chill of terror for the first time" in his life. "This horrible emptiness of blackness bewildered him, and he was afraid." The other scene takes place in a forest bathed in winter moonlight where a group in a sleigh is lost because the snow has magically transformed the familiar wood into a strange place. "Nothing could be more dreadful than fairy-land! Even the beauty that had been made the present scene more terrible to her. There was no beauty now; everything was cold, pale, spectral, and awful!"[40] Again Stockton broaches Poe's most sinister themes; again he, after unveiling the void, returns the curtain and continues his story. The city slicker is rescued from the cave, the sleigh leaves the forest fairyland guided by the horse's instinct. Like Poe, Stockton is conscious of what he called "the deep ravine"; unlike Poe, he wished to gather also the "fair flowers" growing on the ravine's lip.

In addition to theme, the two writers compare in the technique known as "the grotesque," an art term that Poe had used in describing those short stories that concentrate on unusual and hyperbolic but not supernatural characterization and setting. Howells had noted that Stockton's stories contained "Grotesquerie in abundance," and Theodore F. Wolfe referred to "the grotesque mental pictures . . . portrayed upon his page."[41] But where Poe's chief end of the grotesque is horror, Stockton's is humor.

Thus while Poe is Stockton's literary progenitor, Mark Twain is his contemporary cousin, and Stockton, in what may be one of the best early essays on Twain, perceives that Twain's humor is often a mask for dire, Poesque insights. "The humor is merely sprinkled on the rest of the substance," Stockton says of Twain. "It is like the fun of a circus-clown taking the money at the door; he may be a queer fellow, but he means business."[42] Two pages later, Stockton reiterates,

It is well known that the actor of comedy often casts longing glances toward the tragic mask, and when he has an opportunity to put it on, he often wears it so well that one cannot say that he has no right to it. The same pen-point that will make a man laugh out in church, if gently pricked by it, will not only slay a bride at the altar, but will go entirely through her and kill her father who is giving her away. The figure with the tragic mask stalks through much of Mark Twain's works. . . . Long live that comic mask! With such a forest of points for it to catch upon, there will be no danger of its ever being lost, and while Mark Twain lives he will not cease to be the man of the double stroke—the Bismark of humorists.

Twain, Stockton, and Poe shared the dark philosophy of life, but in technique Twain worked in Realism, while Poe and Stockton preferred the Grotesque. In their artistic intention, Stockton and Twain sought to be humorous—Twain broadly so, Stockton subtly—while Poe horrified. All were misconstrued in their times, and the most Stockton's admirers would dare to acknowledge is that one should "look behind the jest" because the "fun is only the color [of Stockton's writings], and not their substance. Their substance is human nature thrown into relief by a glass which imparts a comical hue."[43] Indeed, Stockton saw himself as he saw Twain: a new form of American humorist who not only told jokes but was a philosopher, a narrative artist, and a story-teller as well.[44]

Though Stockton appreciated Poe's philosophy of darkness and his artistic strategy of the grotesque, he shunned what Poe called his "arabesque," his exotic, baroque style. In doing so, Stockton's style is closer to Twain's Realism, though he never abandons the fanciful and the whimsical. As an artist, Stockton had much to say, and the main points can be collected under two headings: the "plain fishing" of narrative style that resembles Twain, and the "grotesque" of technique whereby Poesque horrors are domesticated for the readership of his era.

III *"Plain Fishing"*

Howells, who had championed Twain but had been puzzled by Stockton, wrote in 1897 that the latter had brought his calm and easy comic style "to higher artistic perfection than it has ever had before." Howells compares Stockton's narrative style to "the flavor of honey. . . . He does not give it us in the comb, but filters it through the fine mesh of his fancy."[45] Stockton must have appreciated the compliment, for throughout his career he worked for the development of art while writing popular-selling stories.

While the Naturalists and Realists were redefining "average" to mean lower class, and while James was analyzing highly intelligent and sensitive beings, Stockton focused on the middle-brow middle class. He felt that this social segment provided sufficient material for creativity and opportunities for artistic experimentation, even though in *The Vizier of Alexander* the immortal man admits, "Poor people frequently have more adventures, at least more interesting ones, than those who are in easy circumstances. Possession of money is apt to make life smoother and more commonplace; so, in selecting the most interesting events of my career to tell you, I naturally describe periods of comparative poverty."[46]

His audience's ample leisure time made it possible for Stockton to develop one of his style's most notable features—the "fox chase" of a plot, as Buel puts it, or his ability, to use Howells's words, to "make the turn of the story rather than the crisis of a plot account for everything," where Stockton's immediate wit is independent of any definite conclusion.[47] In a sense, Stockton did for the short story what Montaigne did for the essay: getting there, not arriving, is all the joy. This virtue makes criticism difficult. Stockton's plots are so full of twists, wrinkles, and kinks that they are challenging to summarize clearly.

In "That Same Old Coon," a local color sketch, a wise, old, crusty Virginian, Martin Heiskill, informs Stockton, who appears as a character: "Well, the fun in a coon hunt ain't so much in gittin' the coon as goin' arter him—which is purty much the same in a good many other things, as I tell ye."[48] The point of the story about coon-hunting and literature is limpid, but its complicated plot would require three pages to outline. In the novel *The Merry Chanter* a zany crew has many enjoyable experiences, but they never reach their destination; indeed their ship does not even get free of its harbor of origin. In *The Squirrel Inn* the eccentric design of the hotel mirrors Stockton's art, which takes unpredictable turns and twists. The intricate internal mechanism becomes more intriguing than the story's climax. Sometimes, as "The Lady, or the Tiger?" illustrates, his stories end with no climax at all.

Because he respected his middle-class readers, Stockton cast barbs at writers who did not. In "The Queen's Museum" he attacks elitists who feel people are stupid because they do not share their specialized interests. The populace shunned the Queen's rare collection of buttonholes but flock to the museum when the scope is widened to include something for every worthwhile interest, a scope that Stockton hoped his own literary museum offered. In "The Cot and the Rill" and *The Captain's Toll-Gate* he pokes fun at landscapers who bring in 1200 Italian workers aiming to achieve "the highest grade of true naturalism" in three days, and thus points up a paradox of Naturalism: no matter how objectively the artist tries to portray an undoctored "slice of life," the result is always by necessity artificial.

In terms of his own art, the fact that Stockton did not fall back upon the Pomona stories even though a ready market existed for them argues for his artistic integrity. In *The House of Martha* he assures his utilitarian audience that literature is as worthwhile a profession as medicine. In *The Hundredth Man* his heroines and heroes enjoy photography while superficial people scorn this art, preferring "the real thing" that the camera selected. In *Pomona's Travels* and *The Rudder Grangers Abroad* Pomona argues that literary characters are as real as historical figures, and that literature actually enhances the significance of places, peoples, and times. In "The Conscious Amanda" the narrator says he prefers fiction to other prose writings because it reveals more about the depths of the mind; it allows more room for the expression of deep motives.

Stockton's respect for literary art caused him to experiment. *The Vizier of Alexander* is a post-Modernist work which invites the reader to dream about history. The novel also presents Stockton's greatest experimental interest—point of view and reader perception—a concern he much admired in his favorite poet, Robert Browning, in such works as "In a Balcony" (1855) and *The Ring and the Book* (1869). Stockton's demand that readers interpret "The Lady, or the Tiger?" for themselves was not an anomaly, and he demanded interpretation to various degrees of greater subtlety in many other stories. In *Pomona's Travels* Jonas complains that he feels like a character in a novel, which of course he is. In an interview Stockton claimed that sometimes his characters protested that they wished to behave differently than Stockton intended.[49] "A Landsman's Tale," an anti-adventure story with its anticlimax, offends the listeners who complain about this narrative technique, and the listeners become part of the technique themselves.

Stockton's "Our Story" develops this same technique in a startling way. The narrator tells about the problems and excitement he and his lover share in the literary process when they try to write a story about a man staying at their hotel who also turns out to be an author. Abruptly, in the final sentence, the narrator informs the reader that he and his lover never finished their story, but their character—the author—did write his, and this, "Our Story," is it. The "narrator" and his lover turn out to be the characters, their "character" turns out to be the narrator's persona, and the narrator turns out to be Stockton himself. This experimentation with narrative point-of-view is far more innovative than Stockton's more popular "The Lady, or the Tiger?", and it is a technique Gertrude Stein later used in her *The Autobiography of Alice B. Toklas*.

The Vizier of the Two-Horned Alexander uses narration within narration. Stockton as narrator also listens to the narration of an immortal man. While the immortal's autobiography may have been of prime interest to the adventure-loving segment of Stockton's audience, Stockton as narrator and listener is more interested in the responses of the immortal's current wife, who as a Quaker represents high moral principles. His main interest is in precisely what points of the Vizier's two-thousand-year story defy her tolerance and reveal the idealist's bias.

Throughout *John Gayther's Garden* apperception is the principal theme. As the garden group listens to various stories, they speculate, revise, object, and editorialize. The auditors and the narrators together create the garden of tales. Sometimes they suggest alternate denouements. Sometimes they offer interpretations of what the story truly reveals in contrast to the narrator's expressed intention. Sometimes the theme is so revealing when a comic sketch becomes serious that all shun mentioning it: "This story was not commented upon."[50] The reluctance of the audience to intrude is itself a comment on the forcefulness of the themes, specifically in this case conflict between husband

and wife, the fragility of friendship and other human bonds, the eternal immanence of death.

Finally, Stockton's experimentation demonstrated itself in satire, where he would write a story following the formula of a particular sub-genre like Romance, Gothic, Adventure, Pirate, or Detective Story, and then parody the sub-genre usually by inverting its formula. Such is the point of "Struck by a Boomerang" in which the detective discovers himself to be the unwitting murderer, a satire on the Sherlock Holmes stories. In *The Girl at Cobhurst* Stockton composes the most treacly, sentimental passage ever, not because he was unable to create a love scene but because he intended burlesque. When a man in a garden lets his beloved know he loves her, "She raised to him a face more brightly hued than any peach-blossom—rich with the color of the ripe fruit. Ten minutes after this, two wood-doves, sitting in a tree to the east of the lettuce-bed, and looking westward, turned around on their twig and looked toward the east. They were sunny-minded little creatures, and did not like to be cast into the shade."[51]

An equally maudlin burlesque occurs in *The Hundredth Man* when a jilted lover, who manages a restaurant, arranges his oysters on ice to spell "Gone are all the hopes I cherish." When his former love and his new one come to dine, he gives the oysters in the first three words to his ex-lover and the rest—"the hopes I cherish"—to his new love.[52] Small wonder even perceptive critics like Howells were confused about when Stockton was serious and when satirical. By playing with conventional and popular formulas Stockton made his intention whether of romantic love or gentle humor difficult to interpret.

Such interest in experimentation indicates Stockton might have been quite successful as a modern writer, but he respected the reader expectations of his day too much to range far beyond conventions, and he was well aware of the delicate balance he attempted. In "A Tale of Negative Gravity" the hero hides his new invention because the world is not ready for it, as another hero also does in *The Great Stone of Sardis*. In "His Wife's Deceased Sister" the creator of a superb, new kind of story secretes it because he fears the public's reaction.

That public, as Stockton saw it, wanted well-crafted not avant-garde stories. *The Merry Chanter* insists a good story must be lively. *Mrs. Cliff's Yacht* believes plain writing is the best writing. Madame La Fleur in *The Girl at Cobhurst* is proud of her "culinary art" which is "thoroughly wholesome, delicious, and artistic." These qualities classify her as belonging "to the very smallest class of angels that visits human beings."[53] In *Pomona's Travels* a roast carver believes the proper execution of his craft to be as important as Disraeli's international machinations. In *John Gayther's Garden* Stockton's gardener explains how he prefers close spade work to fancy devices for aerating the soil. In "Our Archery Club" the best archer is disliked by the club because of his unorthodox method; the goal indeed is to hit the target but "in the proper way."

In "Plain Fishing" Stockton defines "the proper way" of his art which is a middle way between hack writers and esthetes. Stockton's persona, Peter Gruse, says the story of a boy who catches many fish with a bent safety pin while a man with a new fishing rod catches none is "a pure lie." In contrast, the fancy fly angler seems to Peter as cruel as a cat with a mouse. The narrator, skeptical of Peter's advice, tries an unnatural-looking fly, but the great fish he seeks "probably considering it a product of that modern aestheticism which sacrifices natural beauty to mediaeval crudeness of color and form, . . . retired without evincing any disposition to countenance this style of art."[54] Esthetics, quiet for nearly a hundred years after the Romantic articulation of Coleridge and Wordsworth, had burst forth during the latter part of Stockton's career. The Pre-Raphaelite movement in England was proving controversial; Henry James, Howells, Norris, Hamlin Garland, and others produced their book-length esthetic declarations. In addition, the magazine critic became a force to be reckoned with. Two years after Stockton's death, his wife commented on this new phenomenon: "There is a great distinction to be drawn in these days between the *reviewing* public and the *reading* public."[55] Since reviewers praised Stockton's posthumous *John Gayther's Garden* while his readership ignored it, the suggestion is that Stockton would have done well with this more critical audience.

But Stockton believed it best to avoid both extremes of advanced stylistic innovation and of formulaic hack writing. His personal artistic conception was to pursue the middle way: " . . . the man that's got the true feelin' fur fish will try to suit his ideas to theirs, and if he keeps on doin' that, he's like to learn a thing or two that may do him good." Stockton ignored hack writers, and he was too genteel to complain about the estheticians except to say: "But what does rile me is the cheeky way in which they [the fancy anglers] stand up and say that there isn't no decent way of fishin' but their way. And that to a man that's ketched more fish, or more different kinds, with more game in 'em, and had more fun at it, with a lot less money and less tomfoolin', than any fishin' feller that ever come here and talked to me like an old cat tryin' to teach a dog to ketch rabbits."[56] Such is Stockton's fictionalized appraisal of his writing career.

But Stockton was not as comfortable with his public as the folksy fish metaphor suggests. In "Our Story" the male writer argues, "Where is the good of a person or persons devoting himself or themselves, with enthusiasm and earnestness, to his or their life-work, if he or they are to be interfered with by the impertinent babble of the multitude?" He is answered by the mother of the artist he loves who is presumably the buyer of his books: "she considered the babble of the multitude a very serious thing."[57]

The one voice in the babble to which Stockton's temperament was attuned demanded that literature be rejuvenating. In his popular fairy tale, "Old Pipes and the Dryad," a dryad, though misunderstood, brings happiness because of her kisses, each kiss making the person kissed ten years younger. In Stockton's "Mr. Tolman," which Howells considered his best "novel," Tolman feels ten years younger for doing good in the world.

Stockton's stories were intended to have an equally refreshing effect. The distinguished critic William Lyon Phelps read *The Adventures of Captain Horn* four times. Howells said "that in a nervous, impulsive, hysterical time like this, when people's intentions so often run away with them, [Stockton] seems almost to have created [his special brand of droll humor] anew. If he has not done that, he has brought it to higher perfection than it has ever had before." Howells's concluding word on Stockton is, "Life cannot be without an object as long as there is the hope of something more from him."[58]

Regeneration was also Stockton's nemesis, for it blinded readers to the complexity of his art. To be sure, one does leave his stories feeling refreshed, but that does not mean they are banal. He did not neglect the philosophical issues probed by the Naturalists and Realists; he only presented them differently. Yet he did paint his flowers to seem so fair that they camouflaged "the deep ravine" of his thought. Like Twain, he wielded what he called "the double stroke." He may seem as gay as a circus clown, but he means business. He believed in "plain fishing," but his hooks were barbed.

IV   Garden of the Grotesque

Marian Stockton said of her husband, "He shed happiness all around him, not from conscious effort but out of his own bountiful and loving nature. His tender heart sympathized with the sad and unfortunate, but he never allowed sadness to be near, if it were possible to prevent it. He hated mourning and gloom. They seemed to paralyze him mentally until his bright spirit had again asserted itself and he recovered his balance. He usually looked either upon the best or the humorous side of life." A *Harper's Weekly* obituary said the unrealism of Stockton's stories "relieved him from the necessity of keeping them true to the ordinary experiences of life and its sarcastic implications." Howells said Stockton "is an author who has done more than any other (except Mark Twain) to lighten the heart of his generation." In "My Well, and What Came Out of It" Stockton portrays himself as an optimist in a world of pessimists, skeptics, and cynics where it is "hard work" to maintain cheerfulness. Stockton's biographer, Martin Griffin, comparing him to G. K. Chesterton, says he "delighted in viewing the absurd and the incongruous and the impossible with a grave, if puckish, wonderment at the essential rightness of the topsy-turvy."[59]

Remembering, however, the metaphors Stockton used to describe Twain, one wonders if these enthusiasts have mistaken the clown's gay colors and funny clothes for the serious business he intends. In Stockton's favorite novel as one example, the same novel (*Ardis Claverden*) that presents two Poesque portraits of nothingness, one in darkness and one in snow, Stockton includes the following: a lynching, a murder, a barn burning, a house burning, two horse thieves, two hangings brought about by the heroine, hints of homosexuality, a duel, and a suicide. This catalogue of catastrophe may cause one to wonder if the characterization of "puckish humor" is entirely correct.

Moreover, the main theme of the novel is sinister, portraying the psychology of its title-heroine who, though seemingly conventional, is driven by dark forces: "Ardis frequently felt herself bored by the effort to establish harmonies, whether between flowers or stars or human souls, but anything of this sort was better than the terrible discordance for which she was constantly looking." One stereotype of the era was that women should be harmonizers, but Ardis felt driven toward destruction and chaos. She feigned acceptance of the stereotype only to hide demonic pressures that may have their root in Oedipal forces which Stockton had already dared to suggest in his short story, "Come in, New Year!"

Though an accomplished painter, Ardis is shown painting only one picture—a woodsy scene depicting her father shooting a rifle at a male figure in retreat. The man she eventually marries, Roger Dunworth ("none of your stuck-up gentleman. He's a plain, common-sense young man."), is the only man in the story who would refuse to pose for her picture. Roger is the only local male manly enough to attract Ardis away from her fixation on her father. Yet the issue is even more complex than that if one follows the sexual imagery, for her last words to her best girlfriend, Norma (for Normal?) are, "My dear child, why didn't you plant gherkins, and then you might have made your wedding-trip ever so much longer. They never grow big." Norma dislikes gherkins: "They can't get bigger than your finger, and how are you to know whether they are young and tender, or old and tough? [Cucumbers] are like human beings ... but gherkins are like imps or dwarfs. . . ."[60] Roger may be manly enough to woo Ardis from Poe's Imp of the Perverse, Freud's Oedipal complex, or masturbatory inclinations, but he is not powerful enough to threaten Ardis's strong egodrives. Her domestic friend, Norma, is the one who marries the other male lead after Ardis rejects him—Jack Surrey, the virile, aggressive urbanite. One of Ardis's favorite pastimes is taming horses; Surrey might be too vigorous an animal to break.

When Surrey sees that Ardis will choose Roger over him, he provokes the other dominant dark chord of the novel by saying, "I imagine it is about as near right as such things generally are." His English friend, Prouter, who develops a homosexual attraction to Surrey, replies, "They are never right. What you read one day is knocked into a cocked hat by what comes along next day. The whole lot is a beastly nuisance."[61] In addition to the imp from within, represented by Ardis, the external universe was chaotic. The internal imp can be split into two forms—biological forces and the death drive. "The Spectral Mortgage" and *John Gayther's Garden* provide two further examples. In "The Mortgage," a sequel to "The Transferred Ghost," the young father yells at a ghost standing on the other side of his child's crib, calling him "you vile interloper." His wife naturally assumes he is addressing their child, and her "mistake" is more revealing psychologically than the surface level of plot. When a woman friend helps the father dispatch the ghost, phallic imagery is again invoked, "the last thing we saw of the once gay Buck Edwards was a dissolving view of the tip-end of a limp and drooping riding-whip."[62]

In *John Gayther's Garden* the sexual imagery of seeds, flowers, and gardens is more positive and natural than the submission-dominance struggle represented by the riding whip and horse breaking. Certainly, Gayther is "intensely jealous" of the Daughter of the House who is young enough to be his daughter, and when he reaches the point when he "would have been very well pleased to break the head of any stray lover who should wander into his precincts," the Daughter reciprocates by telling a role-reversal story of a ten-year-old boy in love with his mother's sister: "I would like to marry Aunt Amanda. I liked her better than anybody else except my mother."[63]

Although the nephew, when nearly grown, foils two of his aunt's romances so that "then my Aunt Amanda had no lover but me," he, of course, is not permitted an incestuous relationship, and his mother and aunt laugh off his queer attraction. The only consolation the Daughter offers is to have the descendant of one of Amanda's lovers marry the nephew's granddaughter, thereby achieving an indirect but ultimate union. Gayther, while rattling some seeds in a pan, is impressed at the Daughter's deep conscious knowledge, points of which she has not the maturity to understand fully. Gayther does, but his libidinal drives toward the Daughter are channeled into performing the role of gardener or teacher and helping her to grow to her fullest potential. Though he can not plant the seed, he takes comfort in cultivating the vine.

This theme is expanded in *The Captain's Toll-Gate*. John Asher has a niece, Olive, who at the age of fourteen had had a crush on Rupert Hemphill, who now clerks for her older confidante's husband, Tom Easterfield. At a marriageable age now, she sees Rupert as little more than a "tailor's model," and feels no attraction to the worldly, oily Emile du Brant, secretary to the Austrian legation, nor to Claude Locker, a would-be Romantic poet of "pickled verse feet," but she resists meeting the son of her uncle's best friend, named Dick, for two reasons. Olive has learned her father is about to marry a girl her own age with whom she had gone to school. Secondly, she erroneously believes her uncle, whom Tom has described as "her truest, best lover," is about to marry. This search for fathers and father-surrogates as lovers is further complicated when Olive learns her confidante, also when fourteen, had loved Olive's father and that Miss Raleigh, her confidante's secretary, had been and perhaps still is in love with her employer's husband, Tom. The many Oedipal variations swirl into a vast complexity of possibilities, but all is resolved genteelly with Olive finally marrying Dick.

The biological-erotic version of the Imp of the Perverse in *The Toll-Gate* becomes the suicidal-destructive variety in *Kate Bonnet: The Romance of a Pirate's Daughter*, the last complete novel Stockton published in his lifetime. The main character is really Kate's father,

Major Stede Bonnet, who, tired of the "humdrum and stupid" life of a plantation owner on Barbados in the early eighteenth century, chooses to become a pirate, not for the reasons Stockton gave—to be independent and to help the poor like Robin Hood—but to engage in "bloody massacres or heartless drownings" and to owe "no allegiance to any man or to any government, [so] that my will is my law and is the law of every man aboard this vessel." The vessel, *Revenge*, becomes feared from Jamaica to New Jersey. Nothing can dissuade Bonnet from this course, not the love of his daughter ("a brave girl who had loved her father with a love which was more than that of a daughter, which was the love of a mother, of a wife."); nor the ridicule of accomplished pirates like Blackbeard; nor the entreaties of his right-hand man, the religious Scot Ben Greenway, to whom even Blackbeard becomes a temporary convert; nor the intervention of the King of England himself.[64]

Bonnet's relative, Felix Delaplaine, established as a foil to piracy, is as "relentless as the bloody Blackbeard" to promote justice and goodness. He tries to adopt the kinder view that Bonnet's drive toward evil is insanity. He tries to believe his kin is "mad as a March hare," but realizes he is in fact sane in the sense of being mentally balanced, yet driven by destructive forces. Ben Greenway suspects this inner impulse is even greater than Satan could feel: "Ye're gettin' wickeder and wickeder; the de'il himself couldna hae taught ye a craftier trick than that."[65] Even when Bonnet is captured and hanging is certain, he goes to the gallows completely unrepentant. His commitment to lawless destruction is total. This wholesale depiction of evil causes barefoot, catlike Dickory Chartes, a personification of the new American as noble primitive awed by civilization's complexity, to exclaim, "But now the blackness of darkness was over everything."[66] This is an era when the reading public was more accustomed to Romantic pirates like Long John Silver in Stevenson's *Treasure Island* (1883) and chivalrous behavior as in Charles Major's *When Knighthood Was in Flower* (1898).

And Bonnet's problem is not his alone; if Stockton makes him unrepentant, he also makes him universal. When Blackbeard makes him his lowly clerk in Belize, Ben mistakes Bonnet's tractable conduct for reform. Bonnet insists it is only want of opportunity that makes him appear civilized. He groans, "I tell you, Ben Greenway, you are mistaken; I am just as wicked as I ever was. And I was very wicked, as you should admit, knowing what I have done."

Captain Christopher Vince, the king's agent who is sent to put down piracy and who falls fiercely in love with Kate, is first seen by Dickory in Vince's fight with Blackbeard as "champion of all good against the hairy monster who struck his blows for all that was base and wicked." But greater familiarity reveals that Vince is as bad if not worse than the evil he was sent to suppress. His posthumous letter to Kate warns, "You have escaped the fiercest love. Had I lived, I should have shed the blood of everyone whom you loved to gain you and you would have cursed me." Dickory sees Vince now as "a viler wretch than even the bloody pirate [Blackbeard] who killed him."[67]

Still Stockton is not done, for the hero who finally puts a stop to piracy, the American captain Ichabod Crane, marries Kate and buys Bonnet's house to begin a family. In the last paragraph, Crane argues with a man that though Bonnet was a dangerous and violent man, his sins have been expiated by the daughter and the house is now blessed, not cursed. His heart rises with his rhetoric until he utters these final lines of the novel: "and if you will not admit, sir, that her sweet spirit and pure soul have not banished from this earth every taint of wickedness left here by her father, then, sir, bedad, stand where you are and draw!"

To defend the goodness represented by Kate, Crane will resort to Bonnet's lethal methods, and the story ends in irony. The extremes personified by Kate, Dickory, and Felix on one side, and Bonnet, Blackbeard, and Vince on the other become blended into one man, who bears the name of Washington Irving's anti-heroic schoolmaster in "The Legend of Sleepy Hollow." But the blend does not produce a golden mean or a happy medium. Has goodness, in Crane's case, converted destruction to its ally? Or does evil use goodness as an excuse to vent its violence? Either interpretation applies; neither excludes the other possibility, an ambiguity that Stockton also exploits in "The Knife that Killed Po Hancy," a deliberate attempt to produce a more complex rendition of the Jekyll-Hyde story.

In two other novels, the battle between good and evil likewise ends ambiguously even though the fight has different dimensions. In *The Adventures of Captain Horn* evil is rampant, and a wrong deed begets more wickedness until it is consumed in its own destruction. The situation looks hopeless for Horn's party shipwrecked on Patagonia, until a crew of criminals led by a servant who has betrayed the Horn party sails into view to kill Horn and his friends and take their treasure. But the cruelty the crooks have shown toward the traitorous guide causes him to turn on them, and Horn is able to slaughter the brigands. Those few who escape are washed away in a flash flood. Nature destroyed Horn's ship, but it also helped him eliminate his enemies. His servant betrayed him, but his second betrayal saved him. The universe on both the human and environmental levels may seem evil, but the evil is either capricious or self-defeating.

In *The Hundredth Man,* to the contrary, the problem is goodness. The entire, complicated plot depends on who can obtain complete rights to a farm to which Hector Twombly, who lives out West, has a legitimate claim though he is unaware of it. Enoch Bulripple, the rural farmer contesting with the urban banker J. Weatherby Stull, who seeks to destroy him, first finds Twombly, who signs over his rights to Enoch, refusing any financial remuneration. Enoch's farm is thus safe, made so by the good offices of generous, kind, unselfish Twombly. However, the problem is that he is so generous that he would do the same for any and all. Had Stull arrived first, Twombly would have signed over his claim just as readily. The pure goodness he represents is not an active force in the universe. It would certainly stand no chance in a battle with the evil depicted in *Captain Horn.* In *The Hundredth Man* goodness is as neutral as the frontier land Twombly seeks to cultivate. Goodness in this novel is as amoral as any natural resource; only the uses to which it is put, usually a result of chance, have positive or negative faces.

This cosmic view differs dramatically from that of the Naturalists with their rigid sense of determinism, and this departure is partly responsible for the neglect of Stockton. Since he did not share the Naturalists' enthusiasm for the science of Claude Bernard as received through the literary techniques of Emile Zola, he has been ignored in this era which has been characterized as the Naturalistic Period, with geniuses like Twain, James, and perhaps Stephen Crane the only exceptions. Such at least is the American view; the British who, as a *Times Literary Supplement* from 1957 admits, do not share "the prevailing mood of American taste for naturalism," are more impressed by writers like Stockton and O. Henry.[68]

Indeed, the mainstays of Naturalism seemed absurd to Stockton. The doctrine of the Survival of the Fittest, for example, struck him as tautological: the "fittest" was that which survived; that which survived was the fittest. To a mind like Stockton's, the concept could have been conceived by Gilbert and Sullivan. On the human level, Stockton felt man as a cultural being was by necessity and definition a gardener or conservationist. He chose what to preserve and what to weed. He showered time, money, and care upon what seemed culturally preferable. The choice may be ultimately arbitrary, even pointless, but within the realm of human values the choice was a choice nevertheless. Indeed, even the choice's arbitrariness highlighted the absurdity of the Survival of the Fittest, since what man chooses to preserve and cultivate becomes the "fittest" by cultural fiat not by blind natural selection.

This attitude emerges in both Stockton's function as a writer and in his philosophy. In *Gayther's Garden* John worries about his reader-patron's response to his tales and flowers. "He knew her so well, and the habits of her mind, that he was fully assured if his fancies should blossom too luxuriantly she would ruthlessly pull them up and throw them on the path. Still he believed she would like fancies, and highly colored ones; but he must be careful about them. They might be rare and wonderful, but he must not give them long Latin names which meant nothing."[69] As a professional, Stockton was well aware that the best stories did not naturally rise to the top of the best-seller list, and that "best" and "fittest" were not synonymous terms. Horatio Alger outsold him; Henry James outclassed him.

In *The Captain's Toll-Gate*, which reads like a precursive satire of Naturalism and Shaw's Life Force in *Man and Superman* (1903), this particular issue is raised to a philosophic level. On one side of her house Mrs. Easterfield prefers weeds to flowers. "The more you think about it," says she, "the more you like weeds. They have such fine physiques, and they don't ask anybody to do anything for them. They are independent, like self-made men, and come up of themselves. They laugh at disadvantages, and even bricks and flagstones will not keep them down."[70] Thus, whenever anything that looks like a flower shows itself, she ruthlessly jerks it out, for she is "determined to acknowledge the principle of the survival of the fittest." By acknowledging it, of course, she determines it. The principle prevails because of her consent.

That choice being made, another is due, one that links weeds with the founding of America, and one that sees beauty in a poisonous, foul-smelling plant that bears prickly fruit. "I also thin out all but the best weeds. . . . Look at that splendid Jamestown weed—here they call it jimson weed; did you ever see anything finer than that with its great white blossoms and dark-green leaves?" Her auditor, young Olive, concludes that Mrs. Easterfield prefers weeds to flowers, but the matter is not that simple. On the shady side of the house Mrs. Easterfield cares for weeds, but on a sunnier side she finds the soil more suited to flowers. "'Everything in its place; weeds are for the shady spots, but I keep my flowers out of such places—this flower, for instance,' touching Olive on the cheek." Stockton thereby brings the subject down from abstraction to the human level where he always plants his garden.

Whereas a Naturalistic writer like Frank Norris in *The Octopus* depicts the abstract principle of the Survival of the Fittest in its relentless operation, Stockton is more interested in considering what fitness is. In *A Bicycle of Cathay* a young man meets many women. Which is fittest? Each has her virtues and flaws. Moreover, the question is relative, both culturally and individually as it applies to the young man and his search for a companion. Love stories have long been spurned as "women's novels," but this slur is unfair with respect to Stockton's novels. On one level, at least, they involve the highly relevant question of what is a fit human being. And that question when suitably answered does not necessarily insure survival. When cultural "fitness" and social or physical survival do not blend, the result is tragedy whose sorrow is ameliorated by Stockton's comic tone.

This is the point of *The Girl at Cobhurst*. By cultural standards, Dora Bannister is clearly head and shoulders above anyone else in the novel not only in height but in financial well-being, social position, breeding, education, intelligence, will power, integrity, and common sense. She is a strong, archetypal woman, and yet in the tepid environment of this novel's universe, with its pettiness, jealousies, bigotries, and insecurities, she can not be a heroine no matter how heroic she is. The novel opens with Dora seeing a doctor because she fears she is losing her mind over being rejected by a suitor whose irrational behavior she can not understand. The problem which even Dora does not realize is that she is not insane, though the world sometimes is. The corollary: in an insane world the sane seem insane, which is much the point of H. G. Wells's *The Country of the Blind* (1911), wherein the one-eyed man is pariah not king.

This issue separates Stockton from the Naturalists so dramatically that the Survival-of-the-Fittest issue seems in comparison a minor skirmish. The Naturalistic mainstay was Determinism, an inflexible cause-and-effect relationship throughout the entire universe under which even chance was subsumed as a special case of causes. Stockton's view of the universe was more like Henry Adams's "vertiginous chaos" in *The Education of Henry Adams* (1907) or like Stephen Crane's cards in "The Blue Hotel" (1899).

Even in his early children's stories he presents this cosmology of chaos. In "Hevi" (1877), "Huckleberry" (1878), and "Sweet Marjoram Day" (1877) from the *St. Nicholas Magazine* the message is that values are relative and contradictory.[71] Which is the greater of life's two largest animals, the elephant or the whale? "Hevi" points out it all depends on special circumstances. In "Sweet Marjoram Day" an isolated city is shrunk by a wizard's pellet, and since shrinkage is uniform in this Lewis Carroll kind of sketch no one notices he is smaller. In "Huckleberry" gnomes give Lois, a goose girl, two bits of advice about life; both bits seem individually true, but each contradicts the other. Lois's plaint is: "How's anybody to do two things that can't both be done?" There is no solution to the chaotic dilemma.

In "The Clocks of Rondaine" (1887) Stockton satirizes Idealists and Naturalists with one sweep. Arla, a fourteen-year-old girl, is bemused that no two of the clocks in her village agree exactly about the time. In order for everyone to celebrate Jesus' birthday at the identical moment, she attempts to set all the clocks the same. She runs into much opposition, many difficulties. She learns about clocks and learns even more about the fallibility, inaccuracy, and irremediable error of human existence. Even her own clock, naturally ten minutes slow, varies its rhythm as it reacts to heat and cold, humidity, and barometric pressure. Overwhelmed by happenstance, she decides to shut her window on the other clocks of the town, and to let her own clock tick erratically along "until sometime when I feel very sure that you are wrong."[72] Stockton urges Idealists and reformers to tolerate human nature with all its many flaws; in the image of the clocks as a mechanical construct that regulates human affairs, he disagrees with the Naturalists' vision of a carefully ordered, precisely regulated, mechanical universe.

Stockton differed from the Naturalists also on the issue of the power of the individual mind and will. Where they saw the individual as an extremely ineffectual entity in the cosmos, Stockton had great faith in him and "faith in the power of mind over mind, of mind over body, and, primarily, of faith in my own mind and will."[73] He believed man's mind could conquer anything, could invent the greatest technological marvel, could accomplish the wildest dream of extrasensory perception. However, Stockton, again like Adams and Crane, felt that though the mind could conquer anything, it could not control the consequences of its creations and actions. Had Stockton lived in this nuclear age, he would have had a timely and relevant metaphor at his disposal.

Such philosophical speculation affected Stockton's esthetics, and

"Derelict, A Tale of the Wayward Sea" (1887) is a fine example in its fusion of three usually distinct if not contradictory fictional modes—the Romantic, the Realistic, and the Absurd.[74] In a tale of shipwreck, nautical details and the presence of sensual items like cigars, books, and brandy create a realistic setting. However, when another derelict steamer appears on the horizon (aptly named *Fidélité* to stand for either romantic faith or realistic fidelity), the extreme improbability of events from which love blossoms is absurd.

In fact, the story has three levels of absurdity. The lowest is the unpredictability of chance, as the aforementioned example illustrates. The second is the absurdity of reason and romance. The hero, Charles Rockwell, whose love (Bertha Nugent of 42nd Street, New York) has been rescued by another captain on another ship, is told by his captain that Bertha will inevitably fall in love with her captain because Captain Guy is very handsome; he wants to marry; he is very attractive to women and could marry every month if he chose; it is a long voyage; Bertha and Guy will be in close proximity, especially in moonlight; and Guy is a notorious lover; he will seem heroic to Bertha as her rescuer. Rockwell listens to these solid reasons without a word and then illogically concludes: "The captain's reasoning seemed to be very fallacious."

On the other hand, Mary Phillips, Bertha's maid, is the strongest character in the story, so capable that it is *she* Captain Guy loves and marries. Mary is also a romantic. When Guy surmises that a shark has probably eaten Charles's floating love note to Bertha, doing no one any good, Mary objects: certainly this lovely message in the shark's innards must have a softening effect on its voracious nature; at least, it is pretty to think so.

But the greatest absurdity is less obvious. Mary has arranged for Charles and Bertha to marry, and rightly so, for in their mutual weakness, incompetence, and selfishness they are well suited. In making the match, Mary, much to Charles's gratitude, has kept some information from Bertha. When the two wrecks were near, Mary had almost rescued them, but Charles's inability to grasp the rope she threw him foiled her efforts. But Mary is unaware of a parallel scene which shows Charles to be worse than she imagines. When he is rescued, his first and only concern is to have his captain sail after his love-note buoy, forgetting all about the *Fidélité* with his loved one aboard. He calls the captain who refuses an "unmanly Fiend!", a name that better applies to Charles. The pair of newlyweds sail to New York on a new ship with Captain Guy in command; the ship's name is ominous—*Glaucus*. Charles and Bertha, in their complete ineptitude, are the true "derelicts" of the title and story. The subtitle pertains to life itself, which is a "wayward sea" where anything might occur, where the best represented by Mary and Guy err, where the two wrecks—Charles and Bertha—might live happily together, where secrets and sinister forces roil beneath glittering surfaces.

When ideas like these are extracted from Stockton's works, they seem gloomy, but that is not the impression when reading them. Even the dismal philosophy in stories like *The Girl at Cobhurst* and "The Derelict" does not sadden the reader, for Stockton's droll comic mask is firmly in place. As a humorist, Stockton has suffered the opposite fate of writers like Emerson and Melville, who have an image of such seriousness that their humor is often missed. Like the early Mark Twain, Stockton is seen as a "circus clown" whose serious business is generally unnoticed. Unlike Twain who, as modern studies have demonstrated, was consumed by the pessimism of his philosophy, Stockton managed what Henry Adams called the primary mood for survival—good temper. The universe might be chaotic, life absurd, mankind driven by biological and destructive forces, disaster and shipwreck always imminent, but fair flowers still bloomed near the deep ravine in his garden. In *The Captain's Toll-Gate*, when the Romantic poet Claude Locker cries out, "Am I not to know whether I am to rise into paradise, or to sink into the infernal regions?", Olive Asher calmly answers, "Don't do either, Mr. Locker. This earth is a very pleasant place. Stay where you are."[75]

CHAPTER 3

Women and Children First

I   *The Spirit of '73*

ONE of the most curious transformations in literary history is how women and children replaced men as fictional subjects in the last part of the nineteenth-century in America. If one recalls literary figures from before the Civil War, one thinks of Natty Bumppo, Ishmael, Ahab, Whitman, and Thoreau. Hester Prynne seems anomalous in this antebellum male pantheon. Emily Dickinson, whose creative powers flourished in the 1850s, was not widely recognized until the 1890s, and she shares fame in that era with James's Isabel Archer, Twain's Huckleberry Finn and Tom Sawyer, and Dreiser's Sister Carrie. Crane's Henry Fleming is certainly heroic, but he is a far cry from the epic heroes he admires. Melville's males reappear in 1891, but his heroes in *Billy Budd* stutter or consign innocents to the hangman. Jack London resurrected the powerful male, but that is in the early twentieth century, and even the autobiographic *Martin Eden* (1909) loses his will to live and commits suicide.

Many reasons have been proffered for this turnabout, some sensible, some specious, and some that mistake cause for effect. The fact that prestigious women's colleges were formed after 1865 seems more a response to than a cause of a new phenomenon. That women bought and read more books than did males from 1870 to 1900 does not account for the change, since that could as accurately be said of the period from 1840 to 1860. That women outnumbered males at the turn of the century—in *John Gayther's Garden* Stockton puts their majority at 16,240—seems statistically negligible since 16,000 in a population of seventy-six million is only .02 percent.[1] So, this startling shift in literary characterization remains a mystery. A brief look at three principal factors can dispel some fog.

First, as Margaret Mitchell's *Gone With the Wind* (1936) makes clear, women during the Civil War discovered they could depend on themselves. The self-reliance Margaret Fuller had preached in the

84

1840s was taught them by necessity in the war. Thus women rose to the fore as ripe subjects for that favorite of American themes—the paradox of self and society, individualism and social responsibility, personal fulfillment and sacrifice, egotism and love. In Stockton's "The Banished King" (1882) a king, worried over his kingdom's problems, takes his cortège of bureaucrats on a visit to other kingdoms. His own kingdom flourishes in his absence under the able administration of his queen. The subjects decide that the king and his cohorts had been responsible for their problems, and they agree that the queen should continue to rule.

If the war taught women they *could* stand on their own, the postwar era told them that they *should*. As many have asserted, men were bungling their management of the society they dominated. The 1872 Crédit Mobilier scandal, the financial panic of 1873 followed by the depression of 1893–1896 which accentuated class divisions, the impasse of the working class and union problems as evidenced by the many, often fatal strikes, political corruption as represented by the Tweed Ring and James G. Blaine's railroad connections, all served to undermine confidence in government as anything but a confidence game. Religious leaders also proved disillusioning. Henry Ward Beecher, the most respected minister of his day, stood trial in 1876 for alleged intimacy with Mrs. Tilton.[2] Ministers as a class, as Ann Douglas has documented, were an endangered species in terms of power and generally resorted to conservatism and reinforced existing stereotypes instead of providing leadership.[3] The most curious thing about "The Lady, or the Tiger?" is that of the millions who must have debated the story, not one has asked the fairly obvious question: Is it not possible that the young man may have "psyched out" the princess? The context of the story rules out giving the male credit for that much intelligence.

Yet some men surely were still successful at politics, business, and exploration. Why did the fiction spotlight pass them by? The answer I propose is the issue of imperialism. Post-Civil War America was growing into a world power, and American writers, as Warner Berthoff explains, were solidly anti-imperialistic because imperialism meant domination through war.[4] Men conventionally have been associated with aggression, dominance, and conquest; women with peace, cooperation, and tolerance. Charles Dana Gibson's "Gibson Girl," tremendously popular especially in the 1890s, may be full of life and vitality and bathe in what some felt was a risqué fashion at the seashore, but she would not set sail in a warship to battle England, France, or Spain. The anti-imperialism of writers like Stockton either coincided with or was interwoven with the rise of feminism. The resistance toward drives for domination manifested itself both on the international and the domestic level. The ethical, moral, and political decision to oppose one world power's intention to subjugate a less powerful nation applied naturally and logically to the tradition of male domination and female subservience.

Such at least was Stockton's connection between the issues. In his anti-imperialist story, "The Skipper and El Capitan" (1898), a strong male character, a Yankee captain, though outgunned, cleverly defeats El Capitan. But the winner loses, and because of a violation of Russia's neutrality rules must pay to have El Capitan's ship repaired; moreover, his daughter, attracted to the underdog, marries the man he defeated. The moral is delivered by the skipper's wife: "It don't pay to conquer," and one is sure her advice is meant to apply to the conventional battle of the sexes as well as to international war.

Similarly, in the Daughter of the House's story in *Gayther's Garden*, her heroine, "The Bushwhacker Nurse," views war and declares, "These two armies are like hordes of demons! Humanity should not permit it!" A deserter, one of three soldiers she has captured, responds, "Humanity has nothing to do with it. A declaration of war eliminates humanity as a social factor. Such is the usage of nations." The Nurse rejects this male advice, just as she has rejected the soldier's advice—a deserter's advice at that—that social restrictions "are often very desirable; they enable us to proceed to a greater distance along the path of duty than we would be apt to go if we could wander from side to side." Instead she chooses to use her pistol to stop the blood and slaughter, and she succeeds, after which she can consider the possibilities of marrying one of her captives, having "liberated" them in all senses of the word. Here in a single story are several interrelated themes: individualism versus conformity; male-female domination; the inhumanity of war and imperialism; peace as an ideal with its emphasis on love, romance, and marriage. One can even say that the quest for ideals shifts from Arthur Dimmesdale's and Ahab's abstract if not mad obsessions to the more domestic ideals of marriage as symbol of communal peace and of the individual as a socially beneficial participant.

It is of further interest that the careers of anti-imperialism and feminism are identical. Willa Cather in *A Lost Lady* (1923) explains that American society opened somewhat to women in the late 1800s before snapping shut in the early 1900s, staying shut until women received the vote after World War I.[5] Likewise, anti-imperialism suffered defeat in the early 1900s when the Rough Rider diplomacy of Theodore Roosevelt became a cult which did not diminish in popularity until the World War. In short, both anti-imperialism and feminism flourished in the last quarter of the nineteenth century, then subsided in influence from about 1900 to World War I, when they finally emerged as powerful social forces with concrete results such as women's suffrage and rejection of the League of Nations.

While the many factors involving the rise of female and child characters in fiction are complex, fixing the date for their liberation is easy—1873, when their editorial declarations of independence were sounded in the founding of *The Woman's Home Companion* (1873–1957) and *St. Nicholas Magazine* (1873–1940). These were the first widely read periodicals specifically for women and children respectively. Earlier magazines had been nominally for them, but the reality was otherwise. *Godey's Lady's Book* (1830–1898), for example, was undistinguished from other magazines feministically. *The Woman's Home Companion*, in contrast, featured popular fiction by women writers. Similarly, N. P. Willis's *The Youth's Companion* (1827–1929) was aimed ultimately at an adult audience as its advertisements show (for unlikely children's items such as clothes, soap, flour, revolvers, Harvard, cemeteries, and body building), and after 1857 was patently a magazine for adult reading; whereas the stated aim of *St. Nicholas* was to print material that children, and only incidentally their parents, could enjoy.

This date in literary history—1873—parallels other feminist events. Besides the founding of women's colleges (Smith founded in 1871, opened in 1875; Vassar 1861, 1865; Radcliffe 1879), the establishment of the Women's Christian Temperance Union, often ridiculed because misunderstood, announced that women meant to take an active, political role which became enough the norm that by the time Stockton writes *The Associate Hermits* (1899) he has a female character attend the feminist convention at Saratoga as a natural and serious part of her role as an educated, thoughtful, and socially involved woman.

Stockton, whose emotion, sensibility, and respect had been directed more at his mother than at his father and older brother, welcomed the rise of children and especially women in literature. He enjoyed the concomitant theme of love not only as what he called "that necessary ingredient" for popular fiction, but also as a vehicle to explore the issues of peace, war, individualism, self-reliance, self-growth, gentility, social duty, and idealism. It is significant that thirty-one of his thirty-two novels have love as a principal theme. That single exception, *The Great War Syndicate* (1889), is thoroughly unromantic. Individuals give way to syndicates, governments bow to faceless business monopolies, heroes are replaced by technology, the entire "males only" performance turns consummately dull and lacks individual vitality.

A similar case pertains to "Mr. Tolman," which presents a successful male. Tolman, however, finds his financially flourishing business enterprise boring and thinks to quit. On vacation, he is much attracted to the extreme coziness which a woman has created in her small bookshop. Tolman can not resist this feminine sanctuary and buys the shop primarily to be able to sit ensconced in the comfortable domesticity of the back room. Alas, he is again successful, and after playing matchmaker for a time, he sells the bookstore to the newlyweds he and the shop have brought together. He returns to his business refreshed, but big business is merely business; it lacks the warm heart of the woman's bookshop.

Stockton's males may be divided into the weak (the larger group) and the strong. Weak male characters are of three types: the quiet narrator, as in *Rudder Grange,* who observes, comments, and records events but who, though he may purchase a house or take the family to Europe, is not an active force, only a minor character; the potentially strong but physically incapacitated, like Peter Sadler, the owner of the large campground in *The Associate Hermits,* who is described in god-like terms as a "king" who "ruled supreme" but whose will is restricted by the mobility of his wheelchair; and finally the physically whole male who lacks spirituality, vitality, intelligence, or common sense. Dr. Lester in *Ardis Claverden* declines to practice medicine because he fears making a mistake. He also loves Ardis deeply, but never works up the nerve to tell her so. He does advise her on other matters, and has been instrumental in dissuading her from pursuing her calling to become a physician. His own weakness has helped to deter a promising young woman from achieving her potential.

Stockton's strong male characters comprise two types. The first becomes either a misfit or a menace. The poet-suitor in *The Captain's Toll-Gate* seems at first a fool, but as the novel unfolds his personality grows. Still, he remains better fit for a reclusive garret than a marriage bed. He continues as an amusement rather than a respected person. Similarly the Thoreauvian male in *The Associate Hermits,* though respected, goes off to try to fulfill his love for nature by working for a railroad monopoly, and the only fit position the Whitmanian Reverend Bishop can find is to be a rich man's librarian. Representing the more dire type of strong male, the powerful businessmen in *The Hundredth Man* and "The Cot and the Rill" have fulfilled Lord Acton's maxim that power corrupts. They are obnoxious, aggressive, and dangerous when not downright evil. Unlike Tolman, they are unmindful of or hateful toward the people around them. If not restrained by a woman's hand, they threaten all society with discord, disappointment, and disaster.

Those strong males who manage to remain uncorrupted serve one of two literary purposes. The lesser may be seen in *The Merry Chanter:* a man assumes he is lord of the manor, even over the *Merry Chanter*, a ship his wife has inherited. One of this novel's objectives is to reveal that though he is legally the head, he is like the wooden figurehead which they keep as "a household god," and his wife is truly the moving force in the family. When the four retired sea captains who are the crew have a question, it is her opinion that they take for law. The other purpose is revealed by the title hero of *The Adventures of Captain Horn*, the best-selling American novel for 1895, and its sequel, *Mrs. Cliff's Yacht.* Horn is far and away the most admirable man Stockton has created in a novel. He is physically powerful, intelligent, honest, experienced, considerate, clever, truthful, and active, and his virtues are rewarded by enormous wealth. Willy Croup, Mrs. Cliff's kin who has only heard about his exploits, imagines Horn to be "a heathen deity who rained gold upon those of whom he approved, and utterly annihilated the unfortunates who incurred his displeasure."[6]

Though Horn might well appear archetypal at a distance, the reader who sees him more closely knows his ideality does not prevent him from being a real, flesh-and-blood character. And yet this paragon's reason for being is arrived at after 770 pages spanning two novels. At a crisis, Mrs. Cliff and Edna, Horn's fiancée, must decide whether to set sail to foil pirates who intend to hijack their hard-earned treasure of Incan gold or to wait for Horn's ship to arrive first. Mrs. Cliff, who has grown considerably into "a true woman," makes the choice: "in the midst of the confused opinions, Mrs. Cliff spoke out loudly and clearly." Her verdict: they should go on without Horn.[7] Thus this paragon of manhood has been established as a mark beyond which women should grow. He is a model women should surpass. In growing fully into independent womanhood, they can leave even the best of males behind.

Stockton's feminism took many years to develop, and one plot device from the Horn-Cliff novels demonstrates the point: the gun, the main instrument of imperialism and also of protection of home, property, and family. Needless to say, it was also a device that social convention banned from woman's use. A gun appears in his first novel, *What Might Have Been Expected* (1874), but it belongs to a boy who sells it to keep an old black woman from the poorhouse. When the boy gets it back, he attempts to teach his sister to shoot a rabbit, but she thinks the animal looks so cute that her heart can not allow her finger to pull the trigger. The feminine stereotype is fulfilled in a young girl; in *The Late Mrs. Null* (1886) another stereotype is echoed by an adult woman whose malicious personality drives her husband to suicide. Since the event takes place at night and the woman is seen running from her house in her bedclothes, one also suspects the problem's cause is sexual.

Nine years later Captain Horn gives Edna a gun to hold, but because of Horn's brave exploits against the enemy, she is not called upon to use it. In the next novel, when the Horn party is again locked in life-and-death struggle, Horn again gives Edna a pistol and "requests her to use it in anyway she thought proper, if the need should come," meaning that she should shoot herself rather than suffer rape.[8] She does use the gun, but not to commit suicide. She shoots it at Banker, the villain of the story, to protect Horn from being ambushed. She misses, but the shots distract Banker enough to save Horn.

By the time of *Kate Bonnet* (1902), the Fate Worse than Death has become a joke, as when Dickory Charter tells his beloved, "should there be need, I will kill you," and the response is "'Thank you very much,' said Lucilla, coolly." Finally, in *The Captain's Toll-Gate* (1903), the heroine, Olive, seizes a gun herself rather than be handed one; she uses it to shoot an assassin through the head, thus saving not only her uncle but the President of the United States. Moreover, though they keep her homicide secret to protect her reputation and to prevent the stock market from falling, her supposedly unfeminine action is not only excused but applauded by the three men whose opinions count most to her.

In Stockton's twenty-nine-year novelistic career much development occurs even with this single device. Yet feminism, sexism, and women's liberation wear many faces, mean many things to many people. Stockton may have been mirroring his readership's changing values, but he had many possible value schemes to choose from. In that way the matter grows complex. Even in *The Captain's Toll-Gate* Olive and her uncle are unable to keep the assassination attempt secret; he tells two people, she three. The uncle declares, "and I suppose that is about the proportion in which men and women keep secrets."[9] A sexist joke crops up in one of Stockton's more feminist novels. Whose bigotry is it—the uncle's whom Stockton is satirizing, or Stockton's in trying to protect his reputation as a humorist even at the cost of cheapening his own values?

Similarly, many of Stockton's heroines attend college, and several are already college-educated: but rarely do any of his women do anything extraordinary with their education. In *The Squirrel Inn* (1891) Ida Mayberry, a teacher and nurse who majored in mental and moral philosophy at Bryn Mawr, shows promise of becoming a successful physician. But other women are suspicious of her. They cling to the stereotype that a woman's heart calcifies if her head is educated, a notion Ida encourages by saying, "if the higher education is of any good at all, it ought to help us regulate our affections." One mother fears leaving her baby in Ida's care because she might quiet the child with laudanum or surgery. The climax comes when the women tease Ida too much about her nursemaid capacity, and she silences them by stating, "learn something about babies! Nobody knows more about babies than I do—I have dissected one."[10]

The joke is admittedly a good one, but who is its target—the sexist women or the liberated professional? The mixed answer comes in *The Great Stone of Sardis* (1898), where Ida reappears as an eminent professor of geology whose opinion is more respected than any male's; but Ida remains oppressed novelistically in that she is not made a main character and culturally in that her professorship is at Bryn Mawr and not at one of the male-dominated universities. The next section examines those feminist issues central to Stockton's art: feminine ideals and stereotypes; marriage as an ideal representing self-growth through union; individualism as it interlaces with social obligation; characters as guides who, unable to achieve full growth themselves, lead others toward self-fulfillment.

II   *Women Young and Old*

When Stockton published *The Late Mrs. Null* in 1886, its sales were described by male critics as "astonishing" and "phenomenal."[11] While it was not as popular as his two earlier successes—*Rudder Grange* and *The Casting Away of Mrs. Lecks and Mrs. Aleshine*—the version illustrated by A. B. Frost sold five thousand copies on the first day and over twenty thousand copies within five months.[12] The male reviewer was mystified over *Null's* success, for it was not as humorous and sprightly as *Casting Away* or *Rudder Grange*. The female reader, on the contrary, knew exactly why she liked the book. A female rebel is the subject of *Rudder Grange*, but she remains a domestic who must depend on the middle class for employment. Lecks and Aleshine are strong but old widows who extol feminine stereotypes. *Null*, however, gave readers a young, active woman who, though marriage becomes her goal, is able to thrive without a man by her side.

Annie Peyton, an employee of a New York information agency, accepts a detective assignment to travel though Virginia and investigate the background of Junius Keswick, who happens to be her long-lost cousin. Because society frowns on a single woman traveling alone, she pretends to be married to a Mr. Null (Nothing), whom she later has to pretend is dead when people wonder why he does not enquire after her. This ruse allows Annie "to go where she pleases and take care of herself." When she describes her nonexistent husband as "He couldn't be better if he tried," she damns every real-life male spouse. "It would be impossible for us to be more attached than we are," she further stresses. "We never have had the slightest difference, even of opinion, since our wedding day. Why, I believe we are more like one person than any couple in the world." This independence makes Annie a woman who "likes to cut her clothes after her own pattern,"[13] which image assured his readers that Stockton had given them a vigorous and self-reliant woman who would not shock them by doing something too extreme. She might create her own dress designs, but she would not, like Kate Chopin's Edna Pontellier, go naked.

Annie, with "the dash, the spirit, and the bravery" of a heroine, still must avoid the extremes of narrow-minded men and vengeful women. One male, Lawrence Croft, carefully calculates that the right mate for him is Roberta Brandon, a dull sort who was named by her mother "as near as she could come to the name of her only brother" and is known by the servants as "Miss Rob." He is ruled by his head and ignores his heart. Annie finally teaches him that emotion is as important a factor as intellect in human relations. While Croft, like Annie, prefers "original and startling" methods to "traditionary and conventional" ones, he is inept at them. He breaks his leg and passes the time reading of "a defeated general who made the cavalry charge into the camp of the victorious enemy."[14] The other leading man, convention-bound Junius, proposes to his beloved Roberta for Croft while the latter is lame. In a reversal of the John Alden and Priscilla Mullins legend, Roberta accepts the proxy proposal even before Junius can finish making it.

Another inversion surrounds Mrs. Keswick, who has driven her husband to suicide, foiled the marriage between Junius and Roberta, whose father had proposed to her unsuccessfully forty-five years earlier, and generally has made herself hateful with her "Amazonian" ways throughout the novel. When the couples are paired off—Croft to marry Annie, Junius to marry Roberta—Widow Keswick (born "Matty Pettigrew," again showing Stockton playing with role reversal through name gender) claims "Bob" Brandon's forty-five-year-old proposal and cleverly traps him into marriage via an old love letter.

Has she been caught up in hymena! euphoria? It seems more likely she has gone mad. But Matty inverts the seemingly inevitable Romeo and Juliet conclusion by jilting Bob at the altar and exclaiming, "Before he was born, his family defrauded and despoiled my people, and as soon as he took affairs into his own hands, he continued the villainous law robberies until we are poor, and he is rich."[15] Instead of the Romeo and Juliet ending where the two houses of Keswick and Brandon are reconciled through romantic love, Matty, like Shylock in *Measure for Measure*, insists on exacting unrelenting vengeance.

Stockton allows the reader to choose how far to extend the moral. The reader can leave it as Matty's blood feud, or she can interpret it as a statement of class struggle, or of sexist domination of women as "my people." One may also wonder if Roberta, to whom Croft has proposed in a letter, will later feel toward him as Matty does toward Bob. The main function of Matty Keswick is to warn Annie against the bitterness of Matty's selfishness and revenge while Stockton urges her to be more liberated than the novel's males and Roberta.

The same technique , a subtler Lady-or-Tiger choice, is at play in the Christmas story, "The Great Staircase at Landover Hall" (1898), in which an ideal woman named Evelyn, or Eve, dies from a fatal fall down the staircase when she trips over a child's toy. Does Stockton suggest that children are impediments to a woman's evolution up the stairway to full growth? He leaves the question to the reader's values to decipher. Will the newlyweds who give the story a seemingly happy ending ascend toward their ideal communion or become stuck on the dull ground of reality? That depends on whether the reader chooses to interpret the name of the mansion as "Land over all."[16] The mother in

Frances Hodgson Burnett's *Little Lord Fauntleroy*, which was published the same year as *Null*, would gladly sacrifice everything to see her son rise socially and materially, a sacrifice that Stockton definitely felt was absurd.

Opposed to woman's total self-sacrifice, Stockton, at least in 1886, was afraid to advise women to be too self-assertive, because of retaliation from a vindictively sexist environment. Even removing one's boot in mixed company, even in the woods on a picnic, was considered socially offensive in Stockton's stories. Calling a person of the opposite sex by his or her first name was tantamount to a marriage proposal. Arthur Thorne in *The Hundredth Man* speaks for many men and women when he asserts that women belong at home and college is a waste. When the narrator's wife in "As One Woman to Another" (1897) learns that Grace, a woman of genius, is being held captive by her mad scientist uncle, she declares, "I do not believe in such imprisonments in this enlightened age, and in this country." Grace is in fact a physical prisoner; worse, though brilliant she is a psychological prisoner, for she will not escape from her uncle because she fears causing a scandal.

In *The Associate Hermits* a man complains that a woman guide he has hired charges as much as a man; Mrs. Archibald, whose conventionality has been tilted askew by her woodsy Transcendental experiment, proclaims quietly but radically: "Why shouldn't she, if she is just as good?" When women behave sensibly, the Master of the House in *Gayther's Garden* laments, they "ruin great ambitions by too much common sense." When they are imaginative, immature males like Ralph in *Captain Horn* complain, "That's just like a woman. They are always popping up with new and different views of things." With men like these, women can not win.

Sometimes sexism is double-barrelled, as in *The Associate Hermits*, where a man is sure a woman will accept his marriage proposal because, "She is only a woman, and can no more withstand me than a mound of sand built by a baby's hand could withstand the rolling wave." In the next paragraph the man's sister summons him, and "He was only a man, and could no more withstand her than a mound of sand. . . . " Sometimes, too, regressive sexism hides behind the mask of liberalism, as in *A Bicycle of Cathay* when the nameless hero is advised—

if you want to be successful in making love, you must change your methods. You cannot expect to step up in front of a girl and stop her short as if she were a runaway horse. A horse doesn't like that sort of thing, and a girl doesn't like it. You must take more time at it. A runaway girl doesn't hurt anybody, and, if you are active enough, you can jump in behind and take the reins and stop her gradually without hurting her feelings, and then, most likely, you can drive her for all the rest of your life.

But the hero has had enough experience with women to know that they are not quite as tractable as dumb brutes:

I did not like to have any one know so much about my mental interior—or to think she knew so much. I did not like to feel that I was being managed. I had a strong belief that if anybody jumped into a vehicle she was pulling he would find that she was doing her own driving and would allow no interferences. I liked her very much, but I was sure that away from her I would feel freer in mind.

Often Stockton will play prejudice off prejudice, as when he puts highly sexist statements in the mouth of a Frenchman who is distrusted because of his foreignness. Though his wife can smoke cigarettes, he by no means considers her anything more than a toy and tells her, "Think of nothing else but your trust in me," while in his heart he believes, "O Woman! What art thou, and of what strange feelings art thou made! Thou hast the beauty of the flower, and the intellect of the leaf."

The Frenchman's American listeners are less sexist, and their diversity of opinion illustrates the issue's complexity. "Each one had his or her own thought. The Master of the House thought: 'What a clever woman!' The Mistress of the House thought: 'Just like a Frenchman!' The Next Neighbor wished she had been in the balloon to pitch the tiger on him. The Daughter of the House was fascinated by the beautiful, ferocious tiger. And John Gayther [jealous that the Daughter may like the Frenchman] thought, as he looked wistfully at the Daughter of the House: 'I am glad he has a wife!'"[17]

Wary of sexism, Stockton often offered coded messages calling for independence. In *Pomona's Travels*, when Pomona's husband ties her tricycle by a cord to his bicycle to control her, she cuts the cord and pedals madly off to forestall a cruel British stag hunt. The reader can blink at the umbilical symbolism if she chooses, even though a hundred pages later Pomona explains how she much prefers her mother's influence and pedigree to her father's. In *Mrs. Cliff's Yacht* Willy (called "William" when proposed to) Croup hurls oaths at the engineer to save the ship from being rammed. The captain insists that the engineer would not have reacted quickly enough had she not cursed, but Willy swears she will never swear again, even to save a ship, and suffers nightmares over her unladylike conduct. Even in the children's story, "The Battle of the Third Cousins" (1885) in which a girl is raised to a cabinet minister's post, her position as the "Minister of General Comfort" is about as powerless as a Vice President's spouse.[18]

The greatest single "code message" Stockton employed was marriage. His conservative readers could rest assured that regardless of how superior and restless an individual will be, he or she will soon settle down to a peaceful marital state. The more progressive reader, on the other hand, could appraise the same marital possibilities in terms of their openness to individualism, their assessment of individuals as social beings, and their relationship to sexuality and emotion.

Simply put, Stockton always maintained that a right marriage offered the surest chance for happiness, and that a mismatch was "a crime."[19] In one of his finest short stories on this subject, "The Christmas Shadrach" (1891), the choice is made clear. Mildred Bounce in her early twenties is "as fine a woman in every way as one would be likely to meet in a lifetime. She was handsome, of a tender and generous disposition, a fine intelligence, and a thoroughly well-stocked mind," but the nameless narrator, though he wants to keep Mildred as his friend, wishes to marry a lesser individual for three reasons. First, she is slightly prettier. Second, since he has known Mildred since they were children, he feels that to choose Janet would be a better demonstration of free will over environmental influence. Third, Janet, in contrast to Mildred, fulfills the stereotype of conservative womanhood by exhibiting "a tender trustfulness, as if I were a being on whom she could lean and to whom she could look up. I liked this," asserts the narrator. "It was very different from Mildred's manner. With the latter, I had always been well satisfied if I felt myself standing on the same plane."[20]

Complications arise when a Dr. Gilbert courts Mildred, when the hero and Mildred exchange books from their ample libraries, and when the hero gifts Mildred with that part of iron ore which passes through the smelter without effect and which supposedly possesses the magical property of giving to humans "something of its power to keep their minds cool when they are in danger of being overheated." When the complications are resolved, the hero does marry Mildred, not the trustful Janet. The story ends with their honeymoon visit by train to an iron works to witness "the wonderful power of man, air, and fire over the stubborn king of metals."[21]

All the marital elements that Stockton would develop at greater length in novels are present here: the conflict of free will and determinism; the stereotype of the spouse represented by the clinging female as opposed to the fully developed woman; the problem of individualism and love; the necessity of achieving a total relationship by blending intellect with passion, intellect symbolized by books, science, and technology (the "iron," which supplants gold as the "king of metals"), and passion signified by air, fire, and magic (the shadrach). By making this a Christmas story, Stockton is saying that a happy reconciliation of the foregoing issues is as serious an event as the birth of Jesus should be to Christians.

In particular, passion (Freud was to publish *The Interpretation of Dreams* in 1900) had to be treated gingerly, since Stockton's culture stressed gentility. *Ardis Claverden* shows how he used indirection to meet the problem. Ardis dons a man's hat and seizes a man's horse to go after a runaway steer.

She put the horse to the top of his speed and dashed up the road. There was no need of urging that animal. Once on fire with the consciousness that he could go as fast as he pleased, he thundered over the ground. Never before had Ardis had such a horse beneath her. She could feel the swift play of his powerful muscles; his hot breath flew past her; her own blood was hot in her veins; it seemed as if she herself were making those bounds—as if she were a wild, free, powerful being, rushing through the sparkling air. Her own riding-mare was a fine animal, speedy and true; but this fellow was a king of horses, and his blood was up.

When her friend, Norma, tries to excuse Ardis's unladylike conduct by blaming it on necessity, Ardis replies, "Necessity! Of course not! I wanted a bit of wild exhilaration to take away the smell of cooked peaches [they had been canning]; I assure you, Norma, it took it away."[22]

Two hundred pages later, Ardis steals her lover's horse from thieves, is pursued, shot at, and Stockton describes her second orgasmic ride in a more modern trope. Roger's Biscay pounded "with such quick and powerful action that Ardis felt as if she were sitting upon a steam-engine working at highest speed, every stroke of which thrilled and shook her." It is curious that Roger is described by relatives as being more fond of that horse "than he would [be] of a wife an' baby."[23] If one remembers the horse-marriage analogy in *A Bicycle of Cathay*, one sees why Ardis chooses Roger instead of the more clever and independent urbanite Jack Surrey. Although Roger may sometimes seem a fool, he loves the power of horses, and he himself is a horse that Ardis can tame.

Still, her choice may not be the right one, for the two desires of excitement and domination are at odds. Her will may tame Roger so well that he might cease to be a "king of horses" and become a "riding-mare." Though they are antitheses, sexuality and willpower have the same root in Ardis's strong attraction to her father. Her Oedipal fixation both intensifies her sexual drive and causes her to castrate men metaphorically, as in the picture she paints which depicts her father shooting at a retreating male's back. Small wonder that in so many of Stockton's stories individuals are reluctant to join in a union which is supposed to be blissful.[24]

A gentler version of this problem occurs in *The Hundredth Man*. Horace Stratford, whose name rings like "Francis Stockton," is smarter than Roger, and Gay Armatt is less volatile than Ardis. Horace shows Gay how to fish. He "took up his rod and began with much dexterity to throw his fly among the ripples at the bottom of a tiny waterfall. In a few moments he caught a trout and threw it out upon the grass; then Gay ran up to it, dropped down on her knees, and was full of admiration for its beautiful colors and spots." When Gay fly-casts for the first time, she catches a large trout and throws it far out on the grass, "the line just grazing Mr. Stratford's hat as it flew over his head." He experiences gladness, not envy, and assures her, "she could fish any day, and that it was ever so much more pleasure to show her how to use the rod than to use it himself."[25]

Because individuals are driven by irrational, psychological, and egotistical forces, a cicerone, a cooler, more experienced head as guide, is often needed to balance emotionalism. The guide's duty is to establish rational criteria for a model spouse, something of a checklist of the ideal which reality often undermines. Seventy-five-year-old Miss Racilla Panney, acting as Dora's docent in *The Girl at Cobhurst*, says a mate should be suited temperamentally and intellectually, should be a person whom one would marry regardless of money, should be one chosen from a wide selection, should be physically complementary so that the couple would make a handsome pair, and should be a choice whereby one will not envy other people's spouses later. Other Stockton characters offer comparable lists.[26] When Miss Panney finds precisely such a male, she tells Dora he "is just floating along, waiting for someone to thrust out a boathook and pull him in," but Dora answers stiffly, "I shall marry no floating log."[27] The problem with lists is that they are too cerebral and neglect human psychology and passion.

Works like the above stress marriage over self-growth; others, like *The Hundredth Man* and *Mrs. Cliff's Yacht*, emphasize the individual, and marriage is incidental. Gay Armatt has two docents with two different purposes. Mrs. Justin makes sure talented young women who lack money are able to receive a college education. She supplies funds and encouragement, especially since society doubts the wisdom of women going to college. Stratford's guidance, on the contrary, is more individualistic, independent of any institution. He seeks to "be able to bring her to look upon literature, philosophy, and science with the eye of an untrammeled thinker." Realizing the head-heart paradox, he views Gay as "this young creature, with the mind of a philosopher and the heart of a girl."[28]

Stockton's feminist evolution can thus be charted. In his first love story, "Kate" (1859), the bumbling male is the main character, the woman merely an ideal who accepts the male for all his ineptitude. *The Casting Away of Mrs. Lecks and Mrs. Aleshine* (1886) does little more than humorously eulogize the values of middle-class, rural, older women. The other novel he published that year is more original. *The Late Mrs. Null* has as main character a young woman who can cope with society without being married, though marriage does ease some of society's friction. The next year, 1887, Stockton hit upon the device of the cicerone in *The Hundredth Man* which enabled him to approach the ideals of the individual and the marriage partner more analytically, as witnessed by the lists. Having established benchmarks of rationality, he then developed characters motivated by irrational forces, as in *Ardis Claverden* (1890), *The House of Martha* (1891), and "The Christmas Shadrach" (1891).

In *Captain Horn* and *Mrs. Cliff's Yacht* (1895, 1896), he could continue this development with Edna, and he could return to the *Casting Away* focus of an older woman and discuss the issue with more sophistication. Finally, in novels like *The Girl at Cobhurst* (1898) and *The Captain's Toll-Gate* (1903), all these elements can be brought together, and the result seems a full-scale war with the heroine suffering defeat or only partial victory, perhaps because society was becoming again more restrictive, or perhaps because Stockton had finally created women characters who, like Chopin's Edna Pontellier and Henry James's Isabel Archer, were now strong enough to encounter life's most

serious problems without having to be rescued through some facile resolution of plot.

In either case, Dora with her docent, Miss Panney, in *Girl at Cobhurst* battle Cicely with her partisans. Though Dora is clearly superior,
she is defeated, and Miss Panney burns her wills, both literally and
symbolically. Olive, in *The Toll-Gate*, achieves happiness with the
people she loves, but to society at large, represented by the press, she
is only a public freak because she has killed a man. When her uncle
blasts a newsman's camera with a shotgun, he blinds that one prying
eye, but the reader knows Olive and her uncle have won only a skirmish in a war that will ultimately defeat them. Though the mood is
always good-tempered, Stockton's development grows from comfortable conventionality to sinister, powerful threats to individualism,
especially with respect to women's self-actualization.

As one example, "The Great Staircase at Landover Hall," which,
published in 1898, is from this late period, suggests that children may
be one major factor that prevents women from self-fulfillment. Where
Stockton hints, the following year Kate Chopin in *The Awakening*
specifies. Stockton's indirection was prudent in that it avoided the out-
rage Chopin's novel provoked. Also, he was less direct because he felt
selfhood could be achieved within the conventional roles. Chopin's
conventional mother figure is dull; her would-be liberated Edna is
exciting but weak, as doomed to suicide as, to use the novel's imagery,
a bird with a broken wing is doomed to fall. Mrs. Cliff, however, "felt
as if she were a bird—a common-sized bird, perhaps, but with enormous wings, which seemed to grow and grow the more she thought of
them, until they were able to carry her so far and so high that her mind
lost its power of directing them."[29]

The danger of her power running amok is controlled not by intellect
but by this woman's good heart. She "was rapidly becoming a different
woman from the old Mrs. Cliff of Plainton," and her newfound power
is channeled to do good in the world despite the natural temptation to
use her wealth for selfish goals. "Not only did this consciousness of
power swell her veins with a proud delight, but it warmed and invig-
orated all her better impulses. She had always been of a generous disposition, but now she felt an intense good will toward her fellow-
beings, and wished that other people could be as happy as she was."
She matches wish with action, dedicating her position toward improv-
ing life "as fervently as if she had been vowing a vow to seek the Holy
Grail."[30] Her near-religious accomplishments include a beautiful pub-

lic park for the use of all residents of her hometown, a seagoing charitable institution, and a foundation both social and political to improve the living conditions of poor people in Peru, the national origin of her wealth. She seeks, in short, to make the world as Edenic as humanly possible.

The Edenic myth is one main theme of Stockton's canon, and it ranges from an indiviaual like John Gayther finding meaningful work in tending his garden to the United States insuring "domestic tranquility" instead of conquering foreign countries. With the subject of women, the myth focuses on human relations of a prelapsarian Adam and Eve in which the Old Adam is defined not as a tendency to violence as the Puritans and Melville have it, but as joy, trust, and love amidst life's complexities, which is how Stockton defines it in "Old Applejoy's Ghost" (1900). In *A Bicycle of Cathay* one never learns the heroine's name, but the meaning of her middle initial is revealed: "E" for "Europa." But the union formed is not founded by rape, a violation of another individual's integrity as in the Greek myth, but in mutual respect where husband and wife honor each other as "collateral intelligences."[31] Significantly, both "E" and her mate become proficient at medicine. Having healed themselves, the message is, they can now attempt to heal the world. The point of the conclusion of *The Associate Hermits* is that while individual growth is important, it is incomplete unless it blossoms in human relationships. In *The Late Mrs. Null* a sylvan scene remains a mere picnic spot for one; only human intercourse can transfigure it into a work of art.[32]

Yet every garden, even Eden, has serpents. Love which spans the gap between individuals can be destroyed by social and environmental restrictions. Peter Sadler, a crippled god-figure of *The Associate Hermits*, represents those social forces that seem as inviolable as the laws of physics. Martin is a college-educated young man of good family who loves nature and loves the heroine, Marjorie, even more. Yet they can not marry because he is poor. Though his occupation of nature guide is a "nobler one than the practice of the law" according to Marjorie, it is not socially respectable. Marjorie explains: "You are as good as other people, although you do happen to be a guide, and perhaps after a while you may be very well off. But, for all that, you are a guide, and you are in Mr. Sadler's employment, and Mr. Sadler's rights and powers are just like gas escaping from a pipe; they are everywhere from cellar to garret, so to speak, and you can't escape them." Sadler explains his opposition to their union by resorting to religion. Since

Martin is poor, "if [Marjorie's] family wanted her to live like a Christian they would have to give her the money to do it with. . . ."[33] Even religion has been subsumed into a system of social etiquette. Moreover, even Martin's "good" points—social class, pedigree, education—are factors that inhibit human relationships.

Were all the class and social restrictions met, deep human relationships as represented by marriage would still be endangered. In *The Hundredth Man* a foursome plays croquet. Though Horace and Gay are the weaker team, they win because Gay "subordinated herself entirely to Stratford." Mrs. Justin "did not demand such subjection from her partner. She let him rely on himself sometimes, and so she found that he had left little on which she could rely."[34] Even in the best of relationships a union of equals seems seldom possible. The logical topic to inspect at this point is that vast body of Americans with whom, because of social factors, one does not play croquet, much less share love.

III   Class and Race

As a middle-class writer, Stockton presented the upper and lower classes as threats to his audience's welfare. In *The Stories of the Three Burglars* the rich are equated with oppressors, while attempts to organize the lower classes as by Socialism are deemed forms of burglary. In *What Might Have Been Expected* the kind, progressive industry of the middle class is undermined by the machinations of capitalists and by the misunderstanding of the poor. And the lower class becomes even more wrongheaded when it is composed of immigrants or blacks because, as Stockton stated as early as 1860 in *A Northern Voice,* America consisted of "two different and new varieties of the Anglo-Saxon family"—by which Stockton meant British ancestry. Americans whose grandparents were not born here never become major characters in Stockton's fiction. However, with American blacks, who are at least as much part of the local color scene as any white, the subject becomes blurred.[35] Let us take the clearer issue of class first.

In *The Hundredth Man* a working-class strike is organized, and the waiters' strike has laudable aims; to show that the restaurant where they work was not "of a low order," and to prove that they possessed "the manhood with which to assert their rights." But Stockton presents a strike only to undercut it in two ways. First, the strike, unlike Eugene Debs' railroad strikes which protested brutal living conditions, has the comparatively trivial purpose of allowing the waiters to wear dress coats instead of jackets and aprons, a demand so tame that only the unreasonable stubbornness of the restaurant's upper-class owner accounts for its not being accepted. The rich owner himself can explain his resistance only for "the principle of the thing." Second, the strike is broken by true-blue Americans who want nothing to do with exotic fashions; if anyone tried to make them wear dress coats, "they would have to call out the army and navy."[36]

Evolving from the American Transcendental tradition of self-reliance instead of from socialist politics, Mrs. Perkenpine's growing awareness of selfhood in *The Associate Hermits* enables this lower-class woman to achieve a better life. But once again factors qualify the achievement: Stockton's praise for her probably stems from his feminist rather than from his class sympathies. That she should be paid as much as a male guide probably means the male guide earns very little, and what happens out in the woods does not necessarily apply to urban workers. In fairness to Stockton, one might say that his cavalier attitude toward the working class may be attributable to his readers' expectation. Norma, who may represent this readership in *Ardis Claverden*, tells Jack Surrey, who plans to do an illustrated article on her town, that he should feature only ladies and gentlemen because she deems the "traits of working people as utterly beneath notice."[37] But nothing in Stockton's letters or biography contradicts Norma's attitude.

The fullest treatment of this issue appears in *Pomona's Travels*, which depicts British as well as American working-class mores. Pomona, too, because upwardly mobile can present a double perspective. When a British earl asks her if she represents the American middle class, she replies, "I don't know 'zactly where society splits with us, but I guess I'm somewhere nigh the crack." Pomona mentions one important distinction between the two countries' classes: in contrast to British domestics, "an American poor girl will work twice as hard in a shop or factory rather than be a first class servant"—which is an odd observation considering Pomona is a servant. But her insight may account for why in 1894 British servants received half the pay of Americans, probably due to American working-class contempt for the career.[38]

As an American servant touring England, Pomona experiences a double prejudice. Because she is foreign, cab distances double for her and her husband, Jonas. When she tries to rent a vicarage, she discovers "it wouldn't matter how nice we lived, or what we had, so long as we was retired servants." She soon tires of this condescension: "We didn't come over here to be looked upon as if we was the bottom of a pie-dish, and charged as if we was the upper crust." She finds particularly galling her husband's meek acceptance whereby "a half-drowned fly put into the sun to dry would be overbearing and supercilious compared to you."

In spite of her good nature and democratic manners, she decides that she and Jonas must fight fire with fire: "We've got to act as if we had always been waited on, and had never been satisfied with the way it was done. We've got to let people think that we think we are a good deal better than they are, and what they think about it doesn't make the least difference. And then, again, . . . we must make people think that we don't think they are quite good enough for us." In a bigoted society Pomona's policy of arrogance proves a success. Class and national bias are not defeated; they only win two new converts. When Pomona and Jonas return to America, they find the same arrogance in customs officials, and the experience makes Pomona want to haul down the stars and stripes. But she merely lowers Old Glory figuratively to half-mast until her husband's empty rhetoric encourages her to raise it aloft once more.[39]

One significant extraliterary note is that the servant girl on whom Pomona is based was German, but Stockton made her ethnicity obscure except to say she rejects her father's name of Dork. Moreover, Stockton makes Pomona enamored of British culture as represented in literature. Though her ethnic roots may be otherwise, her cultural heritage is firmly British. The only servant in Stockton's works who rises to the middle class is Mary Phillips, whose name is Anglo-Saxon and who marries a British captain in "Derelict," which was included in *The Rudder Grangers Abroad* (1891). In these cases, where Stockton presents a lower-class person rising in the social structure, he is careful to enshroud her with British conservatism, so that his readers would suffer no discomfort by seeing that her rise suggests rebellion or a criticism of bourgeois values.

This thorough Anglophilia excludes even the Scots. Ben Greenway in *Kate Bonnet* is Stockton's only Scot, and he is stereotypically religious and prudent. Setting aside the mad villain in *The Great Stone of Sardis*, Colonel Pulaski is Stockton's only Pole; he is an exotic joke in "The Spirit of Washington" (1895) who, as a ghost, teaches Washington's spirit how to pass through walls. A German Jew who appears in "The Knife that Killed Po Hancy" is pushy and obnoxious. A Swed-

ish girl appears in *Mrs. Cliff's Yacht*, but all she does is take a liking
to a black fellow-servant, which Stockton intends as criticism of undis-
criminating Swedes. The Grootenheimers in *The Casting Away* are
described as "the dumbest people in town," and the Austrian statesman
in *The Captain's Toll-Gate* is slick and "oily." No Russian appears at
all, but the hero's twenty-one-day rule in *The Vizier of Alexander*
smacks greatly of the "White Man's Burden" of imperialism, to which
Stockton was usually opposed.

Even the able French cook, Mrs. La Fleur, in *The Girl at Cobhurst*,
to whom one would expect Stockton to be attracted because of his
mother's French ancestry and because she is an artist, is inferior in that
her motives are selfish and she favors the lesser heroine. The case of
the Irish is more involved, but only slightly. In *The Hundredth Man*
Roon, a fruitseller, is a good man whose experience enables Enoch Bulripple to carry out his plans. But in *The Squirrel Inn* Lanigan Beam,
a man of considerable potential, is not able to persevere at any of his
projects because he is wild and capricious; his wildness, Stockton specifies, is a result of Beam's being "half-Irish." Exactly the same promise
and failing is the characterization of Bonnetti, who changes his name
to Bonnet in *Ardis*, although his background presumably is Italian
instead of Irish.

The Italians are the only ethnic group that Stockton develops to
some degree. Apparently they were so abundant that twelve hundred
could be mustered at a moment's notice as unskilled laborers. The Italian in *A Bicycle of Cathay* is illiterate, comic (he has a performing
bear), easily frightened, violent (he is running away from a New York
vendetta), and dangerously inept (he has fatally stabbed a schoolmaster
by mistake). Stockton sprinkles "dago" throughout the story with no
qualm of conscience, and a local black refers to "a Dago, one of these
I-talians" whom the black is unable to identify because Italians,
"They're all so much alike."[40]

Yet when associated with the upper classes, Italian cognomens are
positive, as in Stull's name for his restaurant: "Valtoldi's." In *The
Vizier* Mrs. Crowder, the Vizier's current wife, is enlightened about
feminism. When her husband explains that he ruled Russia when Princess Sophia was regent because "it was absolutely necessary for her to
have a man on whom she could lean," she responds: "I don't think that
is always necessary, at least in these days." She also feels that Mr. Crowder's opportunity to marry the Italian princess Rina of Ravenna was a
fine marital chance.

As she reacts to her husband's story of immortality, Mrs. Crowder is set up as a test of high Quaker principles against her prejudices as a woman from "North 16th Street, Philadelphia." Her test results are clear. Her husband's marriage to an Italian princess pleases her; his marriage to the Chinese Empress Woo causes her to say, "I don't approve of that matrimonial alliance at all"; his possible marriage to a wild African slave girl who could outrun a deer evokes her fearful question, "Fortunately, thee did not—" and she can not finish the statement. Her husband salves her anxiety, "No, I did not."[41] Her bias is less class-based than racial. Had Rina been a peasant and the African a queen, the Quakeress would still have preferred her husband to marry the Italian.

This leads to the one topic that is the most difficult to settle in Stockton's canon, namely to what degree was he a racist or a humorist using racist stereotypes for the purpose of satire? A scene from *The Merry Chanter* represents the problem. Alwilda, an amateur artist, has created a painting of which Lord Crabstairs, a debt-ridden English aristocrat, asks, "Who is that sprawling nigger at the foot of the stone with his head in a brass pan?" "By that," answers Alwilda, "I intended to represent the downfall of an African king."[42] The artist intended nobility and tragedy; the audience perceived a comic cartoon. How much of the misinterpretation was due to the artist's lack of skill, and how much to the viewer's prejudice Stockton does not explain.

A similar technique is used more elaborately in *Ardis Claverden*. Major Claverden, Ardis's father and the most powerful man in Bolton, Virginia, asserts the democratic principle: "judicious admixtures are very valuable. From these have come the first results of civilization." But does a "judicious admixture" include blacks? The description of the town of Bolton presumes so: "There were blacks and whites with all the intermediate shades, and everybody seemed to be acquainted with everybody else." The exact point where a white becomes a black can not be discerned, unless one reasons that to Stockton only the obvious whites were whites. But since Stockton's own appearance placed him in the zone of "intermediate shades," that theory can not apply. According to his close friend, Robert Underwood Johnson, Stockton was "the darkest man of the Caucasian race I have ever seen."[43]

In contrast to the Major's democratic ideas, a group of British emigrants is responsible for the only viciously racist events in the novel. In one, Tom Prouter, a flighty Englishman, finds that a slovenly black woman is buying milk from the route he has established. He smashes her milk pitcher in loathing when she complains that the milk he sells sours too soon: "Now when the idea came to me that I, a gentleman, you know, was making my living by fetching milk to dirty black niggers, it made my blood boil!" The class dimension to Prouter's racist complaint colors his next sentence: "If there had been a mistress behind her I wouldn't have minded."

In the other scene, the British gang flies down the hill to beat up "an old negro and two half-grown boys" for allegedly hunting raccoons on their employer's property. When the blacks convince them they are really searching for a lost pig, the British offer to help and receive this answer: "Much obliged, sah, but I'd recon you'd skeer him wuss dan you'd ketch him," which shows blacks avenging themselves on whites as much as their racist society would directly permit. In *Captain Horn,* when a black servant is asked why he did not help fight the robbers, he explains his fear with this ironic phrase: "I's all w'ite inside."[44]

An important scene from *The Late Mrs. Null* pinpoints the complexity when Stockton portrays a black church service in Virginia's "black belt." He observes that the ceremony seems more African than Christian, representing the heights of its emotionalism in the "Jerusalem Jump," but he in no way satirizes it as Mark Twain, a charter member of the NAACP, had. Indeed, two positive effects derive from the service: Aunt Patsy, a wise old black woman who owes nothing to anyone, dies serenely at the precise moment of most intense spiritualism; Croft and Annie, who witness the rite from a back pew, are moved emotionally so that they come to realize their love for each other. In fact, the only person who denigrates the blacks' religion is vitriolic Mrs. Keswick "who reviled without stint those utterly thoughtless and heedless colored people, who, once in the midst of their crazy religious exercises, totally forgot that they owed any duty whatever to those who employed them." The class basis of Mrs. Keswick's racism is further revealed when she addresses a free black woman, "'Where is your master,' forgetting all about the Emancipation Act."[45]

The most curious esthetic fact about this novel is that the blacks use the same technique of indirection to present important information that Stockton employed as a humorist. When a black woman asks Uncle Isham, Mrs. Keswick's long-time black hand, if Mrs. Keswick would stoop even to murder to effect her will, Isham leaves her house, then returns to say, "Look h'yar, you Letty, I don't want to hear such fool talk 'bout ole miss." He then proceeds to tell her in detail (while telling her not to speak such fool talk) how Mrs. Keswick drove her husband to suicide, and concludes "an' I don' want to hear no fool talk from you, Letty, 'bout her. Jes' you 'member dat!"[46] He has effectually answered her speculation in full while feigning to argue against it. "Fool talk" to Uncle Isham (I Sham?), and possibly to Stockton as well, was talk that was dangerous to speak openly, not talk that was foolish or untrue. The upshot is that Stockton was sometimes clearly racist, sometimes clearly satirizing racism, and sometimes, most frustrating of all, enigmatic.

Some of his black characters are also bigoted. Besides the black in *A Bicycle of Cathay* who could not tell Italians apart because "they looked so much alike," the black minister in "A Dusky Philosophy" is outrageously sexist, and the black servant in *The Girl of Cobhurst* can not abide redheads. Stockton's own deliberate bigotry is revealed in his manuscript revisions of *Captain Horn*. While most of his changes were minor (to vary the use of "then," to liven the prose by putting "tumble" for "fall," and to simplify vocabulary by writing "opening" for "aperture"), only one major alteration involved content, and that was to be more racist. When Maka, a black servant not as depraved as Mok nor as noble as Cheditafa, does not fight, Stockton had originally supported Maka—"for Maka, although a good servant, could not be expected to fight with a man or a beast"—but he changed this passage to read: "for Maka was known to be a coward. . . . " Likewise, Caliban-like Mok was originally called a "very low kind of fellow," which is not as harsh as the revision, "a very low creature." When the Parisian police impartially separate Mok and the evil Banker from fighting, Stockton explains why they did not side with the white man by changing Banker's description as a "white man" to a "white foreigner."[47]

And yet, a New Orleans black is depicted in a local color sketch, "A Romance of a Mule-Car," as honestly as if it were an impartial photograph. Perhaps the answer here is that Stockton believed blacks were equal but separate, as the Supreme Court held until 1954. That at least is what happens in *Captain Horn* when the noble Cheditafa, a Stocktonian version of Queequeg, marries Horn and Edna with a gold ring he has purchased with his own hard-earned savings. Mrs. Cliff's decree on this event is, "He is a good man and he now believes that he has done everything that ought to be done. But you will be married tomorrow [by a white minister in the American legation], all the same, of course."[48] Of course.

Throughout these examples one has surely noticed the triangular interplay of class, race, and nationality. While Stockton addressed his readers on crucial matters nearly as guardedly as an oppressed black had to speak to a white, Stockton so closely identified with the middle class that he would parody rich and poor, bankers and blacks alike. "Funny Darkies" (1897) clarifies the point when Stockton claims that "Million-heirs" (not self-made men, but inheritors of wealth) have much money but can not enjoy life; blacks have no money, but they enjoy life. Neither group, Stockton theorizes, has the capacity to receive the benefits of life as much as the middle class, a theory that his middle-class audience much wanted to hear. He parodied the mean rich and the happy poor in order to flatter his readers.

At least that is what he meant to do, but art at times transcends theory. His artist's eye and ear lent the blacks more life and value than his class prejudices intended. As Clarence Buel and Howells noted, his black characters were often more interesting, complex, and vigorous than his whites.[49] Other stories further develop the issue. "Grandison's Quandary" (1888) and "An Unhistoric Page" (1885) read as if their theme were that hard-working, ambitious blacks will not be able to rise economically because white society has effective safeguards against their doing so, but that may be a twentieth-century interpolation. The fantasy sketch "Ghosts in My Tower" (1900) seems an allegory about how the white race which has conquered the native American now risks being overthrown by Afro-Americans. The pale ghosts in the narrator's tower (mind? social structure?) are frivolous, perhaps reflecting the "Gay '90's" image. They are scared away by "a jet-black demon" which is "dark as a statue in coal." The climax avers, "The advent of the black spirit seemed to have exerted an evil influence over the sprites in gray, and, like the Indian in the presence of the white man, they faded away and gradually became extinct."[50] Was Stockton aware of the sociological message this story seems so obviously to entail, or was he simply making a conscious attempt to write a ghost story without knowing what the dream revealed?

The same dilemma occurs in Stockton's first realistic novel, *What Might Have Been Expected* (1874). The themes of the novel reverberate from the title. "What Might Have Been Expected" is that capitalists would take advantage of middle-class farmers, that boys would exclude a capable girl from their games and business for sexist reasons, and that adults would use children to further their own ends. The logical extension of this formula would be to say that "What Might Have Been Expected" is that whites would exploit blacks, for that is what happens in the novel, but that interpretation seems diametrically opposed to the evidence of Stockton's racism as demonstrated in particular by his revisions of *Captain Horn*. Unlike Stockton's positions on sexism, class bias, and immigrants, which are complex but clear, his racist persuasion remains a puzzle with clearly defined pieces that do not yet form a coherent whole. Perhaps some day a letter or other piece of evidence will surface that will clarify his intentions.

IV *Not for Children Only*

Setting aside "The Lady, or the Tiger?", Stockton ironically is better known today for his children's stories, especially "The Griffin and the Minor Canon" (1885) and "The Bee-Man of Orn" (1883), which are part of a genre for which Stockton had only grudging respect. "The Griffin," which was immediately popular, continues so, as witnessed by its musical adaptation *Good Grief, A Griffin!* (1968) by Eleanor and Ray Harder and by the version illustrated by award-winning Maurice Sendak in 1963, who also illustrated "The Bee-Man" in 1964, a copy highly recommended recently by *Coevolution Quarterly*, an offshoot of *The Whole Earth Catalog*. The only other Stockton children's story that rivals the popularity of these two is "Old Pipes and the Dryad," which was issued with illustrations by Catherine Hanley in 1978.[51]

Despite popular success, Stockton wrote children's stories reluctantly, even though he produced eighteen volumes of them—seven novels, six short-story collections, and five books on science, travel, and sketches—because it was lucrative. In 1890, for example, he could command $500 from a magazine for a ten-thousand-word fairy tale which would later be anthologized for extra money. Yet in *The Youth's Companion* he insisted he did not write "for young readers, nor for those older readers who take pleasure in work designed for the young," and when volume seventeen of his Shenandoah Edition was being prepared in 1900, he demanded that it lead off with "The Griffin" instead of "The Bee-Man," a reversal of their original presentation in 1887, because, as he said, "'The Griffin,' however is of a much more mature character, and is, obviously, for adult readers." When Edith Thomas in 1893 asked Stockton if he even liked children, he replied with a fond story of an American girl who wished to take some birds to London because she heard the city was catless. But since London's polluted air was notoriously inimical to birds at that time, Stockton's anecdote depicts the girl as kind-hearted but dumb.[52]

Probably Stockton's objection was to the concept of the child whose literature was presumed to be simple, safe, sentimental, educational, and moralistic, criteria perfectly met by Mary Mapes Dodge, Stockton's superior on the *St. Nicholas Magazine*, in her *Hans Brinker, or The Silver Skates* (1865). This concept persisted even to 1964 when Stockton illustrator Maurice Sendak was assailed by adults for depicting frightening and abnormal creatures in *Where the Wild Things Are*. In *The Uses of Enchantment* (1976), the psychologist Bruno Bettelheim articulates the controversial theory that fairy tales are a rich genre in that they can present many layers of meaning, beginning with the simplest, and the reader's maturity or anxiety governs what degree of truth he extracts from the story.[53] Stockton was writing for this Sendak-Bettelheim concept of the child, which in his day he took to be an adult image.

This modern audience model of the child would have been admirably suited to his technique, content, and philosophy. The Griffin could remain a griffin unless one chose to see it as a symbol for man's violence and aggression. His chaotic worlds could seem fanciful amusement or a fearsome cosmology. The vein of nonsense and of the absurd was being mined in America by Sarah Josepha Hale's *Poems of Our Children* (1830), which included "Mary Had a Little Lamb," Lucretia Peabody Hale's *The Peterkin Papers* (1880), and in England by Lewis Carroll (Charles Dodgson).

By writing children's literature Stockton could include the fanciful and the exotic without resorting to "adult" melodrama as represented by Lew Wallace's *Ben Hur* (1880) and H. Rider Haggard's *She* (1887). Moreover, the idiosyncrasies of the publishing trade almost forced him into children's writing because, as Stockton explains in a letter, until the magazine *Puck* was founded in 1877 there were few outlets for humorous writing in adult periodicals. It was even more difficult to publish a book-length humorous story unless it had been first serialized, and such were the careers of his first two novels, *Ting-a-ling* (1870) and *What Might Have Been Expected* (1874) which first appeared in *St. Nicholas Magazine* in serial form.[54]

In addition to the points already made about the 1874 novel, a few other issues should be mentioned. *Expected*'s hero, Harry Loudon, is, like Twain's Huck, "a boy of good natural impulses" whose sister Kate chides him for spending money on books while their ancient black friend, Aunt Matilda, risks starvation: "Is that poor old woman to have only half enough to eat, so that you may read twice as much Virgil?"

All the action of the plot is geared to this charitable deed. Harry and Kate are abetted by the hunter, Tony Kirk, spokesman for the peace and freedom of the woods, and hindered by a mean Injun Joe character called George Mason who is capable of murder.

One scene demonstrates Stockton's irony and humanism. At the moment when Harry and Kate finally succeed in making Aunt Matilda's financial situation secure, she is about to die. Kate tries to comfort her by saying she will meet all her friends and relations in heaven, but Matilda responds, "Well, perhaps I shall and perhaps I shan't; dere's no tellin'. But dere ain't no mistakin' 'bout you chillen."[55] Like Aunt Matilda, Stockton has no interest in heaven or hell. The reality of human motivation is what intrigues him, even if that reality, as with the Loudons' goodness, is rendered nearly pointless by death.

"The Bee-Man of Orn" is more philosophical than *Expected*. An ugly, poor, and reclusive Bee-man is quite content living with millions of bees that have become so accustomed to him that they would no more sting him than they would a tree or a stone. A passing Sorcerer, an intellectual type, tells the Bee-man that he has good reason to think a witch has cast a spell on him and transformed him from what he was originally. The Bee-man, going off to search for his true self, happens on an aristocratic party, from which he is booted out. His true self can not be there, he decides, for high society is too cruel.

Next he meets a Languid Youth who lacks all zest for living, and the two enter a network of caves inhabited by various monsters and ruled by the Very Imp, who delights in persuading people to do things harmful to them, thinking the choice is their own free will. Their journey is cut short when the Bee-man rescues a baby from a dragon by hurling a beehive at it. After they restore the baby to its mother, the Bee-man believes he has discovered his original true self; he has been transformed from a baby. The Sorcerer changes the Bee-man back into a baby, and the mother agrees to raise him with her own child. All the serious issues Stockton has led up to topple into nonsense. The questions of identity, social cruelty, monsters within the caves of our subconscious, free will manipulated by the Very Imp of perversity, all are left unanswered.

Many years later the Sorcerer happens by the Bee-man's old cottage, peers in, and discovers the Bee-man again an adult. "'Upon my word!' exclaimed the Sorcerer. 'He has grown up into the same thing again!'" is the last line of the story. The moral seems to be the recidivism of human nature. Given another chance at life, people will become pretty much what they have already been. Except—always the Stocktonian "except"—the Languid Youth's temperament has been totally transfigured by the adventures in the caves. No longer lethargic with no goal in life, he looks upon existence now with great enthusiasm. The moral of his life is the antithesis of the Bee-man's. "Human nature does not change" and "Human nature can change" are the two mutually exclusive truths of the tale.

When Stockton was a child in his strict Methodist home, he was constantly being told what was right and what was wrong. When an adult, he believed that right and wrong, true and false could be consummately ambiguous. Sometimes, as in "The Bee-man," he presented this belief as abstract philosophy; other times, as in "What Would You Have Done?" (1901), he presented it more personally. A father takes his son, Hal, a camera enthusiast, to hunt deer. After a long wait alone, a doe appears, and Hal picks up his rifle for an easy shot, but then the doe's fawn emerges from the wood too, and Hal's heart makes him change the gun for the camera. Then a beautiful, antlered stag appears, and Hal is torn between shooting him with a gun or a camera. At the precise moment when the deer family, frightened, is about to bound off into the trees, he shoots on impulse—and he happens to have the camera in his hands at the time.

Upon returning home, Hal is ridiculed as a "mollydoddy" by his boy friends for not killing the deer. The only way he can preserve his manhood is to fight tough Sam Curtis. He defeats Sam, and the story ends happily for Hal. The story's title and final paragraph put the ethical dilemma in the readers' laps, asking them what they would have done. Would they have chosen to conserve the beauty of nature by hunting with cameras? Or would they yield to social pressures of manhood and kill? Since Stockton was a cult figure, his young readers would have known that when Stockton was a child, slightly built and somewhat lame, Sam Curtis would have thrashed Hal had he a physique like Stockton's.

Accomplishments like these have led some scholars to celebrate Stockton for his "brilliant contribution" to the development of children's literature in America.[56] The problem is that he came to exploit the genre. It was an easy mode for him because he was temperamentally suited to it, but he lacked sufficient respect for the genre as it was understood at the time to work at it conscientiously. His children's stories from *Ting-a-ling* (1870) until 1885, four years after he resigned as assistant editor (1873–1881) of *St. Nicholas Magazine*, are undeniably superb. After 1885, he banked on reprints, wrote fantasy directed more and more at adults, or, worst of all, turned out superficial, formulaic, boy-adventure stories. Had he continued with *What Might Have Been Expected*, his work would have rivalled Mark Twain's. Instead he produced books like *Captain Chap, or the Rolling Stones* (1897) and *The Young Master at Hyson Hall* (1899), which are amusing and adventurous but contain nothing of special interest. To put it another way, *Expected* is a better novel than T. B. Aldrich's *Story of a Bad Boy* (1869) and perhaps even Twain's *Tom Sawyer* (1876), but while Twain improved the genre with *Huckleberry Finn* (1884) Stockton collapsed into facile formulaism. As soon as his first adult novel appeared in 1879 and his name became famous with "The Lady, or the Tiger?" in 1882, he quit writing children's literature of quality.

He wanted to quit as early as a *St. Nicholas* sketch in 1875. A gardener, not a prince, knocks at Cinderella's door. He proffers a request for a spade instead of an invitation to a ball. Cinderella stoops to the menial task of fetching him the shovel despite her sisters' taunts. The moral of the satire is that this event was "only a trial of good nature, but it was all better than a fairy tale."[57] Stockton believed that his exploration of human nature was better suited to adult literature than to the genre of children's literature as it was then conceptualized.

CHAPTER 4

The Fireside, Fantasy, and Science Fiction

I   "Cold Pink"

AS one of the editors of *Hearth and Home,* a weekly journal dedicated to agricultural information and literature for the rural home, Frank Stockton was asked to settle the question, what was the best way to make a farm pay? His answer was terse: "Pave it." His advice was considered inappropriate for a magazine with a farming readership, but *Hearth and Home* did publish several Stockton stories as well as many short paragraphs on home decoration, dressmaking, preventive medicine, handicraft, and rat control, which he included in the "How to" book he wrote with his wife in 1872.[1]

Since he had contributed to nearly every department of the journal, he considered it time to offer a dish to the recipe section: "Take up all the white meat left over from the Thanksgiving Turkey, and chop it up very fine. Pour a thin cranberry sauce over the cold meat. Mix well, put in a china form and set it away to get cold. When cold serve."[2] Even in this recipe for "Cold Pink," salient characteristics of Stockton's art emerge. He chooses not something inherently exotic, a Kipling-esque meal from India, say, or a Stevensonian dish from Samoa. Instead he takes aim at the American holiday bird, the one Benjamin Franklin wanted as our national emblem instead of the eagle, and tries to transform that domestic fowl into something unique. He offers to make the usual unusual, the ordinary extraordinary, the domestic strange.

He also attempts the reverse. Martin Griffin has rightly observed that "The Queen's Museum" for *St. Nicholas* (1884) was one of the earliest groups of stories in which Stockton's desire to "domesticate the incredible" was realized.[3] In a letter the next year Stockton voiced his intention to write a type of fiction that differed from his children's stories when he said of "Christmas Before Last; or, the Fruit of the Fragile

Palm": "It is not a fairy tale, but a 'fanciful story.'"[4] The difference
between the two story types is that Stockton's originality with the
"fairy tale" was to make bizarre dwarfs, giants, genies, and fairies
behave as if motivated by the same impulses that moved one's next
door neighbors. In the "fanciful story" he took more realistic characters, placed them in bizarre situations, and then returned them to
hearth and home, usually with a greater appreciation of life by the
fireside than they had before.

The "fanciful story" in turn can be divided into two sorts, depending
on the realism of the characters, on whether they seem like friends,
neighbors, or even one's self, or whether they are outright types such
as the Sorcerer, Languid Youth, and Very Imp of "The Bee-man of
Orn." Representing Realism in its extreme are "A Piece of Red Calico"
and "Our Fire-Screen," which could have been written by James
Thurber. In these stories the character is Stockton himself, who is overwhelmed by the zaniness inherent in everyday life as he sets out on a
simple domestic mission. At the end of the story, he returns home glad
to be relieved of the Gilbert-and-Sullivan world of topsy-turvyness that
lurks out there.

When Stockton in "A Piece of Red Calico" is sent by his wife to
purchase two-and-one-half yards of cloth to reupholster their couch,
he is unaware of the complexities lying in wait at a large dry-goods
department store in the city. In "Our Fire-Screen," when the whimsy
of fashion dictates that they have to sell all their well-made but out-of-
date furniture at an eighty-seven per cent discount just because it does
not match the new fire-screen his wife has bought, Stockton meekly
complies, though it makes no sense. Ultimately, Stockton buys a whole
house from his friend, Tom, to whom he has sold his old furniture, and
rents his new house replete with modern but less comfortable furnish-
ings to Tom. At story's end, Stockton sits dazed in his old chair as if
awakening from a stupor, wondering like Alice if she has really
plunged down that rabbit hole. It takes only the slightest jar, these stories suggest, to set even the most pedestrian world atilt.

Stories like "The Queen's Museum" and "Christmas Before Last"
begin with less realistic characters, and the world they enter is more
patently fanciful. In "Christmas" Captain Maroots, who takes only
good-smelling things aboard his ship, the *Horn O'Plenty*, is en route
to spend Christmas with his son when he rescues the Boys' First Class
in Long Division from Apple Island. Of the boys' many adventures,
the chief is discovering "the transcendentally delicious fruit" of the

fragile palm. This landfall is not exploited for mere survival as are apples, nor for commercial gain, nor for worldly fame, nor for symbolic possibilities. Instead, the fruit's ultimate purpose is to be shared by all on Christmas at the captain's son's home.

In "The Queen's Museum" more radical changes occur only to insure domestic accord. An itinerant king with the aid of a professional Pupil seeks to help make the Queen's museum, a rare collection of buttonholes, more popular with her citizens and to disprove her undemocratic assertion that "Most people are too silly to be truly interested in anything. They herd together like cattle, and do not know what is good for them."[5] With the help of a Hermit attuned to "the secrets of nature," a wise magian named Alfrarmedj, and a gang of robbers, the King and Pupil stock the museum with a stuffed mammoth, a whale skeleton, and "everything relating to history, science, and art which ought to be in a really good museum." The populace is ecstatic, and the museum is packed from morn to night. The King, of course, marries the Queen, the Robber Captain becomes a hermit, the Pupil takes his place as robber captain and robs only robbers so that every stolen item winds up with its proper owner. With order established, the Pupil-Captain takes his gang off to other kingdoms "to continue the good work of robbing robbers."

In these very different styles of story, varying in setting from a big city department store to mythical kingdoms, the identical function prevails: to merge fancy with the familiar. The stories try to make the fire in the household hearth blaze with a warm, attractive glow. This effort, as William C. Spengemann argues, is as American as the Constitution of the United States, which "was written 'to insure domestic tranquility', for which the Revolution had been fought."[6] Until Spengemann's recent book, *The Adventurous Muse,* the achievement of writers like Stockton has not been fully understood because of a neglect of the tension in American literature between what Spengemann calls the poetics of adventure and the poetics of domesticity. The former stresses individualistic values of change, discontent, daring, aspiration, curiosity, eccentricity, and self-justification, which are diametrically opposed to domesticity; the latter inculcates the predominantly social and familial values of stability, resignation, prudence, modest ambition, acceptance, conformity, and reconciliation. Adventurous themes call for formal experimentation, domestic values are reinforced by conventional sylistics, and a tension in forms mirrors the tension of values.

To put that concept of American literature in a scientific trope, centrifugal forces would spin characters off into the open independence of the sea or of the frontier, but centripetal forces attract these same characters to a still center of peace, tranquility, and contentment within the core of social relationships. In all Stockton's novels the adventurer returns from wildness and exotica to the warmth of a central fireside shared usually with a newfound spouse. In fact, the more adventurous a Stockton novel is, the proportionately stronger becomes domestic attraction. As the hero or heroine encounters increasingly strange and individualistic experiences, the forces which draw him back to hearth and home become more powerful.

In Stockton's most purely adventure novel, *Captain Horn,* he required another entire domestic novel, *Mrs. Cliff's Yacht,* as sequel to balance *Horn's* centrifugal nature. Whereas *Rudder Grange* had many sequels because of reader demand, *Mrs. Cliff's Yacht* was born out of the need for domesticity. That is perhaps the main reason Stockton cited Defoe and Dickens as "My Favorite Novelists." Both are high priests of homely virtues, *Robinson Crusoe* being an effort to transform the unusual and the exotic into a warmly homely experience. The only objection Stockton would have to Spengemann's argument is the latter's saying that since adventure leads away from home to confirm the values of home, it is negatively instructive: "Because it can teach the wanderer nothing he could not learn less painfully at home, it has no original moral power."[7] Stockton's objection would be that travel and adventure do teach precisely that important lesson. Without experiencing adventure, one could not fully appreciate peace. Stockton tempts his characters with great personal power, fame, wealth in order to demonstrate how superior domestic values are. In the science-fiction novel *The Great Stone of Sardis* Roland Clewe stands to win a diamond as big as the moon so that he can learn that love is a greater jewel. In *Kate Bonnet,* as point of contrast, the lesson is not learned by the pirate, Stede Bonnet, and his quest for adventure ends in his being hanged, his captor setting up house in his old home.

Travel can be symbolic as well as literal. It can be an imaginative journey as well as an actual one. It must mean an impulse away from the virtues of the fireside as the nexus of human involvement, and the impulse can be made internally manifest as well as externally demonstrated. "The Knife that Killed Po Hancy" (1889) is an example because it has been grossly misinterpreted. Harry, as a Boston lawyer, represents the civilized man; as an individual, he is reserved and shy and so physically out of trim that one game of billiards exhausts him. A missionary friend has given him a present of a knife from British

Burma, "a rude weapon, with a heavy blade nearly nine inches long, enclosed in a wooden sheath, and with a beautifully polished handle of bone-like wood," which has been used by "civilized Burmese"— "two native spies"—who trapped and killed Po Hancy, a rebel against society and "chief of a band of dacoit robbers."[8]

The symbolism is clear, for the knife which Harry uses to open letters and to sharpen pen nibs—to facilitate human correspondence, a domestic virtue—has "great blotches of rust" on the blade "caused by the blood of Po Hancy," and it is taken by the missionary "as a trophy of the superior valor of the loyal and somewhat civilized natives over that of the outlaws of the jungle." Hence, four levels of civilization are presented, from the blatant jungle outlawry of Po Hancy, through the somewhat civilized natives, through the death-trophy-bearing missionary, to Harry, the sedentary lawyer.

The story's focus is the contrasting extremes of Hancy and Harry, thus inaugurating the theme of the doppelganger or the double personality. Harry says, "The idea struck me that Po Hancy and I were as different from each other as two human beings could possibly be. . . . I had heard a great deal of this tiger-like dacoit, crawling through the jungles for ten, fifteen, or twenty miles, leaping down rocks with foothold as silent and certain as that of a cat, and bounding upon his victims with the strength and swiftness of an untiring beast of prey. How different was I—a languid, soft-fleshed, almost middle-aged lawyer . . . to whom . . . years of too much work of one kind, and too little of another, had made activity a memory, and wholesome exercise a discomfort. Po Hancy was a specimen of perfect animal life, and of the most imperfect life of the mind and soul. My body resembled his mind and soul. Of my mind and soul I will say nothing, being of a modest disposition."

To make the doubleness more entwined, Stockton calls up two recent developments, one in science and one in literature. Harry, an amateur scientist, takes "a great interest in experiments such as those performed by [Edouard] Brown-Séquard and Dr. [Robert] Koch," experts in blood and bacteriology. "If certain physical attributes of one class of living beings could be communicated to another by inoculation, or hypodermic injection, why should not another physical attribute be transmitted in the same way?" When he balances his letter opener-trophy on his finger "as if to weigh this infinitesimal remnant of savage mortality," it slips, cutting his thumb; Po Hancy's blood becomes mixed with the lawyer's.

Within a matter of weeks the effect is noticed by all his friends.

Where he had been lethargic, he was now athletic; where he had been stiff and awkward, now lithe and nimble. Harry likes the taste of his newfound vigor so much that he wants a banquet, and he scrapes more of Hancy's blood from the knife and vaccinates himself with it. The unforeseen result is that the influence of this larger blood sampling is psychological as well as physical. "Had I been contented with the little prick my knife had given me, I might have been no more than the active, healthy gentleman I had always wished to be. But that foolish desire to shine in the athletic games had not only given me an excess of strength, but also the impulses of a jungle sneak."

Thus Stockton capitalizes upon the popularity of Stevenson's *The Strange Case of Dr. Jekyll and Mr. Hyde* (1886). Indeed, Stockton's ambition is to do Stevenson one better. "This robber blood was making a different man of me—a man who ran the risk of ending his life in prison. Sometimes I thought of myself as another Mr. Hyde. But alas! my case was worse than that. I was not sometimes good and sometimes bad. I was under an evil influence which was steadfast and of increasing power, the effects of which, my reason told me, must be permanent. When a Christian gentleman puts dacoit blood into his veins, there is no way of getting it out again, except by letting out all his blood—a remedy I did not fancy."

Having established all the prerequisites for an exciting adventure story, "The Knife" could easily take the sinister turns of a tale by an Edgar Allan Poe. The "poetics of adventure" has been posited, but the "poetics of domesticity" takes over. While the danger has been said to be more severe than in Stevenson's story, "The Knife" veers away from the adventure esthetic and the focus becomes domestic. Stockton depicts three levels of danger aimed at three kinds of reader—call them the boy adventure reader, the middle-class woman, and Stockton himself—and these levels are so distinct that a reader attuned to one level may be blind to the others.

Such is the problem of Richard Gid Powers, the anthologist of Stockton's science fiction, who complains, "there is scarcely an echo of the struggle between the untamable savagery of the hidden self and the fair face we wear for society. . . . With Po Hancy's blood in his veins, Harry becomes a country club athlete whose worst impulse is to push back when jostled on the streetcar (he doesn't because he is afraid he will look ridiculous)."[9] This is Harry's worst impulse only on one reading level, that of the adventure story, and it should be coupled with another incident: Harry plots to burglarize a jewelry store. His plans are so meticulous and his strength so outstanding that doubtlessly he could succeed in the theft. But, as with the man on the streetcar, he does not because his civilized self wins out over the savage self. The desires for personal revenge and wealth are two key elements in the story, but they pertain only to one level, the simplest level of the story.

A second reading level involves his women readers, the ideal of marriage, and sexism. Two women characters are posited; one is Camilla Sunderland, "a leading belle, a dazzling star of the season. She goes everywhere, does everything, drives four-in-hand, plays tennis-matches, is devoted to balls, theatre-parties—why, my dear Harry," says his aunt, "I should think you could not exist with a wife like that." This is the woman Harry is attracted to when he is, as it were, blooded. She is the ideal for a man who combines civilization with barbarism. Because of his savagery, he need not fear being overshadowed by this social star.

Before Harry is influenced by Po Hancy's blood, the ideal is quite different, as represented by thirty-year-old Susan Mooney from Stock-bridge, "the kindest, gentlest, quietest, softest woman in the world. Her disposition was so tender that if one spoke to her of trouble or pain, the tears would almost come into her eyes." Harry saves himself from savage instincts when he inoculates himself once again, this time with Susan's blood. The high civilization she represents neutralizes the dacoit influence. Although returned to his former languid self, he still wants Camilla for his wife. When his aunt avers that Harry's ideal of womanhood has changed, he responds, "I should despise a woman who would tremble at my tread. What I want is a wife who will guide, direct, and lead me, upon whom I can lean and depend; and I think Miss Sunderland is such a woman." Languid Harry has no chance of winning Camilla's hand, and since he has tasted Po Hancy's blood, he has lost all interest in Susan, the girl he would have married had the knife not slipped the first time.

Three types of intimate human relationships are represented—two weak individuals cling to each other for support with one dominant for convenience; two strong individuals lead an exciting but selfish life together; one weak individual defers to a stronger for guidance. The middle type is the conventional ideal; however, the problem is that the strong individuals who make that type of union possible are exactly those responsible for civilization being perverted into imperialism, the bloody Anglo-Burmese wars of the nineteenth century, for example. The women's names suggest this: "Mooney" for blissful idiocy, and

"Sunderland" for civil strife. Each type of union is fraught with its special dangers and failings.

The story appears to end with a clear-cut description of what ideal persons and marriages are; yet that ideal on an international plane is one that Stockton condemns. On a personal level, Harry never attains a balance. He is either listlessly civilized, or his well-being is threatened by selfish energy represented by savage blood. Before the first inoculation he might have led a somewhat happy life with Susan. By the end of the story his situation is worse, for a happy union with either Susan or Camilla is impossible. Hence the story really ends not in didactic instruction but in ambiguous complexity as ironic as the missionary at the outset of the tale who through his gift of the trophy-knife makes the apparatus of the story possible, the man of God who celebrates murder by assassination.

The third level of interpretation which interested Stockton most involves two incidents. The milder one is the imp of perversity, which causes the hero to enjoy placing himself "in opposition, especially if the other party did not know how I stood." Harry chucks distinctions of right and wrong, good and evil, all the superstructure of morality and ethics on which civilization prides itself. He becomes anarchical and dangerous to society. He becomes somewhat like the anarchist assassin whom Olive kills in *The Captain's Toll-Gate*, only Harry as Hancy is even more dangerous because the lawyer maintains the mask of propriety which will keep him off the police docket.

This danger is aptly demonstrated when Harry wrongly suspects a burglar has stolen into his house: "my whole body thrilled with a warm ecstasy.... My eyes must have glistened with the expectant joy of meeting a burglar. What transporting delight it would be to steal upon the rascal and slay him with one blow [of Hancy's knife]! It is so seldom that one gets an opportunity to legitimately slay a rascal, or indeed any one ... how gladly would I exercise my legal rights!" The key phrases are "or indeed any one " and "to legitimately slay." These clauses indicate Harry would gladly seize any pretext of civilization to perpetrate evil. Like the corrupt policeman or the hypocritical politician or even, on a vaster scale, Joseph Conrad's Kurtz in "Heart of Darkness", Harry would give vent to the most murderous impulses under the guise of legality.

This, not the incident of the rude man on the streetcar, is the "worst impulse" of the story. That an intelligent reader might miss it is due in large part to Stockton's technique. Since literature then was still governed by the Genteel Tradition, Stockton would "encode" the most powerful themes. Just as sex would be made most subtly suggestive, the drive to destruction is stated covertly, there for those who wish to ferret it out, hidden to protect gentler souls or those who wish to feign so. By a similar technique of indirection Uncle Isham in *The Late Mrs. Null* tells how his employer, Mrs. Keswick, is capable of murder.

Perhaps the greatest irony of "The Knife" is that Stockton exploits his readers' lust for adventure to attack the spirit of adventure, trying to convert it into a domesticity that has no satisfying resolution. But Stockton is not always so absurdist, and other stories attempt to extract some sanity from the chaotic universe into which his characters are plunged. One such story is "A Sailor's Knot" (1900), whose title is explained in Stockton's introduction. A sailor's knot might appear weirdly complex and impossible to untie, but, as opposed to the Gordian Knot, which must be severed by force, one proper, knowing tug can unravel it.[10] In contrast to a pagan emphasis on the sword of violence to solve life's dilemmas, "A Sailor's Knot" champions reason, experience, and civilization.

Mr. Radnor, a struggling businessman, can not marry his rich lover, Florence Brower, because a codicil in her father's will stipulates she must marry a sea captain to receive the inheritance. The two lovers arrange for Florence to marry old, dying Captain Asa Lopper, who is to be paid two dollars a day for his part in the ruse. But Asa's health improves, and it appears Florence might not become a widow for a decade or two. In the pivotal scene in which Radnor takes Asa sailing, Asa precariously is setting the jib when Radnor lets go the tiller, claiming, "It is likely that I did not comprehend the necessity of grasping it firmly at such a time."[11] The humorous tale turns serious as Asa is flung from the boat and risks drowning. The reader, as with Theodore Dreiser's parallel boat scene in *An American Tragedy* (1925), wonders if the dunking is more "likely" a mistake or whether Radnor's subconscious is directing his acts, fooling his conscious mind.

Asa's opinion is clear; he suspects evil intent. His face held "a look of suspicion, contempt, and hatred. It told me as plainly as if he had spoken that he believed I had purposely let the boat fly around." While Radnor's motivation may be as sinisterly psychological as that of Dreiser's Clyde Griffiths, he does not hesitate like Clyde. To disprove Asa's suspicion of savagery, Radnor plunges into the water and through "superhuman" effort saves him from drowning. A grateful Asa divorces Florence, and the story waltzes on to a happy ending for all.

But the major issue has already been raised. Radnor believes he is civilized, and that belief—though it may be false, though it may be far more complex and impure than he imagines—saves the day. The belief in civilization, the commitment to fundamental domestic values, may be complex, sometimes inadequate, and frequently illusory, but it is the most man has. Egotistical, self-serving Clyde, though not a savage like Po Hancy, has no great concept of civilization and lets Roberta drown; Radnor saves Asa, though he risks death in the effort. In the process, he rescues fragile domestic virtues from shipwreck and from the chaos of the seas.

The most extended development of this theme is found in Stockton's best-selling adventure novel, *The Adventures of Captain Horn,* which can be appreciated by contrasting it with a novel equally popular in its era, B. Traven's *The Treasure of the Sierra Madre* (1927; movie version, 1948). The all-consuming theme of Traven's book is greed and how it destroys four derelicts. In the city they are slowly ground into inhumanity by the quiet bureaucratic greed of monopolistic business companies. When they discover gold in the mountains of a barbaric country, they are endangered from within instead of from without. Their own greed triggers an antisocial selfishness that eventually destroys them socially and individually. The most damning sentence of the novel contrasts these men with their pack animals: "The burros did not mind [the men's quarreling], because they had more sense and besides had been raised on a better philosophical system."[12]

The difference between Traven's *Treasure* and Stockton's *Captain Horn* is night and day, and civilization makes the sun rise. Stockton includes characters like Traven's in persons like George Burke, and they too are destroyed. But Stockton's main interest is not in social rejects but in civilization's flower as represented by Horn. Traven's intent is to show how depraved the social animal called man can become; Stockton's is to demonstrate how successful in a civilized sense man can be despite temptation and threats. Traven, like Huck Finn, greatly resents civilizing influences; Stockton keeps faith with civilization as the best possible ground for mankind's self-culture.

Stockton makes Horn a captain because as a middle-class position it offers more hope than does the lower-class station of Traven's characters and enjoys less debilitating luxury than does an upper-class status. But the main reason is that ships, creations that combine man's skill with nature's resources, are fine analogies for man's control, through cooperation and knowledge, over the tempestuous forces of life. "The captain was a man who, since he had come to an age of maturity, had been in the habit of turning his mind this way and that as he would turn the helm of his vessel, and of holding it to the course he had determined upon, no matter how strong the wind or wave, how dense the fog, or how black the night. But never had he stood to his helm as he now stood to a resolve." [13]

Through a combination of chance, accident, and resolve, he discovers many millions of dollars worth of pure Incan gold that has been cunningly secreted within an enormous mound in Peru. One crisis comes when he has extracted all the gold that he safely can (it later turns to be $200,000,000 worth), but has to decide whether to risk trying to dig out a few million more from this pit that seems to hold an inexhaustible supply. Horn is severely tempted to try for more gold, but after his greed wrestles with his reason he decides, "If I ever come back, I will come back, but what I have to do now is to get away with sound reason and steady nerves. . . . If I permit myself to think of taking another bar, I shall be committing a crime." The crime is the personal one of greed gaining the upper hand over reason, a very real possibility when gold fever is near.

But to Horn and Stockton as civilized men, "sound reason and steady nerves" are more important than kingly wealth. Horn maintains his "maturity" to the extent that he is skeptical even of the blessing of the treasure they have already won. "I made up my mind it would be the worst kind of folly to try and get anything else out of that mound. We have now all that is good for us to have. The only question is whether or not we have not more than is good for us." Stockton witnesses Horn's struggle and announces the benediction when it is over. "It was like leaving behind a kingdom and a throne, the command of armies and vast navies, the domination of power, of human happenings; but he came away." [14]

Contrasted to Horn are Mr. Shirley and George Burke, Horn's first and second mates. Both are threatened by gold fever. Shirley copes with it by brainwashing himself, pretending that the sacks contain coal not gold. Burke, on the other hand, capitulates to greed. When Horn reaches the floor of the mound, he suspects it is false and that even more valuables are hidden beneath. But he resists finding out. Burke, against orders, leaves the ship the night before their departure. He finds the lever that releases the trap door of the mound's false bottom and plunges to his death. Gold was hidden below the floor, true enough; but it was cleverly arranged around the walls of an apparently bottomless pit.

Burke is essentially a decent man, but his greed overcomes him, and his fate is almost as terrible as that of Andy MacLeish, an outlaw who has stolen one bag of gold the weight of which has prevented him from escaping an Indian pursuit. He is buried up to his head in sand to be baked by the sun and/or devoured by ants. The wages of greed are destruction. It is to Horn's credit that he knows this maxim in general terms, though he is unaware of the specific dangers of greed, being ignorant of the fates of Burke and MacLeish.

Still Horn's trials are not over, and he must contend with more organized forms of greed represented by government and the law, a plot the chronological reverse of Traven's *Treasure*. The corrupt Peruvian government lays claim to all the gold Horn's party has discovered even though it was initially ignorant of the treasure's existence and had no part in its recovery. Adamantly resisting, Horn feels that his party's fair share is one fifth or forty million dollars. He refuses to give any of the money to the corrupt government unless it agrees by contract to deploy half of the $160,000,000 for the good of the Incan descendants. It must devote eighty million dollars "to the schools, hospitals, libraries, and benefactions of the kind."

Horn must also stand firm against lawyers who wish to be his champion. They have resurrected some "old Roman law" of salvage rights which would entitle Horn to fifty per cent of the gold. This temptation is nearly as great as the desire to test the false bottom of the treasure mound, but Horn is aware of how lawyers tend to redirect wealth into their own pockets. Horn is shrewd enough to play the lawyers' claim against Peru's without committing himself. He has determined by his own lights that twenty per cent is his party's fair share. Twenty per cent is what his party gets.

Published on the proverbial eve of the Alaskan gold rushes of the late 1890s, *Captain Horn* seems prescient both in terms of personal depravity and institutional greed.[15] Horn is able to transcend gold fever because of his belief in civilization, but that abstraction needs a tangible representation concrete enough to match the equation of gold and greed. Hence Stockton embodies "civilization" in the domestic institution of the family, with the spouse as its most salient emblem. When Horn has finally overcome all obstacles and sails safely with his gold cargo, he enjoys the "consciousness of power," but power does not become arrogant tyranny because it "had nothing definite about it. It had nothing which could wholly satisfy the soul of this man, who kept his eyes and his thoughts so steadfastly toward the north. He knew there were but few things in the world that his power could not give him, but there was one thing upon which it might have no influence whatever, and that one thing was far more to him than all the other things in the world." That one thing was a woman, Edna.

The spirit of civilization which guides him is made manifest in the image of Edna that Horn remembers from their life-and-death struggle against bandits. Her picture was "imprinted on the retina of his soul. There he saw a woman still young, tall, and too thin, in a suit of blue flannel faded and worn, with her hair bound tightly around her head and covered by a straw hat with a faded ribbon. But it was toward this figure that he was sailing, sailing, sailing, as fast as the winds of heaven would blow his vessel onward." When he does reach this figure in the flesh, the treasure becomes secondary. As Edna says, "He scarcely mentioned the gold. We had more precious things to talk about."[16] Civilization, love, and self-fulfillment through human relationships win out over chaos, greed, and self-aggrandizement. The simple straw hat proves more attractive than any amount of glittering gold; precious thoughts from an age long dead.

Such sentiments were dealt a near fatal blow by World War I when people began to doubt whether civilization was worth preserving even if it could be preserved. No Captain Horn or Edna appears in Traven's *Treasure*, and minor characters like Burke and MacLeish take the spotlight. One might even aver that Horn is replaced by the impotent Jake Barnes of Ernest Hemingway's *The Sun Also Rises* (1926) or the ineffectual Nick Carraway of F. Scott Fitzgerald's *The Great Gatsby* (1925). Edna is superseded by Hemingway's charming "bitch" Lady Brett Ashley or by Fitzgerald's Daisy Buchanan, whose voice rings not of civilization but money.

Writing a quarter century before World War I, Stockton enjoyed the luxury of being able to believe in civilization as an effective, reasonable, and admirable bulwark against selfish, irrational forces. But even he, like Hemingway, distrusted inspirational rhetoric when it was lifted to the level of abstraction. Duty, honor, patriotism, and other such chivalrous terms made sense to him only when anchored to the home with its ever-attendant garden. Integral with his anti-imperialistic beliefs was the notion that it was better to plant a garden than to plant a flag, better to return to a home of love than to continue to adventure abroad. The center that holds society from scattering into fragments is the warmth radiating from the domestic hearth.

This theme reverberates through nearly all Stockton's fiction. In *Mrs. Cliff's Yacht* sailors are converted from their wandering life to the domestic model presented by Mrs. Cliff, just as they are in *The Casting Away of Mrs. Lecks and Mrs. Aleshine* and in "The Gilded Idol and the King Conch Shell." In "A Widow's Cruise" the tall, muscular, smart, landlocked Widow Duckett hears out the fictional extravaganzas of four traveling sea captains, then tops their tall tales with her own before going indoors, saying to her friend, "I think we can now say we are square with all the world, and so let's go in and wash the dishes."

In a less nautical vein, the wife in "A Spectral Mortgage" knows that her suitor is a ghost because roses on a bush behind him show through him; no will-o'-the-wisp can lure her from devotion to her home and garden. In *Ardis Claverden* the artistic Chiverleys add houses to their landscapes because they prefer to speculate on what is happening in the homes rather than obey the call of the wild to venture into the wilderness. In "A Borrowed Month" even extrasensory perception is harnessed to serve domestic, familial ends. Throughout Stockton's works the home is presented as an anchor against the swirling chaos of an absurdist universe he spied beyond the garden's verge.

Had Stockton lived through World War I even this anchor might have slipped. Or perhaps he might have emphasized domesticity even more strenuously since the nonfamilial world seemed so corrupt and confused. But even had he pursued this latter course, the result would not have been the same because his concepts of domesticity and civilization were closely intertwined and mutually supportive. His household god in *The Merry Chanter* is a twin of what he so blithely refers to as "The Spirit of Civilization" in *The Great War Syndicate*. A family could still be happy before the hearth, but it lacked the assurance that its joy was synonymous with an overall cultural if not international superstructure.

When Stockton's wife, Marian, was trying to drum up business for his local color sketches of Southern life in 1905, she used the argument of conservation: "The first one he ever wrote 'What Might Have Been Expected' (the *first year* of St. Nicholas!) is the story of a past that is utterly obliterated. Some of it would have to be explained even to Stockton children."[17] The same might be said of Stockton's faith in domesticity as the lynch-pin of civilization. Perhaps his garden, like America's small farms, has become anachronistic. One further wonders how prescient Stockton was when, firmly into the then-new twentieth century, he wrote to his closest friends to describe a nightmare he had had: "Last night, I dreamed a dream to the following effect; my house and everything I possessed burned down and I had nothing left but one suit of clothes."[18] One was not left naked, but one's single suit of clothes was outdated, and there was no longer any archetypal pattern of culture by which the suit could be measured.

II   *Science Fiction*

Nobody and everybody knows when American science fiction began. Leslie Fiedler thinks Melville's realistic portrayal of factory life in "The Tartarus of Maids" and Poe's dialogue between angels in "The Conversation of Eiros and Charmion" are somehow science fiction. H. Bruce Franklin claims everyone in the nineteenth century wrote science fiction although he did not know it.[19] But if a science-fiction fan were to read these purported specimens he would no doubt feel deceived, especially if his concept of the genre requires a fascination with advanced science that creates an aura of the marvelous in both senses of the word—an extrapolation beyond the known science of the day that verges on the magical, and a sense of awe about science as the supreme instrument created by man's hand. By such definition the first American science-fiction story may well be "The Diamond Lens" (1858) by the gifted, short-lived Irish-American Fitz-James O'Brien (1828–1862).

Frank Stockton might quite possibly be America's first science-fiction novelist. His *The Great War Syndicate* (1889) fits even the fan's definition of what science fiction is. While Stockton insisted to his publisher that *The Syndicate* was quite popular, especially in military circles, the market must not have been ripe because Stockton did not duplicate the historical achievement for nine years, when he published his next and only other science-fiction novel, *The Great Stone of Sardis* (1898). His science-fiction career was long and began with the story "The Water-Devil: A Marine Tale" (1874), and continued until "My Translataphone" (1900). During these twenty-six years Stockton wrote enough science-fiction, in addition to his two novels, to fill two complete volumes, and his very popular story, "A Tale of Negative Gravity," appeared at midpoint in his career in 1884.[20] Stockton's evolving science-fiction technique can be charted by examining the stories at the extreme ends of this career, especially since they are so similar that any change is revealing.

In "The Water-Devil" a traveling marine spends the night at the home of a blacksmith named Fryker, his wife, and his daughter,

Joanna, in the landlocked village of Riprock. Also present are the schoolmaster, Andrew Cardly, "an enthusiast on natural history and mythology" who has written an article reconciling "the beasts of tradition with the fauna of to-day," and elderly Mr. Harberry, "a man of substance, and a man in whom all of Riprock, not excluding himself, placed unqualified confidence as to his veracity, his financial soundness, and his deep insight into the causes, the influences, and the final issue of events and conditions."[21] The traveler tells the tale of how his one-thousand-ton sailer-steamer's engine stopped while crossing the Bay of Bengal and the ship made no progress even though its sails were filled with wind.

A superstitious Portuguese sailor tells the crew that they are in the tentacles of the water-devil, "about as big as six whales, and in shape very like an oyster without its shell, and he fastens himself to the rocks at the bottom with a million claws. Right out of the middle of him there grows up a long arm that reaches to the top of the water, and at the end of this arm is a fist about the size of a yawl-boat, with fifty-two fingers to it, with each one of them covered with little suckers that will stick fast to anything—iron, wood, stone, or flesh. . . . As the ship is sinkin' he turns her over . . . and gives her a shake, and when the people drop out he sucks them into a sort of funnel, which is his mouth."

It turns out, the marine claims, that the ship was rendered immobile not by a monster but by electromagnetism. The ship's cargo was electricity stored in strongboxes that leaked, causing the metal machinery of the engine to freeze, and making the iron vessel "an enormous floating magnet" drawn inexorably to a six-hundred-mile-long electric telegraph cable the British had laid on the bay floor.

Science thus spoils the tension of the tale as it routs superstition, and the story is more about the difficulty of telling science fiction than about the monster. The marine, who has his eye on Joanna, introduces an anemic love story for her sake, complete with a naughty joke involving a pun on "dying" for sexual intercourse. His tale bores her. When he rises to go to bed with his gaze fixed on Joanna, she, who represents the coming generation of reader, ignores him, preferring to read the weekly newspaper. Mr. Harberry all along has treated the tall tale as a test of sagacity, a yarn that exposes how wise or gullible the listener is. The blacksmith, Fryker, is the simplest sort of reader; he is interested only in the plot which, for him, should be fast-paced, simple, exciting, and formulaic. His wife is a little more complex. When the marine argues eloquently that science makes as exciting a story as a monster can, she, personifying the present generation of reader, says science fiction still disappoints; she prefers the more conventional monster story.

The most interesting listener is Andrew Cardly, whose reactions reveal much about how exciting and confusing science was in 1874. With his knowledge of mythology, specializing in the relationship of mythological beasts to modern animals, he should have recognized the Portuguese's water-devil as a newer version of Scylla, the torment of Jason, Aeneas, and other legendary sailors, but he did not. The reason is that though he knows much about science—others constantly refer to him as an authority to validate or deny the veracity of the marine's account—science has already become so enormous a field that it is the private domain of specialists. An amateur like Cardly, even though he has published an article on the subject, is no authority. A century earlier, someone like Benjamin Franklin could be a scientist among many other things, but by 1874 the generalist is no longer possible unless in the debased notion of dabbler or dilettante.

Stockton's label for Cardly—an "enthusiast"—is better than "amateur," for it echoes Stockton's preoccupation with the conflict of head and heart. Considering the knowledge explosion in science, a willing heart is no compensation for a well-stocked head. By 1874, the "amateur scientist" was no longer viable; one was either a scientist or not, the word "scientist" itself not having been coined until 1844. So, when Cardly is asked whether he has ever heard of a creature like the water-devil, his honest reply, is "I cannot say that I have. But it is certain that there are many strange creatures, especially in the sea, of which scientists are comparatively ignorant." A humorist with a rawer style would have said, "When it comes to knowledge, the only certainty is ignorance." Comparatively, that is.

One major advance in Stockton's technique over twenty-six years was to elevate a minor character like Cardly to the primary role of narrator, as he does in "My Translataphone" (1900) with John Howard, an elderly professor of mathematics who had been a young inventor. This single change in narrative technique completely alters the texture and tone of the tale. By making the narrator a scientific expert, his facts can be taken for granted and the possibility of his story being a tall tale becomes irrelevant. By making him a truthful guest in *John Gayther's Garden*, his story also becomes more personal; it is a story from the heart with no chance of it being a hoax. The audience of five, the same number as in "The Water-devil," can still question the terms of his narration, but on the more sophisticated level of its wisdom instead of its veracity.

When young, John Howard, fascinated by mechanics and "practical problems in science," invents a translataphone, a tube that resembles a hearing trumpet, which can instantaneously translate any language into perfect English. John shows the tube to his beloved Mary Armat, who has recently returned from Burma as a missionary teacher, but, bored by his scientific interests, she speaks Burmese into the tube before John can explain its function. She confesses she loves John but is exasperated that all he talks about is science. She tells him how much more useful it would be if he would invent something that allowed his eyes to see clearly. If he did, then he would see her love for him and her wish to marry—which is, ironically, precisely what his invention does allow him to understand. Assuming John has not the slightest understanding of Burmese, Mary is quite satisfied with the "peculiar revenge" of her speech. Now ready to hear about John's 'phone, Mary's "knowledge-loving" friend, Sarah Castle, "active in mind and body," comes to visit at this precise moment and saves John from having to explain what has just occurred, and he leaves.

Alone, John contemplates what he should do and ponders many possibilities. He is sure that prying Sarah will insist on knowing the secret of the 'phone. He sees his invention as "a great boon I was about to bestow upon the world", with which a scientist could put himself "into communication with the minds of every grade and variety of humanity." And the thought comes to him that his 'phone might work even with birds, dogs, frogs, and other animals, especially chattering monkeys. "What discovery in all natural history could be so great as this? The thought that these little creatures, so nearly allied to man, might disclose to me their dispositions, their hopes, their ambitions, their hates, their reflections upon mankind, had such a sudden and powerful influence upon me that I felt like seizing my translataphone and rushing off to the Zoölogical Gardens."[22] But he decides, "What was anything a black tube could do for me—what, indeed, was anything in the world—compared to the love of that dear girl?"

The culprit is social convention; should Mary discover she, a woman, had been the first to speak of love, she would have to "fly from me in shame." When an invitation to visit comes from Mary, John is mistakenly sure it was instigated by nosey Sarah. To spare Mary shame, he places the invention on the hearthstone and raises his foot above it. "Here it lay, perfect, finished, ready to tell me more than any man ever has known—a thing of life, and ready to be brought to life by the voice of man or beast or bird, or perhaps of any living thing. Could I have the heart to destroy it?' 'Yes,' said I to myself; 'I have the heart to do anything that will prevent my losing the love of Mary Armat.'" He brings his heel down hard. Then he visits Mary and finds that Sarah indeed is behind the invitation, but as his ally not his enemy. She has chided Mary for taking no interest in a field in which his "whole soul" is invested. They talk of science, briefly, then of their love. They engage to marry.

But the story is far from over. The five auditors in the story now have their chance. The Daughter asks if John ever regretted his decision, and John says no because his marriage was happy until Mary's recent death. The Daughter's father asserts John did the right thing, as would anyone "desperately in love." John Gayther asks if it was "fair to the world to destroy an instrument that might have been of great advantage to science," and Howard retreats into relativity: "It is not easy to decide between what we owe to the world and science, and what we owe to ourselves. You see, I decided in favor of myself."

The Next Neighbor is exasperated by all this talk. As a liberated woman, one of Pomona's favorite readers and one who was infuriated by a Frenchman's sexist story, she thinks Howard's talk and actions are nonsense, and all his "fine-spun feelings were unnecessary." Why, she demands, did he not simply remove the translataphone's internal mechanism, show the plain tube to Mary, propose, and then later reinsert the mechanism and enjoy both Mary and the monkeys? To this astute observation Howard blathers some vague excuses but is mercifully interrupted by the melodious song of a red thrush in the lilacs. The old professor seizes on the song and has the final word: "My translataphone would have been worse than useless here. If I could have heard those words, I should have lost that delicious melody. Doubtless the words were commonplace enough, but the melody was divine. And it was easy to interpret the spirit of it. It was a song of joy for all that is pleasant, and bright, and happy in this world."

According to the conventions of the genre, the "last say" is supposed to be the "right say," but the Next Neighbor has cast sufficient shadow on Howard's wisdom to render his summation doubtful, to turn his statements into questions. Does science in its relentless search for facts and truth spoil beauty? Do the words of a song ruin its spirit because they may be commonplace or not as joyous as man anthropomorphically presumes? "My Translataphone" is a fine science-fiction story because it introduces major epistomological questions surrounding truth and wisdom with science as their core, and concludes with those same unanswered questions. The Next Neighbor sees Howard's antitheses as false dichotomies which were responsible for Howard's conduct: a song's spirit as opposed to its message, truth versus love, head versus heart, mechanics versus mathematics, the world versus the mate, creativity versus social convention, domesticity of the hearth-stone on which the invention is crushed versus the welfare of the world through the progress of science. As a mathematics professor, Howard should be aware of the interdependence of scientific theory and prac-tical application.

If one can not agree with the Next Neighbor that such antipodes are erroneous, one must concede that this particular decision was made by a shortsighted man and woman. Only politeness paid to his age and his wife's death prevents some auditors from being more critical. Had Howard read Stockton's *The Girl at Cobhurst* or "The Christmas Shadrach," he would realize that Sarah, not Mary, is more deserving of his love and respect and would make a better life-mate for a scien-tist. But he prefers Mary because of childhood conditioning, having been friends since they went to school together. Moreover, he should have noticed what the Daughter did, that Mary quickly abandoned her missionary work in Burma when the weather turned bad and the work monotonous. Perhaps the Daughter is too harsh with Mary, but some truth attends her insight: "I do not like her. She had no enthusi-asm, or real goodness, to give up her work so soon and for such reasons."

Finally, somewhat like the two inadequate but well-matched char-acters in "Derelict, A Tale of the Wayward Sea," Howard is inept, even setting aside the question of his wisdom in divorcing personal happiness from the world's benefit. When he decides to propose to Mary with his invention in ruins, his plan is fourfold: he has hopes that his translataphone will win him fame and fortune, he wishes to lay same at her feet, he offers himself for himself alone without fame or fortune; should she then accept him, he will tell her the invention did not work. That seems a rather deceptive proposition; someone like Sarah might call it entrapment.

One last point about this story should be made, particularly since one critic has complained that Stockton "did as much as he could to turn [an action adventure story] into a sentimental romance of man-ners."[23] Blacksmith Fryker from "The Water-Devil" might agree, but certainly not Sarah Castle or John Gayther, or, for that matter, Stockton. In "My Translataphone" manners are indeed the enemy. Guilt and shame over trivialities suppress creativity and individuality, and prevent the world's progress. Stockton's domesticity has nothing to do with etiquette; sometimes they are fatally opposed. His emphasis on the social contract militates against petty convention and narrow-minded preconceptions that hinder the full development of individuals bonded together in a family, a family which ultimately comprises the family of man.

Although Stockton condemned certain dichotomies in "My Translataphone," he realized that head and heart do sometimes pose conflicts. When the choice between science and love must be made, Stockton resolves the dilemma in favor of domesticity, as he does in "A Tale of Negative Gravity" (1884). This story has historical importance in that it anticipates H. G. Wells's *The First Men in the Moon* (1901) by seventeen years. Where Jules Verne in the 1870s had sent his men to the moon by means of an enormous cannon, Stockton and then Wells devise an anti-gravity substance—a machine small enough to fit a knapsack in "Gravity," a metal called Cavorite in *First Men*. But where Verne and Wells reach the moon, the inventor in "Gravity" does not get more than fifty feet off the ground. Indeed he is so domestic that the uses he conceives for his invention are most down to earth: to help invalids and old people move about and to move large loads easily, thus sparing draft animals. Though Stockton had reviewed Verne's lunar story, it had no influence on "Gravity" except possibly for one word, "lunatic." Because he has been seen forcing a pony to pull what seems an enormously heavy load, the inventor has been thought to be a cruel madman. His reputation has caused Mr. Gilbert, the father of his son's ideal mate, to break off their children's engagement. After a mishap in Italy where the hero nearly floats into the vastness of space due to understandable human error, he writes down the secret of the device and leaves it with his lawyer to be given to his son upon his death. Then he screws the machine to its intensest pitch and allows it to rise by itself out of sight into the void.

"Gravity" may be the most domestic science fiction ever written. First, it emphasizes family. The inventor arrives at his decision to hide his invention only after several long consultations with his wife. Unlike John Howard and Mary Armat's relationship, their marriage is open, honest, and collaborative. Heartwarming, too, is the trust they have in their son and his fiancée to make the right decision about the use of the invention once they inherit its secret. Most important of all is the idea that science should be a "domestic," in the definition of the word as a "servant." The inventor has no lust for wealth or fame, and has seen the problems the device caused when his tests were misconstrued and when he nearly died through human error. He is not mad nor messianic. He is sure the world can wait for his invention until the world is ready for it. Like Copernicus, he feels no great urgency that his discovery be acclaimed. If science can serve man well, he will use it; if not, its application will be postponed.

The only use he puts the machine to, besides personal pleasure, is to demonstrate it to Mr. Gilbert to convince him he is not mad nor cruel. When Gilbert is assured the inventor is sane and civilized, he urges his daughter's marriage. The inventor's choice had been between feeling like "a winged Mercury" relieved from "that attraction of gravitation which drags us down to earth" and seeing "the buoyancy and lightness of two young and loving hearts." Science in this story is not an enemy of the family except as it is misunderstood or misapplied. The inventor delights in science and the mental exercises it requires. Indeed, he is much like Stockton the story-inventor, who in parallel fashion locks a story in a strongbox because it threatens family happiness in "His Wife's Deceased Sister" (1884), which was published in the same volume of the same magazine. Any Faustian striving, whether in science or in art, was to be treated warily if it endangered the nucleus of civilization, the family.

Stockton has been said to have seen science as "an imcomprehensible threat to the most central value of gentility."[24] In fact, he, an inventor himself, believed science was no more a threat than the antiscience forces it provoked. The lawyer, again Stockton's symbol for civilization, who narrates "Amos Kilbright: His Adscititious Experiences" (1888), is appalled by Dr. Hildstein, a German scientist, because his complete unconcern for individual human life results from an "inhuman craving for scientific investigation" with "cruel and inhuman designs."[25] Although Hildstein is safe from the lawyer's profession, since his actions are technically legal, the lawyer's wife informs Hildstein he is wrong if he thinks "there is no law that will sweep down" on him who "reduces to nothing a fellow human being, and calls it an experiment." She vividly describes the antiscience savagery that could be unleashed:

"there will be no need of courts or judges or lawyers for you. Like a wild beast you will be hunted down. You will be trampled under foot, you will be torn to pieces! Fire, the sword, the hangman's noose, clubs, and crowbars will not be enough to satisfy the vengeance of an outraged people upon a cold-blooded wretch who came to this country solely for the purpose of perpetrating a crime more awful than anything that was ever known before! Did you ever hear of lynching? I see by your face you know what that means. You are in the midst of a people who, in ten short minutes, will be shrieking for your blood!"

If law is taken as one benchmark of civilized behavior, then clearly Stockton felt the fury of an illegal lynch mob to be as dangerous as lawful scientific experimentation which behind the cloak of objectivity dismisses individual human life as irrelevant.

Science even preserves civilization from war in *The Great War Syndicate*, when a business consortium goes into the anti-war market and ends war between America and England by demonstrating superior weaponry such as a submarine and guided missiles. These ultimate weapons bring peace. Beyond this, little can be said of the novel, except that the price paid for peace is high. The faceless syndicate routs heroism; bureaucracy defeats individualism. The only novel by Stockton that omits a theme of love is also the one where his characters are devoid of personal identity. They are as tame as the bovine Euloi in Wells's *The Time Machine* (1895), and they are even deprived of the Euloi's hedonism. Yet the novel was very popular and inspired that sincerest form of flattery when its idea and title were stolen at least twice in the next seventeen years.[26] Stockton wrote the novel to promote his anti-war, anti-imperialistic beliefs, and to do so he wrote for his simplest level of reader, represented by Blacksmith Fryker in "The Water-Devil," giving him much action and one main theme. It is curious that if compared to his other stories, *The Great War Syndicate* today would seem his most thoroughgoing science-fiction effort. It is also his most superficial.

His next science-fiction novel, *The Great Stone of Sardis*, is more complex than *Syndicate* in that it has two plots—polar exploration and laser research—which move into highlight or background like the double hull of the hero's hydroplane: "Each hull had a name of its own, and so the combination name of the entire vessel was frequently changed."[27] This trope also represents shifting moods because the ship's twin-hulled name, *Thalia-Euterpe* or *Euterpe-Thalia*, shows the novel being sometimes lyrical or poetic (Euterpe) and sometimes comic and action-oriented (Thalia).

One plot involves an imagined attempt by submarine in 1947 to reach the North Pole (something which would not be accomplished historically until 1958). This plot offers much gadgetry. Besides the submarine, Stockton includes snowmobiles, a type of radar, homing devices, an instrument for extracting air from water, gas bombs, directional bombs, and other inventions. He also digresses in what came to be typical science-fiction fashion to comment on historical trends. With ecology, for example, the last two whales in the world were presumed killed in 1935 off Melville Island. The expedition is strongly tempted to bring the sole survivor back as a trophy when they find it near the Pole, but they desist, not being able to bear the responsibility for the death of the last specimen of the world's largest mammal. Yet they are certain a hunting expedition will soon be organized by some hunt club to carry off this prize.

Still the vainglory of the whale hunt is present in the Polar search. Mrs. Sarah Block, who sees the effort as "a sort of congregational suicide," is a genial symbol of those antiscience and anti-adventure forces Stockton criticizes in the novel's opening chapter. The opposite extreme is represented by a Pole, Ivan Rovinski, whose nationality is chosen as a punning link with the Polar quest. Rovinski tries sabotage and deceit and risks death in the frozen wastes just for the personal glory of being the first man at the Pole. He would gladly give his life just to have a Polar sea named after him, a sea that is so foreboding that the crew disdain to name it for their commander ("he's too good a man") and call it "Lake Shiver" instead. Stockton takes some care to point out that Rovinski "was not perhaps a lunatic, but his unprincipled ambition" made him do insane things.[28] He is not a madman but a normal man caught up in a prideful scientific quest that, upon inspection, may seem mad.

The crew at large, even though they gain fame and wealth, come to a similar suspicion about themselves. At the Pole their readings are "longitude everything." Their weathervane points always south no matter which way the wind blows. When they first reach the Pole they are greatly excited, but thrill dissipates when there is nothing to see but flat ice. Nothing marks any particular spot as the precise Pole except mathematical technicality. The title of chapter fourteen seems to capsulate their epochal achievement—they have found "A Region of Nothingness." Other than the fact that they have been there, their efforts have resulted in no real benefit to mankind, even though men have died in the effort.

The Pole plot (North and Rovinski) generates most of the action of the story, but thematically its presence only reflects the dangers and importance of the other plot, in which the thirty-five-year-old scientist, Roland Clewe in Sardis, New Jersey, uses a type of laser to penetrate over fourteen miles into the earth and discovers an enormous diamond, "The Great Stone of Sardis," which discovery argues that the earth was once a comet. Clewe runs no risk of being opposed to science as Sarah Block is. He is Stockton's ideal civilized scientist, "well known as a man of science, an inventor, an electrician of rare ability, and a man of serious purpose and strict probity, but it was possible for a man of great attainments and of the highest moral character to become a little twisted in his intellect."[29]

This "twist" is evident when Clewe invents the laser. He is so intent on using it to discover "the internal structure of the earth" that he is blind to more practical, human-oriented applications of the invention, such as its use in medical surgery. In other words, he risks being caught up in abstractions and losing his link with humanity. Just as Stockton had shown that he himself prefers "Plain Fishing" to Art for Art's sake in his own esthetic, he champions humane science over abstract scientific research related only remotely to man's welfare. Clewe, an ideal scientist, still risks being swirled like Ivan Rovinski into a hysterical obsession with scientific projects.

The person to preserve Clewe from madness is Margaret Raleigh, a widow of a rich scientist who is a scientist herself. Clewe's beam reveals only an impenetrable void that parallels the Pole's "Region of Nothingness." To gain further knowledge, a dangerous personal descent must be made. He puts the problem to his beloved, saying that if Margaret wishes it, he will desist from the descent and cover up the hole. She, unlike Mary Armat, urges Clewe to pursue the quest because, "It holds a love for you which is stronger than any fear or horror or dread." Stockton later explains her behavior thus: "Margaret was not ‚ealous of her rival, science, and if Roland had ceased to be an inventor, a discoverer, a philosopher, simply because he had become a rich and happy husband, he would have ceased to be the Roland she had loved so long."[30] Margaret is the diametric opposite of Rovinski's mad scientific questing; she is also the opposite of Mary Armat's ignorant, selfish conventionality in "My Translataphone."

By descending into the shaft, a deed blessed by the adventurer's loved one, the void ceases to seem a void and becomes an enormous diamond, which creates other problems. To announce this fact would ruin the world's economy, and Clewe and Margaret decide to keep the fact secret, at least for a time. But the descent was worthwhile on a higher plane in that science now knows more about the origin of its planet. It is also certainly rewarding on a personal level in that love and science, domesticity and the adventure of discovery have been happily wedded, as personified by the marriage of Roland and Margaret, which might be seen as Stockton's version of Richard Lovelace's famous proverb, "I could not love thee, dear, so much,/Lov'd I not honor more."[31] It is further significant that after the moment of crisis, when Margaret bids Clewe descend into the shaft, references to Clewe change. Before, he is referred to most often as "Clewe," suggesting a search for clues to knowledge and human character. After the crisis, he becomes "Roland," not Charlemagne's flawed hero nor Browning's seeker at the dark tower but Stockton's civilized hero, whose commitment to adventure is balanced by his devotion to love, whose obsession with the frontier of discovery is tempered by his fondness for a happy home around the fireside.

   The Great Stone of Sardis is a good domestic novel, but a science-fiction failure. It is one that a reader like Joanna Fryker from "The Water-Devil" might appreciate, but not her blacksmith father. The problem is that science fiction and the domestic novel make a bad marriage. As clear proof, one may look at the passage that occurs when Roland and Margaret have overcome all the obstacles to their personal, professional, and philosophic happiness, and Roland points out "three dear little birds," baby robins who have made a nest in "an old tomato-can." Margaret's response is, "Roland, when I first knew you, you would not have noticed such a little thing as that." Roland responds, "I couldn't afford it." "It is the sweetest charm of all your triumphs!" Margaret proclaims.[32]

   This scene is meant to be the crowning touch of domesticity; to a reader like Blacksmith Fryker it would seem sickeningly sentimental. An adventure novel like *Moby-Dick* can be enhanced by the poetics of domesticity, as in the tense moment when Ahab is almost dissauded from his monomaniac quest for the white whale by fond recollections of his family. But science fiction, as a sub-genre of the adventure novel, is more rigid. Its unyielding purpose is, as one famous science-fiction creation has it, "To boldly go where no man has gone before." To take along one's spouse and then to make the familial relationship the cynosure of the story is anathema to science fiction. While there are many adult science-fiction readers, the psychological appeal of the mode is still "adolescent," in that it is predicated on rebellion against the father figure and on discontent with the status quo. Two main themes are anti-utopia (where the evils of civilization's tendencies are protrayed) and the end of the world (where the obliteration of civilization is perceived with a certain amount of glee). With such anti-civilizational characteristics inherent in the genre, Stockton's commitment to the poetics of domesticity must suffer defeat. *The Great Stone of Sardis* is a freakish hybrid; *The Great War Syndicate* is a bore outside its time.

Stockton's science fiction could have been salvaged had he been more imaginative. Intrigued by electricity in *The Great Stone of Sardis*, for example, he can not conceive of a wireless telegraph, and so his submarine must pay out miles of cable to communicate with its base. But Stockton was not imaginative in this way because he had other interests. His main serious question was, "Can and if so how can two people get along?" which is not the stuff from which good science fiction is woven. His interest in invention went no further than its impact on human relationships, as in "My Translataphone" and "The Lady in the Box." His philosophical perspective is voiced by Roland Clewe when he says, "There is nothing regular or exact in nature. Even our earth is not a perfect sphere. Nature is never mathematically correct. You must always allow for variations."[33]

Stockton's imaginative "variations" might include an anti-gravity device, but its purpose is to achieve family happiness, not to seek the moon. Approximately fifty feet from solid earth is about as far as Stockton wishes "to boldly go." Because of his primary values of humor in an absurd if not a chaotic world and of fundamental human relationships, Stockton's science fiction is closer to that of Kurt Vonnegut in *Cat's-Cradle* than to Jules Verne or H. G. Wells.

The nonfictional data support this point. When Stockton patented his parallel-line engraver on February 20, 1886, his device was eminently practical and much used, but it was not particularly startling, as were the inventions of his fellow Jerseyman, Thomas Edison. When he stuck his editor with editing a manuscript of his in 1877, he commented from a steamer that he was "going to set up extensive 'Revise-works,' to be run by steam. English literature demands them." In 1896, when the invention of the bicycle seemed to jeopardize literacy as television does today, Stockton tossed off the threat to his livelihood as a joke: "My recent royalty returns—the smallest I have ever had from your house—have made me fear that there may be some truth in the statement that the bicycle rage has had a bad effect upon the book trade. I suppose that that cannot be helped unless books are protected by a heavy tax on bicycles."[34] A cavalier attitude toward invention does not make good science fiction.

All these factors, which kept Stockton from writing successful science fiction, were boons to his other fantasy efforts. Where science fiction demands dramatic extrapolation—clothing, time machines, bug-eyed monsters, space travel—fantasy permits milder whimsy with respect to the earth's "variations" instead of wild ruptures of normalcy. One of Stevenson's favorite Stockton tales, "The Remarkable Wreck of the *Thomas Hyke*" (1884), is a fine example. Bureaucracy is the context. Five men gather at the Registrar of Woes' shipwreck office, run by a politician who values his country house more than his country. The shipwreck clerk, John J. Laylor, whose age might be twenty-five or forty-five, is putting in his last day at his soft government post because he is about to be replaced by the Spoils System, a prospect he faces with a "quite resigned air." With many issues to attack, from political corruption to the banality of government employment, Stockton chooses to chide the smug arrogance of bureaucratic officials at a time when the word "officious" has shifted from meaning "fawning" to "condescending" or "patronizing." He attempts to shake the clerk from his confidence in the clockwork regularity of his record book, which he believes lists every possible kind of wreck under the sun or in the sea.

Hence the tale is told of cheerful William Anderson, who is drowned in the ocean and yet dry as a chip. His ship's cargo of pig iron breaks loose and rushes to the bows of the ship during a storm. The shift of weight causes the ship to hang perpendicularly in the water with only part of its propeller showing. Since the ship has technically "sunk," Anderson is "drowned." Yet he is dry because of the airtight compartments, and he sets up a pleasant life aboard the "sunken" ship. His rescue comes about when the pig iron crashes through the hull, allowing the ship to bob to the surface and be spotted. The clerk is then challenged to classify this "shipwreck" in his neat, fat record book. But bureaucracy, with time if not tide its ally, wins because the clerk announces, rising from his seat on his last day in office, "Gents, it's four-o'clock, and at that hour this office closes."

The ingredient that makes this story provocative as well as amusing, the factor that makes "The Wreck" as the title says "Remarkable," is that Anderson's mentality is very similar to the clerk's. The character the men create to astound the clerk's smooth complacency is much like the clerk when at the most hopeless point in the wreck Anderson says to his fellow survivors, "What we've got to do is to be content with the comforts we have around us, and something will turn up to get us out of this; you see if it don't."[35] Clearly this is a safe bet, since if something does not turn up to save them, no one will be left alive to complain.

"The Wreck" is a strange story. It starts out to be an attack on the bureaucratic mind. Upon reflection, one feels that the Anderson mind is identical with the clerk's, and their rescues are similar in being timely and fortuitous. A critic confidently asserts this tale is a satire, then he feels compelled to murmur "sort of." At its most sophisticated, Stockton's satire seems sure, but he keeps the butt of the satire ambiguous. One is even tempted to assert that Stockton is at his most impressive when he is satirizing the genre of satire.

The same flip-flop occurs in strictly fantasy pieces with no satirical purpose. In one of the best, "A Philosophy of Relative Existences" (1892), Rupert Vance, an unknown philosopher working on a book with the same title as this story, leaves a hamlet one night to cross a river, and finds himself in a ghost city where he meets a ghost girl who tells him his book is already written and esteemed a classic, though she is sure the book's author is dead. The story's burden is that perhaps real people are figments of a dream much like the characters in dreams dreamers dream. Identity and existence are presented as completely relative. One leaves the story in the eerie mood that no clear demarcation separates the real from the unreal, that the dream and actuality are as intricately interdependent as the mind and the brain. A comment that George Saintsbury made about Gustave Flaubert's dream fiction in contrast to Thomas De Quincey's is highly relevant to Stockton:

> The capacities of dreams and hallucinations for literary treatment are undoubted. But most writers, including even De Quincey, who have tried this style, have erred, inasmuch as they have endeavoured to throw a portion of the mystery with which the waking mind invests dreams over the dream itself. Anyone's experience is sufficient to show that this is wrong. The events of dreams as they happen are quite plain and matter-of-fact, and it is only in the intervals, and, so to speak, the scene-shifting of dreaming, that any suspicion of strangeness occurs to the dreamer.[36]

This unsuspected dream quality of Stockton's art applies as well to his patently realistic sketches, like "Asaph" (1892), whose title character can do "less work in more time than anybody they ever saw."[37] To Stockton, fantasy was a shade of reality, not a separate realism. Just as the color red shades gently into orange and then into yellow, Stockton's fantasy slides smoothly into the unusual and then into the realistic. In contrast to his father's strict sense of right and wrong, righteous and sinful, Stockton's philosophy danced in ambiguity, irony, and complexity. Whereas Melville might view this spectacle as "the blackness of darkness" and Twain might expose it with a knee-slapping joke, Stockton preferred to twirl the cosmic confusion into bright, gay, kaleidoscopic colors.

His most famous story "The Lady, or the Tiger?" demonstrates this point sharply, for ambiguity is rampant, confusion is supreme, and nearly all the principal philosophic questions are swirled into a twilight zone which is neither strictly day nor night. The story takes place in a semi-barbaric, semi-civilized age, but what age is that? Theodore Dreiser describes humanity on the eve of the twentieth century that way, even using the tiger to represent barbarism in Chapter VIII of *Sister Carrie* (1900). The king, too, is ambivalent. He is godlike, his will is supreme in his universe, and his subjects move like orbs in his constellation. More specifically, he is a Christian god whose nature is "bland and genial," whose actions are described in biblical echoes, "for nothing pleased him so much as to make the crooked straight, and crush down uneven places," a borrowing from Luke 3:5.[38]

Within a framework of necessity, the hero, solidly middle class since not a slave or a noble, has free will, though the impulse of love for the princess initially propelled him into the predicament. He must choose between two doors; behind one is a ferocious tiger who would devour him, and behind the other a beautiful lady whom he would marry. But the choice he makes will be a fifty-fifty chance; free will is interlocked with statistical accident. Chance, free will, and necessity become a jumble where it is difficult to separate one from the others.

The princess only confuses matters. "Possessed of more power, influence, and force of character than anyone" and possessed also of a "moiety of barbarism," she solves the riddle of the doors through the "power of a woman's will" and with the help of gold, the obvious symbol of economic persuasion which rules society as much as free will, chance, or necessity. She discovers not only which door the lady stands behind but the lady's identity as well.

As the sole source of information upon which the hero can base his decision and exert his will over chance, the princess is corrupt. She hates the lady and is jealous of her hero-lover because "Often had she seen, *or imagined she had seen*, this fair creature throwing glances of admiration upon the person of her lover, and *sometimes she thought* these glances were perceived and even returned" (italics mine). An intelligent decision must be based on reliable intelligence, yet in this case at least there is no assurance that the source of information is trustworthy. The science enthusiast in "The Water-Devil" has already made the point that data is seldom complete.

The ending of the story is left for the reader to interpret, yet three main points are clear. One is that the godlike king in "his barbaric idealism" has attempted to create a system of "perfect fairness," which is undermined by an astute individual whose beliefs and free will are founded on the flimsiest of facts where misperception may be the basis of misconception. The second point is that the hero is a fool who accepts the princess's decision without any reflection on whether she in jealousy might send him to the tiger. He opens the door she indicates "without the slightest hesitation," and she makes the signal again "without the slightest hesitation" because she has spent "days and nights of anguished deliberation." Perhaps Stockton's point, reinforced by this echo phrase, is that whether choice is made in blind trust without thought or whether choice is made after anguished deliberation with undependable information, they often come to the same fate in the end.

The third point is that the story is clearly divisible into two main interests—development and conclusion (or inconclusion). The former is cosmic, the latter internal. The one depicts the confused, chaotic universe in which man is a force buffeted by other various, powerful, inscrutable forces. The other, in the story's words, is "a study of the human heart which leads us through devious mazes of passion, out of which it is difficult to find our way."[39] The fact that Stockton originally titled the story "In the King's Arena" suggests he was more interested in the cosmic issue. That he tamely submitted—presumably "without the slightest hesitation"—to William Carey's suggestion as editor of *Century Magazine* that a better title would be "The Lady, or the Tiger?" the dilemma he suffered as a practicing writer is evident. As author, he was treated as whimsically as he trapped his blameless, foolish, anonymous hero.

Yet Cary's title with its redirection of attention toward the story's conclusion proved a boon, since everyone from Chicago schoolchildren to Robert Browning to Hindu sages debated the question of which door

was opened, the lady's or the tiger's. But the boon was a bane in that it channeled interest away from Stockton's primary to his secondary concerns. What fame he has today is based on what he only incidentally intended. His reputation as a widely popular author in the late nineteenth century has eclipsed the fact that he was also a serious writer, just as his fame as a humorist has made people blind to his serious statements. Stockton would have appreciated this irony, for it was the very stuff of his philosophy and art. In the last section of "The Lady, or the Tiger?" the third-person narration falls away and Stockton addresses the reader directly. It is time that we address the matter of reader perception just as directly.

CHAPTER 5

All in All: Conclusion

I *The Holt Tower*

STOCKTON'S audience read him essentially for one reason: to be refreshed by wit so that they could return to their business with renewed vigor. They expected his art to be like the magic kiss in "Old Pipes and the Dryad" which makes the recipient ten years younger. They went to his books as later audiences went to the silent screen comedies, not for art nor for philosophy but for humor and escape. They formed "Pass-it-on Societies" to spread "The Buller-Podington Contract," not because the story was a plea for people even of antipathetic interests to cooperate but because they thought the plot was funny. They loved "The Lady, or the Tiger?" not for its cosmology, nor for its depiction of the joy and terror of sex, nor for its concern whether passion and selfishness or reason and morality were the greater forces in human behavior, but because the story gave them an excuse to debate among themselves, perhaps peppering their remarks with sexist or anti-sexist jokes. They read about Pomona because she was eccentric, not because she raised questions of feminism, class bias, or American culture. If this audience were told that Gertrude Stein, an admirer of Stockton's, had borrowed the inversion of point of view he used in "Our Story" (1883) to write her famous *Autobiography of Alice B. Toklas* (1933), they would shrug their shoulders politely; they would not be impressed.[1]

This audience also liked its literature to be straightforward. When Stockton in "The Knife That Killed Po Hancy" (1889) set out deliberately to render the split-personality concept of Robert Louis Stevenson's Jekyll and Hyde (1886) in a more complex fashion, his audience considered the complexity a distraction instead of an asset; they much preferred Stockton's earlier, less complex efforts such as "The Transferred Ghost" (1882) and "The Spectral Mortgage" (1883). They favored Charles Dickens's "A Christmas Carol" (1843) over Stockton's "The Baker of Barnbury" (1884), in part because Scrooge's belief that

Christmas is a humbug is proved wrong, whereas the baker's suspicion is more sinister. He believes Christmas celebrants are hypocrites and their celebration a fraud.

Similarly, when this audience praised Stockton's women, they were far more generous to his conventional characterizations of older widows, as in *The Casting Away of Mrs. Lecks and Mrs. Aleshine* (1886), than to his vigorous, aggressive, sexually charged young heroines, as in *Ardis Claverden* (1890)—a response that was in inverse proportion to Stockton's own evaluation of these two books. That they recognized the significant contribution to the development of the short story achieved in "The Lady, or the Tiger?" (1882) is to their credit, but they were unable to perceive Stockton's far more subtle and sophisticated use of this technique in *John Gayther's Garden* (1902) and *The Vizier of the Two-Horned Alexander* (1899). When Stockton introduced genuine tragedy into the comic texture of *The Girl at Cobhurst* (1898), he confused his audience. Even today when people study his evil women—and he has created some truly fine ones—they highlight characters like Maria Port in *The Captain's Toll-Gate* (1903) who is rendered innocuous by the other women in the novel, and they ignore more menacing females like Mrs. Keswick in *The Late Mrs. Null* (1886) who is capable of destroying people and driving some to suicide.[2]

This audience preferred the obvious to the complex, the simple to the sinister, because they and their families, to paraphrase Victoria, wished to be amused. Consequently, anything beyond the frankly humorous had to be buried in the substrata of the story for the appreciation of that minority within his popular audience whom Stockton called "a chosen few." *Ardis Claverden's* sexual drives were described in terms of thrilling horseback rides or seemingly innocent paintings. Sexuality is discussed in an apparent digression about the relative merits of cucumbers and gherkins. Marriage on the rebound to an unsuitable mate is characterized by the wedding gift of a corkscrew. The age-old double entendre of "dying" to mean sexual intercourse is so deftly interwoven into "The Water-Devil: A Marine Tale" as to be unnoticed on first glance, even though flirtation is an obvious element of the story.

Stockton's stint at the children's magazine *St. Nicholas* was a useful apprenticeship for this type of work because children's literature provides many levels of interpretation, from the most innocent to the dangerously profound, and the reader, depending on his maturity, can probe as deeply as he dares. Writing adult literature at a time still influenced by official and social censorship, Stockton encoded his stories with suggestive themes and let the reader decide whether to decipher them.

As it was with sex, so it was with other taboos. The void—or the meaninglessness of existence—and the absurd—or the vision of a universe of total ambiguity—intrigued Stockton as it did Melville, Hawthorne, and Poe, but where the last three faced the void and absurdity full face, sometimes even revelling in them, Stockton gave them only passing glances. He would nod an acknowledgement of their presence and then get on with his plot. In *Ardis Claverden* he gives two portraits of the void, one in black, the other in white; one in a cave, the other lost in a snowy wood. Having presented these pictures of nothingness, he quickly extricates his characters and hurries them into the complexities of an everyday world that seems significant by comparison because it is all they have. Stockton assures them and his readers, quite as quickly, that that world is more than enough.

I call this technique indirection; the most serious statements are made covertly, by suggestion, clue, hint, innuendo. It is the essence of the Western Tall Tale, but Stockton knew it better in the guarded speech of oppressed American blacks such as Uncle Isham in *The Late Mrs. Null.*

One might imagine that the limits imposed by his middle-class, middle-brow audience would have greatly frustrated Stockton. Sometimes he did see these limits as an unavoidable prerequisite of his craft, but generally he identified closely with the values of middle-class Americans. Where Walt Whitman might sing the praises of the divine common and Frank Norris might view mankind as so many stupid sheep, Stockton genuinely liked his bourgeois readers. He saw their values as a necessary bulwark against greed and selfishness, privilege and riot, monopoly and chaos.

He saw middle-class women especially as the one sane sector in a world bent on destruction and war. Much has been made of this era of "bloomers," symbol of increased mobility, but Stockton also liked the top part of the Gibson girl's outfit: the tie, the blouse with broad shoulders or enlarged arms symbolic of a willingness to carry the weight of the world or to do the world's work, and her hat—no floral, awkward, immobilizing hat, but a plain, direct statement that she was ready to do the right thinking society required. This thinking involved an opposition to war, imperialism, monopoly, wealth, sexism, selfishness, ignorance, and oppression, and promoted those genteel virtues necessary to make a garden flourish, to put a house in order, to allow a family to grow.

Stockton's auctorial posture was as though he were regarding this pageant from the Kitchell astronomical observatory in the tower of his beloved home called "The Holt." Theodore Roosevelt had played there when a child, and the two sides of Roosevelt—the conservationist, "Teddy Bear" side, and the aggressive "Big Stick" side—aptly pinpoint Stockton's allegiance: firmly opposed to imperialism, positively in favor of conserving the most humane elements of American civilization. His narrative persona may seem detached as if in a tower, but his concern was immediate as if he spent countless hours behind a telescope making close scrutiny of society's complex activity. The noted critic Edmund Gosse reported that Robert Louis Stevenson had "adored these tales of Mr. Stockton's, a taste which must be shared by all good men," little knowing that in the twentieth century the concept of the "good man" would be ridiculed as incredibly naive or woefully inadequate.[3]

Stockton felt that of all segments of society his middle-class readership was the most admirable, even though they had many faults. His identification with this class provided many of his strengths and some of his most glaring weaknesses. By allying himself with this social stratum, he developed a distaste for the powerfully rich, believing with Lord Acton that power corrupts. His bourgeois sympathies made him neglectful of the lower classes at the other end of the social scale. In his essay "Funny Darkies," for example, he dehumanizes both rich and poor. He satirizes "million-heirs" who have inherited wealth but can not enjoy life and contrasts them with poor but happy blacks.[4] A medium between the two extremes would theoretically be the middle class.

Such wholehearted identification with the bourgeoisie made him dislike immigrants of all ethnic persuasions, including the British, as well as blacks, labor unions, and the working class in general. Occasionally, as with Pomona in a series of novels and with the heroine of "Derelict: A Tale of the Wayward Sea" (1891), he would sympathize with individuals in the lower class as he did with the upper classes in *The Great War Syndicate* (1889); but generally his values lay with the new phenomenon of the vast middle class which bought his books.

Although Stockton liked middle-class values, he would sometimes criticize them, but his delicate satire was easy to miss. In two cases, for example, he uses a nest of birds to cap the contract between his hero and heroine to begin a family. In *The Girl at Cobhurst* the scene is intentionally overwritten as a parody of the Sentimental Romance; in *The Great Stone of Sardis* (1898) a similar bird scene is meant as an honest tribute to the couple's love and their individual growth.

The same quiet satire can be seen at work in the one political issue Stockton felt strongly about—imperialism and its handmaiden, war. He attempted to nudge his readers gently from the path of imperialism. People who smiled at a humorous story were not in the mood, he hoped, to wage international war, a prospect that loomed inevitable to his generation. An enthusiast about the conservationist dimension of Teddy Roosevelt and America, he loathed the "Big Stick," "Rough Rider," and "Great White Fleet," which he saw as the Hyde half of America's national character. Stockton stood for what he called "the Spirit of Civilization," little suspecting that this virtue, like Stevenson's "good man," would so soon be seen as a farce, as when D. H. Lawrence in the early 1920s proclaimed, "Civilized society is insane."[5]

If by "civilized society" Lawrence meant etiquette, narrow conventionality, and suppression of individualism, Stockton would agree, since he himself criticized those qualities as threats to self-growth, in "My Translataphone" and "Derelict," for example. But Stockton would draw the line where self-growth risked becoming self-indulgence. To him, sound civilization was based on its elemental nucleus—the individual who has come to a sufficient understanding of himself or herself that he or she can enter into a mutually rewarding relationship with another human being. In "Derelict" he presents two couples—one has achieved this monad of civilization; another has merely become married.

In stories like "The Christmas Shadrach" (1891) and "The Magic Egg" (1894) Stockton demonstrates exactly how difficult this twin goal of self-understanding and growth through human relationships can be. In novels like *Ardis Claverden* and *The Girl at Cobhurst* he shows that the goal is especially difficult, since the human imagination can so easily fool itself that it has accomplished what it has not. The goal is also imperative since society seemed about to fall apart, as the frequent shipwrecks in Stockton's stories suggest. This concern for an imperiled civilization led Stockton to follow the success of *The Adventures of Captain Horn*, the best-selling American novel for 1895, with a sequel, *Mrs. Cliff's Yacht* (1896), in an effort to channel the spirit of adventure in the direction of domesticity. He hoped he could help make the common problem of living well seem as exciting as any great enterprise from Polar exploration *(The Great Stone of Sardis)* to piracy *(Kate Bonnet,* 1902). His characters, as in *Kate Bonnet,* are motivated by complex, powerful forces which sometimes resemble Poe's Imp of the Perverse. Their universe seems often corrupt, chaotic, or absurd. Small wonder Stockton saw civilization as no easy or cozy quest.

In 1936, Walter L. Pforzheimer declared about Stockton, "The people who know the author know the epoch [1880–1900], and the two are interchangeable; the author is the age incarnate; rarely has a man so reflected his period." This assessment is probably hyperbolic, and the opinion expressed in *Harper's Weekly* in 1902 is more balanced: Stockton "was as distinct an embodiment of the American spirit in one sort as Mark Twain was in another."[6] The safest statement is that Stockton does reveal much principally about the middle-class, middle-brow, generally female audience of his day. While Richard Harding Davis's women were striving to become regal, as in *The Princess Aline* (1895), and while Frances Hodgson Burnett's mother would sacrifice anything to see her American child become an aristocrat in *Little Lord Fauntleroy* (1886), Stockton's women were becoming self-reliant individuals, his children realistic American children. Of his thirty novels, only one—*The House of Martha*—seems boring to modern readers, and that is because it is a creature of its time. Widely popular in 1891, *Martha* is a reverse of *Pygmalion* or *My Fair Lady;* a woman who lives like a reclusive nun doffs her cap to reveal hair as rich as Hester Prynne's and becomes a doctor and a lover. Unlike Hawthorne, Chopin, and James, Stockton celebrates the transformation without ambivalence.

Reading Stockton can reveal much about the era, its values, customs, economy, fashions, problems, housing, transportation. His children's novel, *What Might Have Been Expected* (1874), a forerunner of *Huckleberry Finn* (1884), tells how much flour costs, how Christmas was celebrated, how sumac was collected and processed for tanning, and other practical information. To me, however, the most fascinating quality of Stockton's art is how conscious he was of his readership, an attention that foreshadows recent trends in recreative fiction and apperceptive criticism wherein what the reader does with the book before him is of great importance.

In the assembly of auditors in *John Gayther's Garden,* as one example, we learn how diverse his audiences were even when they shared the same socioeconomic class. They range from the liberated Next Neighbor, to the conventional Master of the House, to the astute but conservative Mistress of the House and her Daughter, who shows much promise and much confusion as a representative of the next generation of reader. In *The Vizier of the Two-Horned Alexander* the wife takes no part in the action, yet she is the focus of the novel as a test of whether her idealism or her local prejudices will win out, a trial that mirrors Stockton's conception of his readers' possible responses.

To his further credit, it is clear these achievements were deliberate, not happenstance. In a series of writings, ranging from stories like "The Pilgrim's Packets" (1873) to sketches like "Plain Fishing" (1888) to articles like "Mark Twain and His Recent Works" (1893) to his introductions to story collections like *Afield and Afloat* (1900) and *A Story-Teller's Pack* (1897), he makes clear what he believes are the special qualities of his art. He acknowledges that his uniqueness prevents him from being classed easily in any of the literary movements of his era—not strictly a Naturalist, Realist, Western humorist, local colorist, satirist, nor regionalist—although his work touches upon each of these categories. He will not risk losing his audience by indulging in the literary experimentation of a James or a Crane, and yet he will not stoop to the hack writing of a Davis, an Alger, or a Burnett. He realizes that because his writings are generally humorous their deeper philosophy will be ignored. He knows his artistry seeks to gather "fair flowers that verge on the deep ravine" and that many will not see the philosophical abyss because of the floral display. In a nightmare he had toward the end of his career, he dreamed that the house of fiction he had built up had burned down, but I doubt he suspected how complete the conflagration would be. He went from being as widely known as Mark Twain and as highly respected as Henry James in his day to all but total obscurity in modern times.

For one who accomplished so much and knew what he was doing, such neglect is unjust. The British marvel that Stockton is better known and esteemed in England than he is in his native land.[7] Specialized book-length studies, which a knowledge of Stockton could enrich, pay him only passing notice.[8] Unless the effort is made to preserve Stockton for American literary culture, he may continue to suffer what Frederick Lewis Pattee feared in 1923: "He has receded far into the shadow, the gloom of which bids fair to become total."

II *Tending Garden*

Among Stockton's contemporary admirers may be counted Robert Louis Stevenson, Mark Twain, William Dean Howells, James Russell Lowell, Rudyard Kipling, Robert Browning, Edmund Gosse, Edward

Eggleston, Arthur Quiller-Couch, Mary Mapes Dodge, and Gertrude Stein. Librarians in 1893 reported that only Twain and Frances Marion Crawford were more popular than Stockton. *Century Magazine* in 1901 considered him, along with Joel Chandler Harris and Mark Twain, one of America's finest writers.[9] A name everyone recognized in the Gay 90's, "Stockton" then seemed immortal.

As early as the 1920s, that name faced its demise. Although people like F. L. Pattee, Robert Underwood Johnson, William L. Werner, and Arthur Quiller-Couch still sang his praises, the mood was that "Stockton" would soon become a forgotten word. Quiller-Couch said Stockton's characters are "about the most genuinely American things in American fiction," and he mused over Stockton's predicament: "Everyone has read *Rudder Grange, The Lady or the Tiger?* and *A Borrowed Month;* but somehow few people seem to think of them as subjects for serious criticism. And yet these stories are almost classics. That is to say, they have the classical qualities, and only need time to ripen them into classics. . . . Originality, good temper, good sense, moderation, wit—these are classical qualities; and he is a rare benefactor who employs them all for the amusement of the world."[10]

But the decades marked by the hedonism of the 1920s, the Depression of the 1930s, and the War of the 1940s were not conducive to an appreciation of Stockton's ironic wit. In fact, his works went out of print, despite the call for reissues by people as illustrious then as Alexander Woolcott, Christopher Morley, and Eleanor Roosevelt.[11]

The modern situation is not as grim as the 1930s nor as gay as the 1890s. Stockton continues to find champions like Maurice Sendak, who has illustrated two of his stories; Edmund Wilson, who was impressed by the quality of Stockton's stories; and Cornelia Meigs, who has ranked Stockton's children's literature with Kipling's, Kenneth Grahame's, and Beatrix Potter's, saying that his tales "were among the glories" of *St. Nicholas'* early years.[12] Librarians still honor Stockton, but to rank his work among "20,000 Vital Titles" is a demotion from his repute among "1000 best books" in 1924 and among "200 best books" in 1928.[13]

The National Union Catalog indicates that in the last twenty years Stockton has been fairly well represented by reprints and reissues, but these are difficult to obtain except for collections like *The Story-Teller's Pack, A Frank R. Stockton Reader* (New York: Charles Scribner's Sons, 1968) and *The Lady or the Tiger and Other Stories* (New York: Airmont, 1968). More usual is his republication by coteries of fans, as with the hundred-copy edition of *The Magic Egg* (London: Covent Garden Press, 1970) or the microtransparencies (1974) of *The Casting Away of Mrs. Lecks and Mrs. Aleshine, The Girl at Cobhurst,* and *The Great Stone of Sardis* by—ominous-sounding enough—the Lost Cause Press.

Some writers are lost due to the whim of history; others for understandable reasons. Stockton belongs to this latter class of victim. Eight major factors can be cited as cause for his obscurity. First, he was enormously popular, and for many decades popular writers have been disdained. While this problem has been rectified somewhat since scholars have discovered they can learn much about American culture by studying its popular literature, the focus remains on lesser writers than Stockton like Crawford, Davis, and Alger. Ironically, had Stockton been a hack writer, he might be better known today. But he insisted on quality within the limits of his middle-brow audience. This audience may have lacked the sensitivity, education,and energy to appreciate Henry James fully, but it resented literature that was trashy, facile, or formulaic.

Second, Stockton was basically a humorist, and for years because of some puritanical twist it was thought that if some one is funny he can not be serious; if the reader laughs, he can not be learning—a rupture of the Lucretian dictum that good literature should entertain and instruct. Even Mark Twain's philosophy was long neglected because he seemed a comedian, and it required the effort of Stockton as well as others like Howells to argue that humorists too have serious statements to make.

Paradoxically, Stockton's efforts on Twain's behalf may have helped plunge him into Twain's shadow. Twain's humor is of the broad, Western variety, whereas Stockton's is subtler, gentler, more Eastern. One knows when Twain has made a joke, but can not always be sure with Stockton. Howells referred to the sweet, refined honey of Stockton's humor and, in another simile, likened him to "an exceedingly clever juggler, who rolls up his sleeves . . . puts on an innocent face, deprecates the slightest appearance of deception, and then performs his extraordinary feats. There is a nimbleness of movement, an imperturbable air, and the thing is done."[14] F. L. Pattee praises Stockton's uniqueness in being a humorist but at the same time an artist who is able to show "restraint and refinement and yet to be truly funny."[15] It took Howells more than a decade to figure out Stockton's humor completely; the majority of the world has not yet caught on. In a epoch noted for humorous literature Stockton with Harris and Twain is one of the most notable humorists.

That epoch is a third reason for Stockton's obscurity, because for most of this century it was seen, as Henry Seidel Canby remarks, as "a small town joke" or as a germinal phase before Naturalism. But America in the last quarter of the nineteenth century was fraught with significant issues, such as industrialization, the rise of labor unions and the city, the influx of immigrants, social mobility, the "Negro question" and the "servant question," the threat of war, and America's growing stature as a world power.

In fact, two cultural issues are so major as to be classed by themselves as causes of Stockton's obscurity—the neglect of feminist history and the poetics of domesticity. For the first half of this century there was no wide interest in the history of feminism; Kate Chopin, Stockton's contemporary, for example, was not seriously studied until 1956.[16] I know of no American writer who investigates the question of women's liberation in so many permutations who has been as summarily neglected as Stockton. Perhaps with revitalized interest in this subject the error will be remedied.

Domesticity as a literary subject has suffered as much neglect as feminist history, in part because we have not had adequate tools to analyze this esthetic, although William C. Spengemann's 1977 book has made a valuable contribution. Indeed, the poetics of domesticity might strike some as Stockton's most fascinating quality. Again, he is poles apart from Twain, whose Huck Finn makes "sivilizin'" sound like some dread disease. In contrast, Stockton may be the last capable American author to be a stalwart defender of civilization not as an abstraction but as a concrete manifestation in the form of love, marriage, and the family—a belief that literature appears to have abandoned, though it has its champions in the other arts, as witnessed by the sculptor Henry Moore.

Stockton's uniqueness is the sixth cause for his neglect. Though he confronts social determinism and evolution, he is not a Naturalist. Though he captures places in points of time, he is no local colorist and no regionalist. Though he gives accurate portraits of people and places from New England, New York, and the Old South, he is too inventive to be a staunch Realist alone. As he specified in "The Pilgrim's Packets," he fits none of the categories of the period's literature. Dreiser's *Sister Carrie* (1900) does triple duty; in reading it, one knows the novel, has a taste of Dreiser's entire canon, and gains a sense of what

Naturalism is. By reading Stockton's *The Girl at Cobhurst*, one knows only that novel, and can not be sure that his next chronological production will be similar. In fact, *Cobhurst* is followed in a span of three years by the science-fiction novel *The Great Stone of Sardis*, then the history of piracy *The Buccaneers and Pirates of Our Coast*, then the fantasy novel on immortality *The Vizier of the Two-Horned Alexander*, and the satire on Transcendentalism in *The Associate Hermits*, then the facile children's adventure story *The Young Master of Hyson Hall*, followed by one of his best story anthologies *Afield and Afloat*, which is equalled in quality by the picaresque romance *A Bicycle of Cathay*, and so forth.

The seventh major shortcoming is that Stockton wrote no single novel that stands head and shoulders above the rest. Melville's *Moby-Dick*, Hawthorne's *The Scarlet Letter*, Dreiser's *Sister Carrie* are essential to their canon and are the foundation for much of their reputation. Henry James's *The American*, *The Portrait of a Lady*, and *The Ambassadors* are convenient novelistic shorthand which represent his three major phases. With Stockton, no one novel is preëminent. To understand his canon, one must read his canon. To comprehend adequately his views on feminism, at least half a dozen volumes must be perused.

To augment the problem, somewhat encouraged by his being paid by length and by his audience's leisurely reading habits, his style is often prolix. When a witty conceit strikes him, he will take a few paragraphs to explore it. Some of his crucial scenes, as when John Asher in *The Captain's Toll-Gate* confronts the evil Maria Port, could be reduced from four paragraphs to four lines by a writer like Hemingway. Indeed, Stockton's willingness to give a leisurely cast to his novels is his one true fault as an artist. They lack the terseness, concision, and economy modern reading tastes demand.

For that reason, a beginning Stockton reader should start with his short stories, which are tighter than his novels. Some suggestions are "The Magic Egg," which stands comparison with Sherwood Anderson's "The Egg"; "The Knife That Killed Po Hancy," which can be compared to Poe and Stevenson; "Mr. Tolman" as Stockton's peculiar form of Realism; "The Christmas Shadrach" as a study of psychology and feminism; "Ghosts in My Tower" as a study of racism; "The Philosophy of Relative Existences" as a fine philosophical fantasy, "Our Story" as an experiment in point of view; "Derelict: A Tale of the Wayward Sea" which plays with the modes of Realism, Romance, and Absurdism; and "The Wreck of the *Thomas Hyke*" which demonstrates Stockton's quirky perspective on reality.

The eighth and final point highlights Stockton's technique of "indirection," by which much of his serious matter is hidden behind the humorous gloss which sold his books. Irvin Ehrenpreis has recently offered a useful terminology by which this trait may be understood, though he modestly applies it exclusively to poetry.[17] He distinguishes between "the poetry of limits" and "the poetry of extremes," in which the former "depends on form, on gradations of tone, on language that is deliberate, obviously selected," whereas the latter "depends on deep, often shocking images, on sudden leaps of mood, unpredictable reversals of tone, on language that sounds uncalculated." The poetry of limits "suggests clarification emerging from uncertainty; the poetry of extremes suggests mysterious emotions in conflict."

When one recalls Stockton's essential belief that the universe is likely a vertiginous chaos of absurdity, one can appreciate Ehrenpreis's belief that, "In the poetry of limits the common relation between form and meaning is ironical. The form is tangible and suggests design bringing order to chaos. The meaning suggests chaos pressing against form." While the "poetry of limits" seems a valuable construct for appreciating Stockton's work, Stockton complicates the matter by being a humorist to boot. The challenge about humorists as with their satirist cousins is knowing when they are being flippant and when they have discovered the still, oracular balance. One way to view Stockton is as a Henry Adams in motley, however much such a metaphor helps.

Stockton would be best served by being thrust into the throes of objective criticism. He sorely needs a test conducted by a number of informed minds to determine just how important a writer he is. No doubt he would emerge as one of the finest humorists, Twain and Harris included, of the last twenty-five years of nineteenth-century American literature. Among his contemporaries, Stockton is not as fine an artist as Henry James nor so idiosyncratically a genius as Stephen Crane, but that is no reason he should be totally discarded. Of the hundreds of writers who flourished in America in the last decades of the nineteenth century listed in Howells's *Literature and Life* and in Thomas Beer's *The Mauve Decade*, very few deserve immortality. Stockton is one who does. Were his entire canon matched against Twain's, Stockton would emerge a close rival, although no one of his books can match the greatness of *Huckleberry Finn*.

Certainly in terms of scope Stockton is impressive. Consider the gamut he ranges in *A Chosen Few* (1895): the local color sketch "Asaph" and the speculative philosophy of "Relative Existences," the science-fiction story "A Tale of Negative Gravity" and the fairy tale "Old Pipes and the Dryad," the ghost story "The Transferred Ghost" and the realistic, Thurberesque "A Piece of Red Calico," even the significant triumph of "The Lady, or the Tiger?" whose popularity and problems Stockton commented on in "His Wife's Deceased Sister." If one desired a literary garden filled with everything from discrete purple violets to tall, bold sunflowers, few candidates could emulate Stockton's achievement. My hope is that this slim book will plunge him into "The King's Arena" of close literary criticism, whether to be devoured by tigers or to be embraced in admiration, but in any case to be rescued from the oblivion and from the naive enthusiasm he does not at all deserve.

Notes and References

Chapter One

1. Clarence Clough Buel, "The Author of 'The Lady, or the Tiger?'" *Century Magazine*, X (July, 1886), 406–07; hereafter cited as Buel.; for different opinions on how Stockton became lame, see Martin I. J. Griffin, *Frank R. Stockton, A Critical Biography* (Port Washington, New York; 1965), p. 8, hereafter cited as Griffin.

2. Buel, p. 405; see also Thomas Allen Glenn, *Some Colonial Mansions and Those Who Lived in Them* (Philadelphia, 1899).

3. Buel, p. 406; William L. Werner, "The Escapes of Frank Stockton," *Essays in Honor of A. Howry Espenshade* (New York, 1937), pp. 21–45.

4. Buel, p. 406.

5. Reverend Dr. Thomas Hewlings Stockton, *Sunday Newspapers in Conflict with the Law of God and the Welfare of Man* (Philadelphia? 1865).

6. Thomas H. Stockton, *Poems, with Autobiographical and Other Notes* (Philadelphia, 1861); Griffin (p. 14) gives 1862 as the date for this book, so it may have been reprinted.

7. Frank Stockton, "The Battle of the Third Cousins," *The Novels and Stories of Frank R. Stockton* (New York, 1899–1904), XVII, 170; hereafter this twenty-three volume Shenandoah Edition will be cited as *Novels*.

8. Stockton, "How Three Men Went to the Moon," *Tales Out of School* (New York, 1891), p. 97.

9. Marian Stockton, "A Memorial Sketch of Mr. Stockton, "*Novels*, XXIII, 189–206; Henry C. Vedder, *American Writers of To-Day* (New York, 1894), pp. 288–300.

10. Edwin W. Bowen, "Frank R. Stockton," *Sewanee Review*, XI (October, 1903), 474.

11. Stockton, *Stories of New Jersey* (New Brunswick, 1961), p. 251.

12. Stockton, "New Jersey and the Land of Gold," ibid., pp. 246–54.

13. Except for one novel and several stories, Stockton's science fiction has been collected in *The Science Fiction of Frank R. Stockton*, ed. Richard Gid Powers (Boston, 1976).

14. William Dean Howells, "Stockton's Stories," *Atlantic Monthly*, LIX (January, 1887), 130–32; Howells, "Stockton's Novels and Stories," *Atlantic Monthly*, LXXXVII (January, 1901), 136–38; Buel, p. 405.

15. Griffin, p. 5.

16. Buel, p. 407.

17. Griffin, p. 6; Thomas Stockton, *Poems*, pp. 292–93.

18. Griffin, p. 19.

19. Ibid., p. 7.

20. Stockton, *Mrs. Cliff's Yacht, Novels*, X, 175–76.

21. Stockton, *The Captain's Toll-Gate, Novels*, XXII, 312–27.

22. Stockton, *The Girl at Cobhurst, Novels*, XII, 404.

23. Griffin, p. 9.

24. Stockton's classmates, according to Griffin, p. 9, include: William H. Ashman, Judge of the Orphan's Court of Philadelphia and a lifelong friend; James G. Barnwell, philanthropist; Samuel S. Fisher, U.S. Commissioner of Patents; P. A. B. Widener, financier; W. W. Keen, surgeon.

25. Edith M. Thomas, "Frank Richard Stockton," *McClure's Magazine*, I (November, 1893), 469.

26. Buel, p. 407.

27. Ibid.

28. Thomas, p. 477.

29. Stockton, "Tickled by a Straw," *Roundabout Rambles in Lands of Fact and Fancy* (New York, 1872), p. 305.

30. Marian Stockton, pp. 192–93, and Griffin, p. 12, say it was *Paradise Regained;* Buel, p. 407, claims it was "one of Milton's short devotional poems."

31. Though this first publication has been alluded to often, the story has not been found; see Griffin, pp. 11–12.

32. Stockton letter to Laurens Maynard, now in the Pierpont Morgan Library, New York, as quoted in Griffin, p. 16.

33. Philip B. Kunhardt, "Images of which History Was Made Bore the Mathew Brady Label," *Smithsonian*, VIII (July, 1977), 28.

34. Buel, p. 408, mentions the poet, John A. Dorgan; the marine painter, W. T. Richards; Professor Riché; Judges Mitchell and Ashman; and Frank's brother, John.

35. Stockton, "What Can I Do For An Old Gentleman?" unpublished manuscript in possession of Mrs. George E. Cantrell, as quoted in Griffin, pp. 13–14.

36. Stockton, "The First Beefsteak," as quoted in Griffin, p. 12.

37. Griffin, pp. 21–23.

38. Stockton, *A Northern Voice for the Dissolution of the Union of the United States of America* (Philadelphia? 1861), p. 5.

39. Stockton also notes that England buys $100,000,000 of cotton from the South yearly; *Northern Voice*, p. 7.

40. "A Real Union" was offered at auction on October 13, 1932; *Stockton: First Editions and Literary Autographs of American and English Authors* (Newark, 1932).

41. *Stockton: First Editions*, entries 177, 182.

42. Stockton, *The Spirit of Washington* (Morristown, 1895), p. 10.

43. Griffin, p. 116.

44. Stockton letter to Robert Underwood Johnson, December 29, 1889; to Johnson, March 7, 1890; a specimen postcard is included in the Stockton manuscripts and letters, Barrett Collection, Alderman Library, University of Virginia, Charlottesville.

45. Stockton letter to Johnson, March 6, 1891; April 11, 1891; Barrett Collection.

46. Stockton letter to Johnson, April 14, 1896; September 29, 1896; Barrett Collection.

47. Stockton, "The Governor-General," *The World's Great Masterpieces in History, Biography, Science, Philosophy, Poetry, Drama, Travel, Adventure, Fiction, etc.*, ed. H. T. Peck (New York, 1898–1901), XXVIII, 10283–10303.

48. Buel, p. 408.

49. Thomas, p. 468.

50. Warner Berthoff, *The Ferment of Realism: American Literature, 1884–1919* (New York, 1965), pp. 14–15.

51. Griffin, p. 116.

52. Ibid., pp. 119–20.

53. Buel, p. 409.

54. Frank and Marian Stockton, *The Home, Where It Should Be and What To Put In It* (New York, 1873), pp. 109, 127; the six-page list is at the end.

55. The idea and some episodes for *Ting-a-ling* were conceived while Stockton participated in the "Forensic and Literary Circle" in the 1850s.

56. Others include Howard Pyle, James Whitcomb Riley, Sidney Lanier, Julian Hawthorne, Joaquin Miller, Mary Wilkins Freeman, Rose Terry Cooke, Richard Harding Davis, Frances Hodgson Burnett, and Dodge; see Henry Steele Commager, *The St. Nicholas Anthology* (New York, 1948), pp. 24–33 for Stockton; for still others, see Griffin, p. 36.

57. Alice Barrett Howard, *Mary Mapes Dodge of St. Nicholas* (New York, 1943), p. 202.

58. Anna Lorraine Guthrie, *Index to St. Nicholas: Vols. I-XLV, 1873–1918* (New York, 1920), index.

59. Stockton, *Tales Out of School* (New York, 1891), p. 156.

60. Buel, p. 409.

61. *Stockton: First Editions*, entry 192.

62. Stockton letter to Julius Chambers, undated but bearing the Centennial watermark, Barrett Collection.

63. Stockton letter to Charles Scribner, April 20, 1880, Scribner Archives, Princeton University Library.

64. Stockton letter to Scribner, February 21, 1881, Scribner Archives.

65. "Frank Stockton," *St. Nicholas*, XXIX (June, 1902), 766.

66. Stockton, *Rudder Grange* (New York, 1905), p. 40.

67. Stockton letter to Scribner, February 21, 1881, Scribner Archives.

68. Stockton's engraving of Turner's "Virginia Water" is reproduced in Griffin, following p. 14.

69. James Herbert Morse, "Authors at Home," *Critic* (April 16, 1898). p. 261.

70. Many sources discuss the response to "The Lady, or the Tiger?" but the most detailed, which also includes samples of political cartoons, is Walter L. Pforzheimer, *Stocktoniana: an Essay* (New York, 1936), pp. 9–31.

71. Buel, p. 405.

72. Robert F. Young, "The Arena of Decisions," *Amazing Stories: Fact and Science Fiction*, XXXVIII (March, 1964), 7–25; Steven Sabo brought this version to my attention.

73. Charles L. Webster letter to Scribner, October 14, 1887, Scribner Archives.

74. Stockton letter to Scribner, March 3, 1894, Scribner Archives.

75. J. B. Bartley letter to Stockton, August 4, 1899, Scribner Archives.

76. Mrs. Frederick Gotthold letter to Stockton, November 3, 1900, Scribner Archives; Stockton, *The Lost Dryad* (Riverside, Connecticut: 1912).

77. Stockton letters to Scribner, April 15, 1886, and October 2, 1897, Scribner Archives; Stockton, *Kuriose Geschichten von F. R. Stockton*, tr. Margaret Jacobi (Stuttgart, 1898).

78. Etta De Camp, *The Return of Frank Stockton* (London, 1913).

79. Ada McQuillin letter to Charles Scribner, August 3, 1926; Eugene L. Brewster letter to Scribner, December 8, 1926, and November 23, 1927; A. L. Stone letters to Scribner, August 2, 1926, and August 22, 1926; Scribner Archives.

80. Stockton letter to Mrs. F. Gotthold, August 19, 1897, Barrett Collection; Griffin, p. 112.

81. Olivia Taylor, "Dear Ghosts of Lego and Monticello," *Papers of the Albemarle County Historical Society*, III (1942–1943), 17–32.

82. Theodore F. Wolfe, "Where Stockton Wrote," *Lippincott's Magazine*, LXIV (September, 1899), 367–76.

83. Marian Stockton, pp. 203–05.

84. Charles F. Richardson, *American Literature: 1607–1885* (New York, 1886), p. 521.

85. Stockton letters to Scribner, April 28, 1899; to H. E. Scudder, March 6, 1893; to Scribner, January 9, 1889; March 9, 1886; September 9, 1896; Scribner Archives.

86. Thomas Beer, *The Mauve Decade* (New York, 1926), pp. 49–50.

87. Frederick L. Pattee, *The New American Literature: 1890–1930* (New York, 1930), p. 236.

88. Stockton letters to Scribner, May 20, 1885, January 5, 1889, and July 16, 1891, Scribner Archives.

89. Howells, *Literature and Life* (Port Washington, New York: 1968), pp. 173–86.

90. Stockton letter to Scribner, February 17, 1887, Scribner Archives.

91. Marian Stockton letter to Scribner, January 14, 1903, Scribner Archives.

92. Stockton letter to Scribner, June 5, 1899, Scribner Archives.

93. Other illustrators include C. M. Relyea, Clyde De Land, R. F. Zogbaum; Frost's son became a student of Henri Matisse and a friend of Gertrude Stein.

94. Scribner ledger for Stockton royalties (August 1, 1900, to February 1, 1903), Scribner Archives; royalties from the Shenandoah Edition of *Ardis Claverden* were $538.20, from the popular editions $34.20—fifty dollars behind *The Late Mrs. Null*, the next better selling novel.

95. Cassell and Company letter to Scribner, December 10, 1902, Scribner Archives.

96. William Stockton letter to Scribner re Boy Scouts of America, June 16, 1913; six letters and wires from movie agents to Scribner re Stockton, August 3, 1926, to November 23, 1927; E. May Cross turns "Old Pipes and the Dryad" into a play with two songs, letter to Scribner, May 19, 1926; Elizabeth Seitz Denig turns "Old Pipes" into a three-act play, letter to Scribner, October 10, 1911; Scribner Archives.

97. Marian Stockton letter to Scribner, August 15, 1905; William Stockton letter to Scribner, June 8, 1907; Scribner Archives.

98. Marian Stockton letters to Scribner, March 21, 1905, and September 15, 1906, Scribner Archives.

99. Marian Stockton letters to Scribner: December 3, 1902; August 15, 1905; Spring, 1906; Scribner Archives.

100. William Stockton letters to Scribner, March 28, 1909, and October 26, 1911, Scribner Archives.

101. Stockton letter to Johnson, November 5, 1900, Barrett Collection.

102. Henry Seidel Canby, *The Age of Confidence* (New York, 1934), p. 260.

103. "Francis Richard Stockton," *Harper's Weekly*, XLVI (May 3, 1902), 555.

Chapter Two

1. Canby, p. 260; Larzer Ziff, *The American 1890s* (New York, 1966); Warner Berthoff, *The Ferment of Realism* (New York, 1965); Jay Martin, *Harvests of Change: American Literature 1865–1914* (Englewood Cliffs, N.J. 1967).

2. Berthoff, p. 126.

3. *Newsdealer* (New York, September 1, 1891), clipping re Stockton's works in Scribner Archives.

4. Mrs. Bobbs' letter to Scribner, December 28, 1905; Miss Mary E. Burt letter to Stockton, February 21, 1893; Scribner Archives.

5. Stockton letter to Edward Seymour, April 11, 1870, Scribner Archives.

6. Stockton, "How I Served My Literary Apprenticeship," *Youth's Companion* (March 5, 1896), p. 119.

7. Canby, p. 190.

8. Stockton, *Afield and Afloat, Novels*, XIX, vii–viii.

9. Manuela Soares, *The Soap Opera Book* (New York, 1978).

10. Stockton, *The Casting Away, Novels*, XIII, 155.

11. Stockton, *The Hundredth Man, Novels*, IV, 120.

12. Stockton, *The Captain's Toll-Gate, Novels*, XXII, 39.

13. Canby, p. 197.

14. *Hundredth Man, Novels*, IV, 113.

15. Ibid. p. 79.

16. *Captain's Toll-Gate*, pp. 328, 305.

17. Angus Wilson, *The Strange Ride of Rudyard Kipling* (New York, 1978) , pp. 191–92.

18. Epigraph to Beer, *Mauve Decade*.

19. Howells, *Literature and Life*, p. 21.

20. Stockton, *John Gayther's Garden, Novels*, XXI, 72–73.

21. H. E. Scudder letter to Stockton, March 6, 1893, Scribner Archives.

22. Ann Douglas, *The Feminization of American Culture* (New York, 1977).

23. Stockton, "Our Story," *The Lady or the Tiger and Other Stories* (New York, 1968), pp. 89–90.

24. Buel, p. 407; Werner, p. 35; Howells (January, 1887), p. 132; Stockton letter to Clarke re Archery Prize, September 15, 1878, Barrett Collection.

25. Thomas, p. 472.

26. Stockton, "The Pilgrim's Packets," *Scribner's Monthly*, V (January, 1873), 333; "How I Served," p. 119.

27. William Phelps, *The Advance of the English Novel*. (New York, 1916), pp. 149–50.

28. Stockton, "My Favorite Novelist and His Best Book," *Munsey's Magazine*, XVII (June, 1887), 351.

29. Stockton, "Mark Twain and His Recent Works," *Forum*, XV (August, 1893), 673.

30. Howells, *Harper's Weekly* (May 29, 1897), p. 538.

31. *Hundredth Man*, p. 26.

32. "My Favorite Novelist," p. 16.

33. "Francis Richard Stockton," *Harper's Weekly*, XLVI (May 3, 1902), 555; Howells, "Stockton's Novels," *Atlantic Monthly* (January, 1901), p. 138.

34. *Hundredth Man*, pp. 30–31.

35. Some other writers are Tennyson, Keats, Scott, Chaucer, Jonathan Edwards, Shakespeare, Herodotus, Petrarch, Cooper, Milton, Mary Wilkins Freeman, and Hans Christian Andersen.

36. Stockton, "The Lady in the Box," *Gayther's Garden*, pp. 72–105.

37. Stockton, "The Magic Egg," *Novels*, IV, 1–22.

38. Stockton letter to Charles W. Kent, October 2, 1899, Barrett Collection.

39. Stockton, *Ardis Claverden*, *Novels*, V, 229.

40. *Ardis*, pp. 130–31, 264–65; Stockton also read the same theologians and scientists that influenced Poe as in *Gayther's Garden*, p. 346, when he refers to "Buck's *Theological Dictionary*" and "Dick's *Future State*."

41. Howells (January, 1901), p. 138; Wolfe, p. 370.

42. Stockton, "Mark Twain," pp. 678–79.

43. Buel, p. 411.

44. "Mark Twain," p. 677.

45. Howells, *Harper's Weekly* (May 29, 1897), p. 538.

46. Stockton, *The Vizier of the Two-Horned Alexander*, *Novels*, XIII, 276.

47. Howells, *Atlantic Monthly* (January, 1887), p. 130.

48. Stockton, "That Same Old Coon" *Novels*, XV, 106.

49. Griffin, p. 100.

50. Stockton, "The Vice-Consort," *Novels*, XXI, 338.

51. Stockton, *The Girl at Cobhurst*, *Novels*, XII, 364.

52. *Hundredth Man*, p. 328.

53. *Girl at Cobhurst*, pp. 170, 97.

54. Stockton, "Plain Fishing," *Novels*, XVI, 323, 333.

55. Marian Stockton letter to Scribner, August 11, 1904, Scribner Archives.

56. "Plain Fishing," pp. 335, 341–42.

57. "Our Story," p. 92.

58. William Lyon Phelps, *The Advance*, p. 150; Howells, "A Story-Teller's Pack" *Harper's Weekly*, XLI (May 29, 1897), 538.

59. Marian Stockton, "A Memorial Sketch," p. 205–06; "Francis Richard Stockton," *Harper's Weekly*, XLVI (May 3, 1902), 555; William Werner, "The Escapes," p. 37; Griffin, p. 11; "My Well, and What Came Out of It," *Novels*, XVIII, 195–201.

60. *Ardis Claverden*, *Novels*, V, 173, 41–48, 324, 530.

61. *Claverden*, pp. 500–01.

62. Stockton, "The Spectral Mortgage," *Novels*, XV, 63, 68.

63. Stockton, "The Conscious Amanda," *Novels*, XXI, 259, 262, 272.

64. Stockton, *Kate Bonnet*, *Novels*, XX, 11, 232, 40, 346.

65. Ibid., pp. 277, 229, 85.

66. Ibid., p. 209.

67. Ibid., pp. 117, 212, 292, 297.

68. "The Art of the Short Story," *American Writing Today*, ed. Allan Angoff (Washington Square, 1957), p. 182.

69. Stockton, "The Lady in the Box," *Novels*, XXI, 72–73.

70. Stockton, *The Captain's Toll-Gate*, *Novels*, XXII, 42.

71. Stockton, "Hevi," *St. Nicholas*, IV (July, 1877), 589–92; "Sweet Marjoram Day," V (December, 1877), 111–22; "Huckleberry," V (February, 1878), 274–78.

72. Stockton, "The Clocks of Rondaine," *Novels*, XVII, 14.

73. Stockton, "A Borrowed Month," *Novels*, XV, 206.

74. Stockton, "Derelict, A Tale of the Wayward Sea," *Novels*, XV, 132–82.

75. *Captain's Toll-Gate*, p. 188.

Chapter Three

1. Stockton, *John Gayther's Garden*, *Novels*, XXI, 50.

2. Jay Martin, *Harvests of Change*, p. 22.

3. Ann Douglas, *The Feminization of American Culture* (New York, 1977).

4. Warner Berthoff, *The Ferment of Realism*, pp. 14–15.

5. Willa Cather, *A Lost Lady* (New York, 1972), p. 112.

6. Stockton, *Mrs. Cliff's Yacht*, *Novels*, X, 292.

7. Ibid., p. 222.

8. Ibid., pp. 253–78.

9. *Captain's Toll-Gate*, p. 331.

10. Stockton, *The Squirrel Inn*, *Novels*, II, 142, 156, 130; Ida becomes Professor of Geology at Bryn Mawr in *The Great Stone of Sardis*, *Novels*, II, 208.

11. Wolfe, p. 372.

12. Charles Scribner letters to Stockton, March 3, 1886 and August 9, 1886, Scribner Archives; 9,000 copies were published in German by Robert Lutz, Stuttgart, Stockton letter to Scribner, April 15, 1886, Scribner Archives; by 1891, twelve years after its first printing, *Rudder Grange* still topped Scribner's sales list, Stockton letter to Scribner, March 2, 1891, Scribner Archives.

13. Stockton, *The Late Mrs. Null*, *Novels*, I, 96, 100–01, 406.

14. Ibid., pp. 420, 3, 263.

15. Ibid., pp. 307, 431, 437.

16. Stockton, "The Great Staircase at Landover Hall," *Novels*, XIX, 277.

17. Stockton, *The Hundredth Man*, pp. 280, 155; "As One Woman to Another ," *Novels*, XVI, 230; *The Associate Hermits*, *Novels*, XIV, 106; *John Gayther's Garden*, p. 364; *Captain Horn*, p. 253; *Associate Hermits*, p. 149; *A Bicycle of Cathay*, *Novels*, XXIII, 168; "My Balloon Hunt," *Novels*, XXI, 216, 218–19.

18. Stockton, *Pomona's Travels, Novels,* VIII, 89, 195–96; *Mrs. Cliff's Yacht,* p. 283; "The Battle of the Third Cousins," *Novels,* XVII, 185.

19. Stockton letter to William Henry Rideing re marriage, January 23, 1887 , Barrett Collection; *Hundredth Man,* p. 177; *Captain Horn,* p. 417; the moral of "Our Archery Club" is that marrying well is better than fame.

20. Stockton, "The Christmas Shadrach," *Novels,* XVII, 281, 286.

21. Ibid., p. 306.

22. *Ardis Claverden,* pp. 77, 79.

23. Ibid., pp. 305, 312.

24. Reluctant lovers: "My Unwilling Neighbor," *Novels,* 215–52; "A Romance of a Mule Car," *Novels,* XIX, 27–46; "A Sailor's Knot," *Novels,* XIX, 202–51.

25. *Hundredth Man,* pp. 131–32.

26. Lists: *Girl at Cobhurst,* p. 391; *A Bicycle of Cathay,* p. 140; *John Gayther's Garden,* p. 328.

27. *Girl at Cobhurst, p. 261.*

28. *Hundredth Man,* pp. 36, 74.

29. *Mrs. Cliff's Yacht,* p. 7.

30. Ibid., pp. 113, 17.

31. Stockton, "Old Applejoy's Ghost," *Novels,* XIX, 88; *Bicycle of Cathay,* p. 183; *Ardis Claverden,* p. 426.

32. *The Associate Hermits,* p. 240; *Late Mrs. Null,* p. 313.

33. *Associate Hermits,* pp. 175, 182.

34. *Hundredth Man,* p. 72.

35. Stockton, *The Stories of the Three Burglars, Novels,* VI, 175, 166; *A Northern Voice,* p. 5.

36. *Hundredth Man,* pp. 54, 59, 113.

37. *Ardis Claverden,* p. 104.

38. *Pomona's Travels,* pp. 260, 59, 26.

39. Ibid., pp. 26, 9, 11, 10, 206.

40. *John Gayther's Garden,* p. 119; see also *The Captain's Toll-Gate,* p. 40, and *A Bicycle of Cathay,* pp. 69, 129, 133.

41. Stockton, *The Vizier of the Two-Horned Alexander, Novels,* XIII, 262, 338.

42. Stockton, *The Merry Chanter, Novels,* II, 370.

43. *Ardis Claverden,* pp. 35, 18–19, 30; Robert Underwood Johnson, *Remembered Yesterdays* (Boston, 1923), p. 104.

44. *Ardis Claverden,* pp. 181–83; *Captain Horn,* p. 119.

45. *The Late Mrs. Null,* pp. 333–43, 350, 397.

46. Ibid., pp. 47–49.

47. *Girl at Cobhurst,* p. 244; "Captain Horn" manuscript revisions, pp. 13, 493, Barrett Collection.

48. *Captain Horn,* p. 422.

49. Stockton, "Funny Darkies," *Youth's Companion,* LXXI (November

11, 1897), 564; Buel, p. 409; Howells, "Stockton's Stories," *Atlantic Monthly*, LIX (January, 1887), 132.

50. Stockton, "Ghosts in My Tower," *Novels*, XIX, 290.

51. Eleanor and Ray Harder, *Good Grief, a Griffin*, Anchorage, Kentucky: Anchorage Press, 1968; Maurice Sendak, *The Griffin and the Minor Canon*, New York: Holt, Rinehart, and Winston, 1963, *The Bee-Man of Orn*, New York: Holt, Rinehart, and Winston, 1964; Carol Scott Van Strum, "On Story Telling," *Coevolution Quarterly* (Spring, 1978), p. 124; *Old Pipes and the Dryad*, Catherine Hanley, illustrator, New York: Watts, 1969.

52. Stockton letter to McClure, October 25, 1890, Barrett Collection; Stockton, "How I Served My Apprenticeship as a Man of Letters," *Youth's Companion*, LXX (March 5, 1896), 119; Stockton letter to Scribner, July 5, 1900, Scribner Archives; Edith Thomas, "Frank Stockton," *McClure's*, I (November, 1893), 474; "The Griffin" first appeared in book form under *The Bee-Man of Orn and Other Fanciful Tales* (1887).

53. Bruno Bettelheim, *The Uses of Enchantment*, New York, 1977; children's literature later became established with the following events: the first "children's corner" was founded in a Rhode Island library in 1877; the Pratt Institute began to train children's librarians in 1898; the American Library Association opened the first children's literature section in 1900.

54. William L. Werner, "The Escapes of Frank Stockton," *Essays in Honor of A. Howry Espenshade* (New York, 1937), p. 33.

55. Stockton, *What Might Have Been Expected* (New York, 1898), pp. 12, 72, 290–91.

56. Stockton, "What Would You Have Done?" *Youth's Companion*, LXXV (November 2, 1901), 612–13.

57. Stockton, "Cinderella," *St. Nicholas*, II (April, 1875), 330.

Chapter Four

1. Robert Underwood Johnson, *Remembered Yesterdays* (Boston, 1923), p. 106.

2. As quoted in Griffin, p. 28.

3. Griffin, p. 76.

4. Stockton letter to Mary Mapes Dodge, July 30, 1885, as quoted in Griffin, p. 77.

5. Stockton, " The Queen's Museum," *Novels*, XVII, 73.

6. William C. Spengemann, *The Adventurous Muse* (New Haven, 1977), p. 79.

7. Ibid., pp. 69, 72.

8. Stockton, "The Knife That Killed Po Hancy," *Novels*, VI, 242–64; *The Science Fiction of Frank R. Stockton*, Richard Gid Powers, ed., (Boston, 1976), pp. 135–56, hereafter cited as Powers.

9. Powers, p. xiii.

10. Stockton, "A Sailor's Knot," *Novels*, XIX, 202–51; "introduction," p. ix.

11. Ibid., p. 230.

12. B. Traven, *The Treasure of the Sierra Madre* (New York, 1968), p. 242.

13. *Captain Horn*, p. 188.

14. Ibid., pp. 189, 281, 191.

15. Theodore Roosevelt and Gifford Pinchot were instrumental in preventing the takeover of Northwest gold mines by business monopolies.

16. *Captain Horn*, pp. 417–19.

17. Marian E. Stockton letter to Scribner, August 15, 1905, Scribner Archives.

18. Stockton letter to R. U. Johnson, November 5, 1900, Barrett Collection.

19. Leslie Fiedler, *In Dreams Awake* (New York, 1975), p. 9; H. Bruce Franklin, *Future Perfect* (New York, 1966), p. 18.

20. Richard Gid Powers includes *The Great Stone of Sardis* and six science fiction short stories in his *The Science Fiction of Frank R. Stockton* (1976). He omits *The Great War Syndicate* because it appeared as a Gregg Press reprint in 1970. He gives reasons (p. ix) for omitting stories that have only "a tangential relationship" to science fiction, but that he excludes stories like "The Lady in the Box" is inexcusable.

21. Stockton, "The Water-Devil, a Marine Tale," *Novels*, XI, 221–69; Powers, pp. 3–49.

22. Stockton, "My Translataphone," *Novels*, XXI 279–303.

23. Powers, p. xxi.

24. Powers, p. xi.

25. Stockton, "Amos Kilbright," *Novels*, XVII, 229–71; Powers pp. 85–131.

26. George Griffith write *The Great Pirate Syndicate* (1899) and *The Great Weather Syndicate* (1906) as noted in Powers, p. xviii.

27. Stockton, *The Great Stone of Sardis, Novels*, XI; Powers, p. 211.

28. *Great Stone*, p. 402.

29. Ibid., p. 413.

30. Ibid., pp. 375, 421.

31. Richard Lovelace, *To Lucasta: Going to the Wars* (1649), Stanza III.

32. *Great Stone*, p. 424.

33. Ibid., p. 339.

34. Stockton letter to William Fayal Clarke, September 2, 1877, Barrett Collection; Stockton letter to Scribner, September 9, 1896, Scribner Archives.

35. Stockton, "The Remarkable Wreck of the *Thomas Hyke*," *A Chosen Few* (Freeport, New York: 1895, 1969), p. 160.

36. Arthur Quiller-Couch, "Mr. Stockton," *Adventures in Criticism* (New York, 1925), p. 213.

37. Stockton, "Asaph," *A Chosen Few*, p. 48.

38. Stockton, "The Lady, or the Tiger?" *Novels*, XV, 3–14.
39. Ibid., p. 13.

Chapter Five

1. Gertrude Stein, *The Autobiography of Alice B. Toklas, Selected Writings of Gertrude Stein*, ed. Carl Van Vechten (New York, 1946), p. 208; in *Patriotic Gore: Studies in the Literature of the American Civil War* (New York, 1966, p. 140), Edmund Wilson tries to explain Stein's admiration for Stockton.
2. This phenomenon holds true today, as seen in Ernest Jackson Hall, *The Satirical Element in the American Novel* (New York, 1969), p. 16.
3. As quoted in Quiller-Couch, p. 211.
4. Stockton, "Funny Darkies," p. 565.
5. D. H. Lawrence, *Lady Chatterley's Lover* (New York, 1959), p. 7.
6. Walter L. Pforzheimer, *Stocktoniana: An Essay* (New York, 1936), p. 17; "Frank R. Stockton," *Harper's Weekly*, LXVI (May 3, 1902), 555.
7. *American Writing Today: Its Independence and Vigor* (excerpts from the London *Times Literary Supplement*), ed. Allan Angoff (Washington Square, 1957), pp. 177, 182–83.
8. Judith Fryer, *The Faces of Eve: Women in the Nineteenth-Century American Novel* (New York, 1976); Dorothy Yost, *The Stereotype of the Single Woman* (New York, 1951), p. 143; Ernest Leisy, *The American Historical Novel* (Norman, Oklahoma, 1952), p. 222.
9. See advertisement with photographs for *Century Magazine in 1902: A Year of Humor* in *Youth's Companion*, LXXV (November 7, 1901), 596.
10. Quiller-Couch, p. 212.
11. William L. Werner, p. 44.
12. Cornelia Meigs et al., *A Critical History of Children's Literature* (London, 1969), pp. 257, 402.
13. *Basic Books for Junior College Libraries: 20,000 Vital Titles*, ed. Charles L. Trinker (Northport, Alabama, 1963), p. 706; C. Lewis, *100 Best Books* (New York, 1928), p. 247; Asa D. Dickinson, *1000 Best Books* (New York, 1924), pp. 242–43.
14. Howells, "A Story-Teller's Pack," *Harper's Weekly*, XLI (May 29, 1897), 538; "Stockton's Novels and Stories," *Atlantic Monthly*, LXXXVII (January, 1901), 136.
15. Frederick L. Pattee, *The Development of the American Short Story: An Historical Survey* (New York, 1923), p. 298.
16. See the historical background provided by Margaret Culley's editorial note to Kate Chopin, *The Awakening* (New York, 1976), p. 143.
17. Irvin Ehrenpreis, "At the Poles of Poetry," *The New York Review of Books*, XXV (August 17, 1978), 48–50.

Selected Bibliography

Were all Stockton's writings collected, they would amount to over fifty volumes, including twenty-nine novels, about fourteen volumes of short stories, eight books of travel, history, and natural philosophy, and five or more volumes of essays, letters and various manuscripts. The "complete" bibliography Marian Stockton placed at the end of Volume XXIII of the Shenandoah Edition is not at all complete; Martin Griffin's bibliography in his *Frank Stockton, A Critical Biography* is detailed and reliable although he uses an antiquated bibliographical method. The selected bibliography below excludes specific works already collected in the twenty-three volume Shenandoah Edition and includes only those other works deemed especially important.

PRIMARY SOURCES

1. Books (in order of publication):

A Northern Voice for the Dissolution of the Union of the United States of America. Philadelphia: privately printed, 1861.
Ting-a-ling. Boston: Hurd and Houghton, 1870.
The Home—Where it Should Be and What to Put in It (with Marian Stockton). New York: G. P. Putnam, 1872.
Roundabout Rambles in Lands of Fact and Fancy. New York: Scribners, 1872.
What Might Have Been Expected. New York: Dodd, Mead, 1874, 1898.
The Floating Prince and Other Fairy Tales. New York: Scribners, 1881.
Personally Conducted. New York: Scribners, 1889.
New Jersey, from the Discovery of the Scheyichbi to Recent Times. New York: Appleton, 1896.
The Novels and Stories of Frank R. Stockton (Shenandoah Edition, 23 vols.). New York: Scribners, 1899–1904. Contains 21 novels, 66 short stories, Marian Stockton's memorial sketch, and a partial bibliography.

2. Uncollected Essays and Short Stories:

"Cinderella." *St. Nicholas,* II (April, 1875), 329–30.

"A Few Words to Begin with." *A Story-Teller's Pack* (New York: Scribners, 1897), introduction.

"Funny Darkies." *The Youth's Companion*, LXXI (November 11, 1897), 564–65.

"The Governor-General." *The World's Great Masterpieces in History, Biography, Science, Philosophy, Poetry, Drama, Travel, Adventure, Fiction, etc.* ed. H. T. Peck, New York: American Literary Society, 1898–1901.

"Hevi." *St. Nicholas*, IV (July, 1877), 589–92.

"Huckleberry." *St. Nicholas*, V (February, 1878), 274–78.

"How I Served My Apprenticeship as a Man of Letters." *Youth's Companion*, LXX (March 5, 1896), 119.

"Kate." *The Southern Literary Messenger*, VIII (December, 1859), 415–21.

"Looking Back at Boyhood." *Youth's Companion*, LXV (April 28, 1892), 213–215.

"Mark Twain and His Recent Works." *Forum*, XV (August, 1893), 673–79.

"My Favorite Novelist and His Best Book." *Munsey's Magazine*, XVII (June, 1897), 351–66; *Booklover*, VIII (May-June, 1901), 312–29.

"A Philippine Embarrassment." *New York Sunday World* (November 12, 1899), p. 3.

"The Pilgrim's Packets." *Scribner's Monthly Magazine*, V (January, 1873), 333–36.

"Sweet Marjoram Day." *St. Nicholas*, V (December, 1877), 111–22.

3. Manuscripts and Letters:

University of Virginia, Charlottesville. Sixty-nine manuscripts and letters in the Clifton Waller Barrett Collection and five at large, including eighty-eight manuscript pages of "The Merry Chanter" (called "Marry Chanters") and the complete manuscript of "The Adventures of Captain Horn." See *The Barrett Library's Frank Richard Stockton: A Checklist of Published and Manuscript Works of Frank Richard Stockton in the University of Virginia Library*, ed. Lucy T. Clark, Charlottesville: University of Virginia Press, 1963.

Pierpont Morgan Library, New York. Important letters and manuscripts from this collection are quoted in Martin Griffin, *Frank Richard Stockton, A Critical Biography*, Port Washington, New York: Kennikat Press, 1965.

Princeton University Library, Princeton, New Jersey. Four folders of two-hundred-forty-two letters from Stockton and two-hundred-sixteen about him and his works (1871–1913) and one folder of miscellaneous material in Box 145 of Scribners (Authors Files) Archives.

4. Anthologies (offering readily available Stockton writings):

The Bee-Man of Orn. Illus. Maurice Sendak. New York: Holt, Rinehart and Winston, 1964.

The Best Short Stories of Frank R. Stockton. New York: Scribner, 1957.

Buccaneers and Pirates of Our Coast. New York: Macmillan, 1963, 1967.

A Chosen Few. Freeport, New York: Books for Libraries Press, 1969.

The Great War Syndicate. Boston: Gregg Press, 1970.

The Griffin and the Minor Canon. Illus. Maurice Sendak. New York: Holt, Rinehart and Winston, 1963, 1968.

The Lady or the Tiger and Other Stories. New York: Airmont, 1968.

Old Pipes and the Dryad. Illus. Catherine Hanley. New York: Watts, 1968, 1969.

The Science Fiction of Frank Richard Stockton: an Anthology. Ed. Richard Gid Powers. Boston: Gregg Press, 1976.

Stories of New Jersey. New Brunswick, New Jersey: Rutgers University Press, 1961. Introduction by Mary V. Gaver.

A Story-Teller's Pack, a Frank R. Stockton Reader. New York: Scribners, 1968.

SECONDARY SOURCES

ALDISS, BRIAN W. *Billion Year Spree: The True History of Science Fiction*. New York: Schocken, 1973. Says Stockton's name grows faint but he still reads pleasantly.

ANGOFF, ALLAN, ed. "The Art of the Short Story." *American Writing Today: Its Independence and Vigor*. New York: Washington Square Press, 1957. London *Times Literary Supplement* praises Stockton's contribution to the development of the short story.

ANONYMOUS. "Frank Richard Stockton." *Harper's Weekly*, XLVI (May 3, 1902), 555. Calls Stockton "as distinct an embodiment of the American spirit in one sort" as Mark Twain was in another.

BEER, THOMAS. *The Mauve Decade: American Life at the End of the Nineteenth Century*. New York: Knopf, 1926. Gives inside view of the publishing business during the Gay Nineties.

BERTHOFF, WARNER. *The Ferment of Realism: American Literature, 1884–1919*. New York: The Free Press, 1965. Historical view is particularly useful for chapters on the rise of magazines and middle-brow audience.

BETTELHEIM, BRUNO. *The Uses of Enchantment: The Meaning and Importance of Fairy Tales*. New York:Knopf, 1976. Explains how children's literature offers many levels of interpretation.

BUEL, CLARENCE CLOUGH. "The Author of The Lady, or the Tiger?" *Century*, X (July, 1886), 404–08. One of the best interviews with Stockton; gives important biographical and esthetic information.

CALLOW, JAMES T. and ROBERT J. REILLY. *Guide to American Literature from Emily Dickinson to the Present*. New York: Barnes and Noble, 1977. Links Stockton with F. Marion Crawford.

CANBY, HENRY SEIDEL. *The Age of Confidence: Life in the Nineties*. New

York: Farrar and Rinehart, 1934. Explains what was read by whom in
this era Canby insists is not a "small town joke."

CAWELTI, JOHN G. *Adventure, Mystery, and Romance: Formula Stories as
Art and Popular Culture*. Chicago: University of Chicago Press, 1977.
One of the major recent works on popular literature; concentrates on the
function of formulas in genre writing.

COMMAGER, HENRY STEELE. *The St. Nicholas Anthology*. New York: Random
House, 1948. Includes Stockton's "The Griffin" with other *St. Nicholas*
writers like Eudora Welty, Bret Harte, Louisa May Alcott, many others.

DE CAMP, ETTA. *The Return of Frank Stockton*. London: W. Rider and Son,
1913. Offers stories De Camp says Stockton dictated to her from the
spirit world.

DICKINSON, ASA D. *1000 Best Books*. New York: Doubleday, Page, 1924.
Includes Stockton among the thousand best from all times, all countries.

DOUGLAS, ANN. *The Feminization of American Culture*. New York: Knopf,
1977. History of feminism, especially linked with the clergy; decides
Herman Melville and Margaret Fuller were most enlightened on this
score.

FRANKLIN, H. BRUCE. *Future Perfect: American Science Fiction of the Nineteenth Century*. New York: Oxford University Press, 1966. Says everyone in the nineteenth century wrote science fiction, though they might
not have known it.

GLENN, THOMAS ALLEN. *Some Colonial Mansions and Those Who Lived in
Them*. Philadelphia: Henry T. Coates and Co., 1899. Includes Copley
painting of Stockton's ancestor, Anice Stockton, as well as other data
about Stockton's background.

GRIFFIN, MARTIN I. J. *Frank Stockton; A Critical Biography*. Port Washington, New York: Kennikat Press, 1939, 1965. Good biography and bibliography of Stockton, though tends toward plot summary and avoids critical analysis.

GUTHRIE, ANNA LORRAINE. *Index to St. Nicholas: Vols. I-XLV (1873-1918)*.
New York: H. W. Wilson, 1920. Indexes all entries from this period.

HACKETT, ALICE PAYNE. *Seventy Years of Best Sellers: 1895-1965*. New York:
Bowker, 1967. Establishes that Stockton's *Captain Horn* was the best-
selling American novel for 1895, the first year accurate seller lists are
possible.

HALL, ERNEST JACKSON. *The Satirical Element in the American Novel*. New
York: Haskell House, 1969. Feels there is "some slight social satire in
nearly all" Stockton's novels.

HOWARD, ALICE BARRETT. *Mary Mapes Dodge of St. Nicholas*. New York:
Julian Messner, 1943. Focus on Dodge, but much information on
Stockton.

HOWELLS, WILLIAM DEAN. *Literature and Life, Studies*. Port Washington,
New York: 1902, 1968. Like Beer, an inside view of literature in the last
part of the nineteenth century.

———. "Stockton and His Works." *Book Buyer,* XX (February, 1900), 19.
Along with the next three essays, these articles are the best contemporary
criticisms of Stockton's art.

———. "Stockton's Novels and Stories." *Atlantic Monthly,* LXXXVII (January, 1901), 136–38.

———. "Stockton's Stories." *Atlantic Monthly,* LIX (January, 1887), 130–32.

———. "A Story-Teller's Pack." *Harper's Weekly,* XLI (May 29, 1897), 538.

JOHNSON, ROBERT UNDERWOOD. *Remembered Yesterdays.* Boston: Brown, Little, 1923. Unofficial poet laureate of America has chapter on Stockton
called "A Joyous Humorist."

JORDAN, ALICE M. *From Rollo to Tom Sawyer.* Boston: Horn Book, 1948.
Cites Stockton's "significant contribution to the golden era" of children's
literature of the 1880s.

KNIGHT, GRANT C. *The Strenuous Age in American Literature.* Chapel Hill:
University of North Carolina Press, 1954. Says Stockton's Stede Bonnet
was a real pirate.

LEISY, ERNEST. *The American Historical Novel.* Norman: University of Oklahoma Press, 1952. Believes *Kate Bonnet* is an historical novel.

MARTIN, JAY. *Harvests of Change: American Literature, 1865–1914.* Englewood Cliffs, New Jersey: Prentice-Hall, 1967. Especially relevant to
Stockton is the chapter on "The Rise and Relevance of Mass Literature."

MEIGS, CORNELIA. *A Critical History of Children's Literature.* London: Macmillan, 1969. Claims Stockton's children's stories were "among the glories" of *St. Nicholas'* early years.

MORSE, JAMES HERBERT. "Authors at Home." *Critic* (April 16, 1898), pp. 259–61. Folksy interview reveals many details of Stockton's life and writing
habits.

PATTEE, FREDERICK LEWIS. *The Development of the American Short Story:
An Historical Survey.* New York: Harper and Brothers, 1923. Asserts
that Stockton "was a humorist, but at the same time he was an artist."

———. *The New American Literature: 1890–1930.* New York: Century,
1930. Pattee's respect for Stockton persists while his fame wanes.

PFORZHEIMER, WALTER L. *Stocktoniana: an Essay.* New York: privately
printed, 1936. Enthusiastic review of Stockton, especially his "The
Lady," avers that "the author is the age incarnate; rarely has a man so
reflected his period."

PHELPS, WILLIAM LYON. *The Advance of the English Novel.* New York:
Dodd, Mead, 1916. Great respect for Stockton, especially *The Casting
Away* and *Captain Horn.*

QUILLER-COUCH, ARTHUR THOMAS. *Adventures in Criticism.* New York: Putnam's, 1925. Calls Stockton's works classics, is puzzled why Stockton
receives so little critical attention.

RICHARDSON, CHARLES F. *American Literature: 1607–1885.* New York: G. P.
Putnam's 1893. Calls Stockton, Twain, and Harris the "Reigning Favorites" of the epoch, feels they are slighted because humorous.

SCHLESINGER, ARTHUR MEIER. *The Rise of the City, 1878–98.* New York: Macmillan, 1933. Cites the fact that in 1893 only Twain and Crawford were more in demand than Stockton at American libraries.

SHAW, JOHN MACKAY. *St. Nicholas: an Illustrated Magazine for Young Folks.* Tallahassee: Florida State University Press, 1965. Index that updates the Guthrie book.

SPENGEMANN, WILLIAM C. *The Adventurous Muse: the Poetics of American Fiction, 1789–1900.* New Haven: Yale University Press, 1977. Discusses major and minor American literature in terms of the tension between the poetics of adventure and domesticity.

Stockton: First Editions and Literary Autographs of American and English Authors. Newark: Newark Galleries, 1932. Auction catalog gives information unknown to previous Stockton scholars.

STOCKTON, MARIAN. "A Memorial Sketch of Mr. Stockton." *The Novels and Stories of Frank Stockton* (Shenandoah Edition), XXIII, 189–206. Personal reminiscence by Stockton's wife.

STOCKTON, THOMAS HEWLINGS. *Poems, with Autobiographical and Other Notes.* Philadelphia: 1861. Autobiography by Stockton's older half-brother; includes engravings by Stockton.

TAYLOR, OLIVIA. "Dear Ghosts of Lego and Monticello." *Papers of the Albemarle County Historical Society,* III (1942–43), 17–32. Gives pleasant account of Stocktons' stays at Jefferson's "Lego," where "The Lady, or the Tiger?" was written and recited.

THOMAS, EDITH M. "A Dialogue between Frank R. Stockton and Edith M. Thomas." *McClure's Magazine,* I (November, 1893), 466–77. Flirtatious interview with Stockton as a cult figure gives special insight.

TRINKER, CHARLES L., ed. *Basic Books for Junior College Libraries: 10,000 Vital Titles.* Northport, Alabama: Colonial Press, 1963. Stockton still ranks among world's great literature.

VAN STRUM, CAROL SCOTT. "On Story Telling." *Coevolution Quarterly* (Spring, 1978), p. 124. *Whole Earth Catalog* coterie praises Stockton's children's stories.

VEDDER, HENRY C. *American Writers of To-Day.* New York: Silver, Burdett, 1894. An esteemed critic places Stockton, though unique, with Wilkie Collins, Defoe, Edward E. Hale.

VOSS, ARTHUR. *The American Short Story: A Critical Survey.* Norman: University of Oklahoma Press, 1973. Opinion that Stockton "was mainly a facile journalist and entertainer" compares with Voss's incorrect date for "The Lady" of 1862, twenty years off.

WASSERSTROM, WILLIAM. *Heiress of All the Ages: Sex and Sentiment in the Genteel Tradition.* Minneapolis: University of Minnesota Press, 1959. Compares Stockton's "The Lady" with James's *Daisy Miller* and says that Stockton allegorized for his generation the abiding question whether sex is delightful or devouring, beneficent or consuming, good or evil.

WERNER, WILLIAM L. "The Escapes of Frank Stockton." *Essays in Honor of A. Howry Espenshade*. New York: Thomas Nelson and Sons, 1937, pp. 21–45. Interesting casual discussion of Stockton, though it never quite gets to the point.

WILSON, EDMUND. *Patriotic Gore: Studies in the Literature of the American Civil War*. New York: Oxford University Press, 1966. Documents Gertrude Stein's admiration for Stockton and expresses Wilson's own.

WOLFE, THEODORE F. "Where Stockton Wrote." *Lippincott's Magazine*, LXIV (September, 1899), 367–76. Prose-poem on Stockton's house, sources, writing habits.

YOST, DOROTHY. *The Stereotype of the Single Woman in American Novels; A Social Study with Implications for the Education of Women*. New York: Crown Press, 1951. Thinks *Rudder Grange* and *The Casting Away* are amusing.

Index